To John and A a dying breed but young in spirit.

With best wishes to you both.

Winifred
10.4.06

A HISTORY OF LUDGERSHALL

by Winifred Dixon

© 1994 by Winifred Dixon.

This book is copyright under the Berne Convention.
No reproduction without permission. All rights reserved.

Published in the United Kingdom by the Highfield House Trust.

Highfield House
Ludgershall, Andover
Hants, SP11 9QD.

ISBN: 0 9524273 0 3

British Library Cataloguing in Publication Data
A catalogue record for this book is available from the British Library.

Typeset and printed by Hobbs the Printers of Southampton

Contents

		Page
Acknowledgements		iv
List of Illustrations		v
Abbreviations		vi
Chapter One	Before the Norman Conquest	1
Chapter Two	Ludgershall at the time of Domesday	7
Chapter Three	The Castle and John the Marshal	11
Chapter Four	Castle and Forest, 1165–1216	17
Chapter Five	The Archaeological Record	23
Chapter Six	Henry III and the Dowagers	31
Chapter Seven	The Church of St. James	37
Chapter Eight	Church and People	43
Chapter Nine	Biddesden House	49
Chapter Ten	Ludgershall's Members of Parliament, 1295–1791	53
Chapter Eleven	Ludgershall MP's: the last thirty years	61
Chapter Twelve	Crime and Public Order	67
Chapter Thirteen	Everyday Life and the Poor Law	73
Chapter Fourteen	Tithes and Enclosure	81
Chapter Fifteen	The Railway and the Army	89
Chapter Sixteen	The Railway from 1918 to closure in 1964	97
Chapter Seventeen	Ludgershall's Schools from the beginning to 1920	103
Chapter Eighteen	Ludgershall Schools after 1920	109
Chapter Nineteen	Utilities	115
Chapter Twenty	Fire!	121
Chapter Twenty One	Chapels, Halls and Monuments	127
Chapter Twenty Two	Roads, Streets, Councils and Land	135
Chapter Twenty Three	Village Life between 1895 and 1939	143
Chapter Twenty Four	Ludgershall after 1939	151
Appendices		155
General Index		177
Index of Names		183

Acknowledgements

This history of Ludgershall would never have been begun but for the efforts of those who have gone before in attempting to record events. The Rev. Peter Chesters, a former Rector of the Parish now retired, started me on the long road of enquiry with his own interest in the subject, and I thank him for it. I have visited a great many libraries in the course of my investigations and have invariably found the staff to be most helpful. I should particularly like to thank Paul H. Robinson, Curator of the Wiltshire Archaeological and Natural History Society Library, and Pamela Coleman, the Sandell Librarian. Staff at both the County Libraries at Trowbridge, Wiltshire and at Winchester, Hampshire and the local libraries at Salisbury, Andover and Ludgershall have patiently and kindly assisted me.

Isobel White of the House of Commons Library supplied much useful information concerning the Members of Parliament who represented this ancient borough. The Librarian and Keeper of the Muniments at Salisbury Cathedral Library, Suzanne Edward, assisted in the search for the seal of Milo of Gloucester, and staff at the British Library helped in this matter also. My thanks go to Deputy County Archivist, R. J. E. Bush, of Somerset Record Office who traced the Heneage Deeds which bear the seal of the town of Ludgershall, the Ministry of Defence Assistant Land Agent, G. A. Heard, regarding Manor Farm at the time of its purchase by the War Office, and H. J. New, archivist for Stone, King and Wardle, Solicitors for the Diocese of Clifton, concerning the Catholic Church in Ludgershall. Bryan Guinness, the late Lord Moyne, shared his library and his enthusiasm for that great soldier, General Webb, and pointed me in the direction of further study of his career. John J. Selwyn wrote at length about his famous ancestor, George Augustus Selwyn, and led me to look further afield. Mr David Faber of Ampfield gave his valuable time to talk to me concerning Walter Vavasour Faber, the founder of Faberstown.

The original pencil drawings that so beautifully illustrate the book are by the talented young artist, Gareth Copping, and this history would most certainly never have been completed without the professional skills of my husband, Conrad Dixon, who expertly edited and indexed the bulky manuscript which I had amassed. Finally, to the many people of Ludgershall who offered information and spoke freely to me of their memories of life in the village, I can only say a heartfelt thank you, and I hope you will enjoy reading the result.

Winifred Dixon
September 1994

List of Illustrations

	Page
1. Ludgershall and nearby pre-historic and Roman sites	3
2. Seal of Milo of Gloucester	14
3. Ludgershall Castle in 1994	24
4. St James' Church	38
5. Biddesden House	52
6. Tomb of Sir Richard and Lady Jane Brydges	54
7. Erskine House	61
8. The *Crown* and the *Queen's Head*	64
9. Lynton Cottage and Perry's Cottage	74
10. Merle Cottage and the Doctor's House in St James' Street	75
11. Parish of Ludgershall in 1841	82
12. Centre of the village in 1841	84
13. The *Prince of Wales Hotel*	93
14. Old School House in Butt Street and St. James' Street School	106
15. Captain Faber's water tower	116
16. The Preaching Cross	129
17. The War Memorial	132
18. Allotment Rules	138
19. Highfield House, home of Mary Ann Selfe	143
20. Burials and Baptisms, 1621–1850	173

Abbreviations

AJ	*The Archaeological Journal.*
BCA	Book Club Associates.
comp.	compiler.
DNB	*Dictionary of National Biography.*
ed. eds.	editor; editors.
gen. ed.	general editor.
HMSO	Her Majesty's Stationery Office.
IHR	The Institute of Historical Research.
MA	*Mediaeval Archaeology.*
RIBA	Royal Institute of British Architects.
RIBAJ	*Royal Institute of British Architects Journal.*
VCH	*Victoria County History.*
WANHS	Wiltshire Archaeological and Natural History Society, Devizes.
WAM	*The Wiltshire Archaeological and Natural History Magazine.*
WRO	Wilts Record Office, Trowbridge.
WRS	Wilts Record Society.

CHAPTER ONE

Before the Norman Conquest

The open and often windswept area of chalkland known as Salisbury Plain has attracted settlement since prehistoric times, and the causewayed camps, long barrows, round barrows and henge monuments scattered over the area are a lasting record of the people who first made their homes in this part of the county of Wiltshire. At the beginning of the period known as the Neolithic (or New Stone) Age, some five thousand years before the birth of Christ, great forests covered the whole of Britain: there were huge tracts of deciduous forest consisting of oaks, elms, alders and limes in southern Britain; denser growths of oaks on the heavier clay soils of the Midlands, and birch and pine in the north. The first settlers chose the easier open sites, felling the trees and burning off the brushwood to open up small plots of land for cultivation; with hunting, fishing and fowling to vary the diet.

Between 4300 B.C. and 3300 B.C. forest clearance was on a much larger scale, and by the end of the period large tracts of chalk hill country were open. The chalk uplands were attractive to farmers because the soil was light and easy to manage with the simple implements that they made, and the fields thus cleared were initially very fertile. Chalkland pastures were also easy to turn over to grazing cattle and sheep, and cereals were grown as early as 4200 B.C. at Hembury in Devon. From the remains found on these Neolithic sites it can be seen that the early farmers grew emmer wheat, einkorn wheat, barley and flax.

Sheep were reared; a small scrawny breed similar to today's Soay sheep, and at Durrington Walls, some ten miles south-west of Ludgershall, pig-rearing was carried out. These pigs were smaller, heavily spotted, and longer in the snout than modern pigs. The remains of big dogs were also found at Durrington; the breed resembled the Labrador and they were probably used for guarding, shepherding and hunting. Forest clearance was accomplished using stone axes which were ground and polished to give a fine edge, and harvesting was done with stone sickles mounted in wooden hafts.

These Neolithic settlers buried their dead under longbarrows of the type surviving at East and West Kennet, which they dug out using antler picks and the shoulder blade bones of deer. Their grave goods were few; combs of antler horn, trapezoidal-shaped arrow-heads and round-based bowls which they decorated by impressing small objects into the still-damp clay. They dug out ditches, and banked the soil inside to form great circles which were situated on commanding hill-tops and known as causewayed camps. It is thought that they were used as fortified camp sites, stockaded enclosures for animals, or sometimes for ceremonial occasions. Windmill Hill, a few miles to the north and west of Avebury, is the type site for these camps, being dated to 3500 B.C.

In the middle Neolithic period the design of the enclosures changed. Situated now on the lower slopes of the terrain, they were built with an external bank and an inner ditch with fewer breaks in the bank, and became known as henge monuments.

The most famous is at Stonehenge, south-west of Amesbury and some twelve miles from Ludgershall, where the circular bank and external ditch were dug around 3000 B.C. with the stone circles added later. Avebury, situated some fifteen miles north-west of Ludgershall, is also a henge monument, albeit a huge one. Situated on a low-lying site just above the flood plain of the River Kennet, it is thought to have been used for predominantly religious occasions. Durrington Walls, south-west of Ludgershall, is also situated on low ground beside the River Avon, and by 2500 B.C. it was a substantial settlement.

Life for the early inhabitants of the Plain was made possible because of the rivers that flow from north to south across it. They are the Avon, which is joined at Bulford by the Nine Mile River, the Bourne which rises to the north of Ludgershall and passes through the Collingbournes and on southwards through North and South Tidworth, while to the west is the River Till which joins the Wylie at Stapleford. Bronze Age settlers arrived around 1900 B.C. and brought with them a richer culture. They were able to work tin, copper and gold and mixed the first two metals to make implements and weapons, burying their dead in circular-shaped mounds which can be seen dotted all over the Plain; many have been excavated to reveal fine flint arrowheads, knives and daggers of bronze, bone and jet buttons, jet beads and basket-shaped earrings made of gold.

A few miles west of Ludgershall in the parish of North Tidworth there stands the fortified height known as Sidbury Hill Fort. Heart-shaped, surrounded by double banks and ditches and positioned on the highest point of Salisbury Plain, it was a good defensive position and as such was occupied by man for thousands of years. It possibly began as a causewayed camp, and was certainly used by Bronze Age settlers for among the finds from the site are a Bronze Age celt or axe, a number of bronze pins and a stone axe-hammer. Closer to Ludgershall itself are the two Bronze Age tumuli on Windmillhill Down that stand in silhouette to the west of the village and another tumulus on Pickpit Hill near the Ludgershall-Tidworth road. An earthwork from the same period extends over Perham Down in a north-east direction and pointing towards Ludgershall. The best artifacts from this time, however, were found on Snail Down just north of Sidbury Hill, in 1805 by the Wiltshire antiquarian, Sir Richard Colt Hoare.

He found a bronze chisel fitted into a stag's horn handle, a bone wristguard and three bone lance or arrow heads. Nearby was a whetstone, grooved in several places, and obviously used to sharpen the arrowheads. The artifacts belonged to the Beaker Folk who lived on Salisbury Plain during the early part of the Bronze Age. They were a round-headed people who were immmigrants from the European mainland, and they got their name from the vase-like pots used as drinking vessels and storage jars and found as grave goods. A looped and socketed axehead from a slightly later part of the Bronze Age was found in Ludgershall about a hundred years ago, and it demonstrates the weakness of Bronze Age technology. Bronze weapons cannot be sharpened to take a permanent edge, and the era ended with the arrival of a new wave of settlers whose long iron swords were sharp and guaranteed success in battle.

The Celts moved into Southern England in significant numbers around 500 B.C. A long-headed race, warlike and industrious, they ushered in the Iron Age and better farming methods. They introduced a field system that encouraged crop rotation, and traces of it can be seen to the north and west of Sidbury Hill. They lived in roundhouses and ploughed the land. Their remains are less evident than those for the Bronze Age, but a good idea of how Celts lived and worked may be gained from a visit to the Butser Iron Age Farm near Petersfield in Hampshire. Cereal production seems to have averaged out at around two tonnes per hectare, and with no land shortage at this period the standard of living may have been relatively high.

The coming of the Romans to Salisbury Plain around A.D. 45 brought a new element to the landscape—roads. Trackways had existed from time immemorial, but there were no all-weather, well-drained, firm-surfaced roads before the Roman occupation. Initially, the Roman road served to give armies quick passage into areas of unrest, but with pacification accomplished a second generation of roads was constructed to link centres of population and assist trade. In south-western England there were four groups of roads, but the one that concerns us most ran from London to Silchester and then split to service Winchester, Exeter and Bath, Gloucester and South Wales. The Port Way near Andover was one branch; the Silchester to Old Sarum road another, while at Chute Causeway, a few miles north and east of Ludgershall, the road curved round the top of an escarpment to link Mildenhall and Winchester.

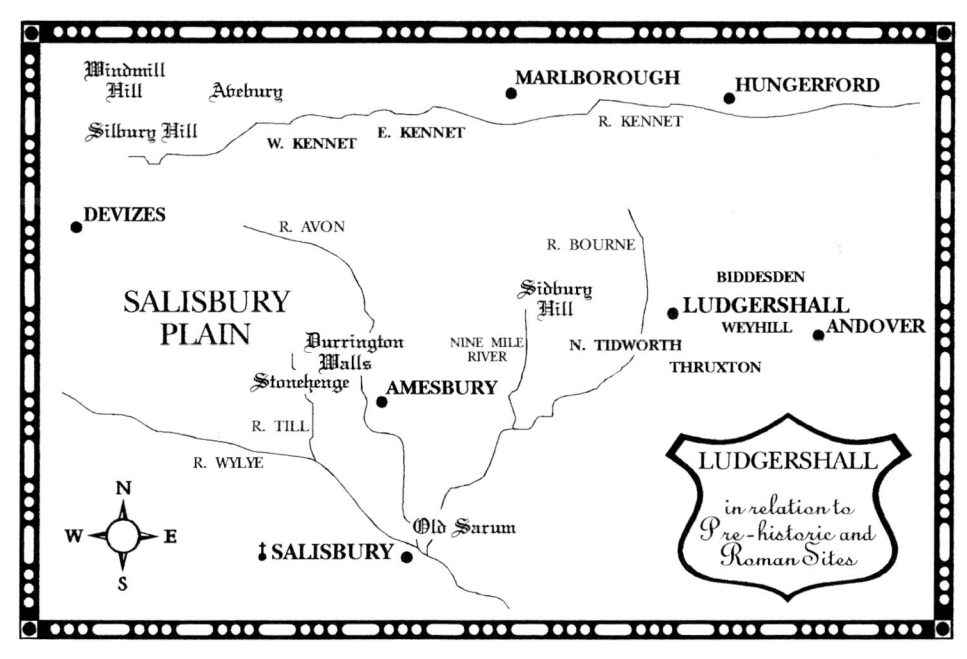

Ludgershall and nearby pre-historic and Roman sites.

Prosperous Romano-British citizens who had done well out of the stable trading conditions created by the *Pax Romana* built homes near these roads. A villa site at Lambourne's Hill near Biddesden Bottom was excavated in 1830. The dig produced evidence of a large and imposing residence. There was a gateway of green sandstone blocks, and columns with well-cut capitals and bases. Another villa site has been discovered just off the present-day A342 main road near Weyhill. A hoard of pewter vessels was unearthed in 1897; two of them bore the Christian symbols of a fish and a Chi-rho indicating a late fourth-century date. Another villa near Thruxton, some two or three miles south of Ludgershall, contained a mosaic 16ft × 16ft with the figure of the god Bacchus seated on his tiger and was dated by means of coins found nearby at around A.D. 350. On two sides of the square is an inscription which reads *Quintus Natalius Natalinus et Bodeni*. In the north-east part of the parish of Ludgershall at Coldridge Down a find of Roman coins and roofing tiles show habitation in the period, while the fragments of Roman pots found on old plough-soil at the base of the northern ringwork of Ludgershall Castle confirm settlement and agriculture on a village site from an early date.

The break-up of Romano-British civil government may have led to the abandonment of town life in the fifth century A.D. but changes in the countryside were much less dramatic. Wattle-and-daub huts are easily rebuilt after the passage of raiders, and the coming of the Saxons around A.D. 495 seems to have increased the importance of the settlement. Excavations in the 1960s show that a massive timber structure had lain under the southern ringwork of Ludgershall Castle and pre-dates the Norman structure on the northern ringwork. The indications are that this was a Saxon hall, and further evidence for Saxon presence may be found in the parish church of St. James. On the south wall of the nave, very near the door, is a fragment of a crucifixion carving from the Saxon period, and it seems to be a stone rescued from an earlier building—probably a small chapel on the same site. Before the arrival of the Normans the settlement had acquired its first name. In the year 1015 it was known as Lategaresheale, and this is the first recorded version of the name. There are so many variations and changes to reach the present spelling of Ludgershall that Appendix One is dedicated wholly to the subject, and to follow that part of our story you must look there.

The appearance of the village in the half-century before the coming of the Normans may be deduced from surviving documents and excavations of Saxon villages in continental Europe. A substantial farmer would have lived in a wood-framed long house with a steep-pitched roof of thatch or shingles. The Roman writer Tacitus suggests that the walls of wattle hurdles daubed with mud were coloured, while low interior screens divided the family from the aniamls. In summer, a hole in the roof would allow smoke from a central fire to escape; in winter it would be stopped up so that smoke trickled through the thatch and kept the living space warm. Aelfric, a monk at Winchester, tells us that society was chiefly composed of *'eorles'* and *'ceorles'*, with the former able to rise to be *'thegns'* or thanes if the village possessed a church, a king's hall or a kitchen—which was probably a communal bakery. The *'ceorles'* lived in smaller huts with a single room, and if land workers were called *'bordars'*, *'villans'* or *'cottars'*. Under King Canute even the slaves had rights. A slave woman working the land was entitled to eight pounds of corn, a sheep or three silver pennies for winter subsistence, a measure of beans during Lent and whey in summer, or an extra penny in lieu. We know that immediately before the Norman Conquest the village was held by a thane named Elward and that he paid taxes on about fifty acres. In the next chapter when dealing with the Domesday survey of 1086 it will be possible to expand on this outline and draw a firmer picture of the village under its new Norman overlord.

SOURCES FOR CHAPTER ONE

CASTLEDEN, Rodney	*The Stonehenge People*. (Routledge and Kegan Paul, London and New York), 1987.
CHILD, Melville T. H.	*Andover in Hampshire; life in the town and its neighbourhood before 1720*, Andover, 1969.
COLLIER, C.	'Andover and its Neighbourhood', *WAM* volume 21, July 1883, 293–314.
DOUBLEDAY, H. Arthur (ed.)	*Hants and the Isle of Wight, VCH*, volume 1.
FOX, Aileen	*South West England*. (Thames and Hudson, London). 1964.
GODDARD, E. H.	'Notes on Implements of the Bronze Age found in Wiltshire, with a list of all known examples found in the County.' *WAM* volume 37, June 1911, 108.
GODDARD, E. H.	'A list of Prehistoric, Roman and Pagan Saxon Antiquities in the County of Wilts Arranged under Parishes.' *WAM*, volume 38. December 1913, 153.
GRUNDY, G. S.	'The Ancient Highways and Tracks of Wiltshire, Berkshire and Hampshire, and the Saxon Battlefields of Wiltshire' in *AJ*, volume 25 (second series), March–December 1918, 69.
HAMPSHIRE COUNTY COUNCIL	*Hants Treasures*. Local history collection compiled by Hampshire County Council, 1983. Copy in Andover Public Library.
HASLAM, Jeremy and EDWARDS, Annette	*Wiltshire Towns: The Archaeological Potential*. (*WANHS* Devizes), 1976.
HOARE, Richard Colt	*The History of Modern Wiltshire: Hundreds of Everley, Ambresbury and Underditch*. London, 1826.
QUENNELL, Marjorie and QUENNELL, C. H. B.	*Everyday Life in Anglo-Saxon Times*. (Transworld Publishers Ltd., Ealing, London), 1972.
REYNOLDS, Peter	*Iron Age Farm: the Butser Experiment*. (British Museum Publications, London), 1979.
WANHS	*Catalogue of the Stourhead Collection*. (*WANHS*, Devizes), 1896.

CHAPTER TWO

Ludgershall at the time of Domesday

Duke William's victory at Hastings in 1066 did not give him immediate and uncontested mastery of England, for in 1068 Harold's sons raided into Somerset from Ireland and a year later the inhabitants of Northumberland slew the earl that William had placed over them and hundreds of his followers. When the Danes arrived on the east coast they were welcomed by the Anglo-Saxons, and a combined host stormed the city of York. The pacification process lasted many years, and it was not until the winter of 1085–86 that William was able, in the words of a Saxon chronicler, to send:

> *'men all over England, into every shire, and cause to be ascertained . . . what property every inhabitant of England possessed in land or in cattle, and how much money this was worth.'*

The purpose, of course, was to exact taxes, and the name Domesday Book was coined to demonstrate that the enquiry was to be so searching as to resemble the day of judgment from which, as all Christians would be aware, there was no escape. The main text was contained in two volumes covering all of England except the four northern counties, and Wiltshire was also dealt with in a parallel work called the Exeter Book. Scholarly opinion today maintains that this latter work was a draft for the main manuscript. The passage for Ludgershall reads as follows:

> *Ipse Edwardus tenet* LITLEGARSELE. *Elwardus tenuit tempore Regis Edwardi, et geldabat pro 1 hida. Terra est 3 carucatae. In dominio sunt 2 carucatae, et 3 servi; et 8 coscez, cum 1 carucata. Ibi pastura 3 quarentenis longa, et una quarentenis lata. Silva dimidio leucae longa, et 2 quarentenis lata. Valuit 100 solidos; modo 6 libras at 10 solidos.'*

When translated, the entry reads:

> *Edward himself holds Litlegarsele. Elward held it in the time of King Edward, and it paid geld for 1 hide. The land is 3 carucates. In demesne are 2 carucates and 3 serfs; and there are 8 coscets, with 1 carucate. There is pasture 3 furlongs long, and 1 furlong broad. The wood is half a mile long, and 2 furlongs broad. It was worth 100 shillings; it is now worth £6–10 shillings.'*

We can start with a very clear picture of who was lord of the manor in 1086. Edward of Salisbury was the second largest land-owner in Wiltshire after the king; he was the son of Walter de Ewras, Earl of Rosmar, who had been given Salisbury and Amesbury for his services during the Conquest. Edward's name is often given as Edwardus Sarisberiensis, and one account says that he was born in the city. He was standard-bearer to Henry I during the Normandy campaigns of 1105 and 1106, and owned land in Surrey, Hampshire, Dorset, Somerset, Middlesex, Oxfordshire and Hertfordshire as well as Wiltshire. The family maintained its status for several centuries, for a great-grand-daughter married the son of Henry II. Edward also enjoyed a lucrative government post. He was sheriff of the county, and as such claimed a third of all fines levied in the king's courts. Problems of interpretation of the Domesday Book passage dealing with Ludgershall begin with the end of the first sentence, but a rough estimate of population and animal power available can be made from the entry. Richard Colt Hoare interpreted this section as reading—

> *'Here are three plough lands. Two of the plough lands are in demesne, with three servants, and eight cottagers occupy the other.'*

A plough team usually consisted of eight oxen, and it seems likely that the number of people in eleven households might amount to about fifty, with twenty-four draught oxen to do the heavy work.

The term *'in demesne'* is straightforward, meaning that portion of the manor that was cultivated for the lord's own use. Measurement of the land is far more complex; the terms *'hide'* and *'carucate'* have caused much controversy amongst scholars, and the figures vary widely. The word *'ploughland'* sounds likes the amount of land which could support a plough team, but these ploughlands vary in different regions and do not always match the actual number of teams recorded on the manor. It is today considered that the hide and the carucate must originally have been linked to agricultural potential and used solely as units. Scholars in the nineteenth-century estimated that the hide varied between one hundred and twenty acres and one hundred and sixty acres. In the twentieth century, at least for the county of Wiltshire, they have adjusted the figure to a mere forty-eight acres. Hence, in the previous chapter, the hide of land that Elward possessed has been put down as approximately fifty acres.

The animal-pasturing area is in furlongs, a measurement used until recent times and equalling one-eighth of a mile. There were twenty shillings to the pound, but values should perhaps be uprated by a factor of about fifty thousand to get somewhere near the present worth. A comparison with neighbouring manors gives relative land values. Todeworde (Tidworth) was reported to be worth sixty shillings, but Colingeburn (Collingbourne) was far richer than both Tidworth and Ludgershall together, being valued at sixty pounds. Collingbourne had seventy-five households, arable land amounting to forty-five carucates and a pasture two miles long and a mile broad.

Forest land was included in the assessment because it has a dual product—game and firewood. Woods also provided building materials and food for the small herds of swine that rooted for acorns under the trees in autumn. Huntsmen who managed forest land were people of consequence, and three of them with local associations are known to us by name. Croc held a virgate of land at Tidworth (about seven acres), and ten hides and half a virgate at Collingbourne, but there seems to have been some quarrel with Edward of Salisbury. The Domesday Book entry is laconic about the dispute. It says baldly:

> *'In TODEWORDE is one virgate of land which Croc claimed as belonging of right to him. This land, however, Edward holds.'*

Croc may have been a Saxon from his name, and another such was Aluric, warden of Savernake Forest. After Domesday the post passed to Ricardus Sturmid who held land at Burbage, and whose family became hereditary wardens of the forest over many generations. Finally, there is Waleran, one of King William's principal huntsmen, who held land in Dorset, Hampshire and Wiltshire. A descendant, Robert de Walleran, succeeded to the governorship of Ludgershall Castle in 1206.

We know from Domesday Book that the forests contained alder, ash, oak, thorn and willow, and that a technique of *'asarting'* was employed to clear the trees and make more productive land. Such clearances were very strictly controlled because William the Conqueror loved hunting and imposed harsh anti-poaching laws on his subjects in consequence. It seems almost poetic justice that his oldest son, William Rufus, should die from an arrow wound received while hunting near Brockenhurst, and wholly in the pragmatic spirit of the times that Henry, his younger brother, should at once ride to Winchester to seize the treasury and persuade the Witan to elect him, and then gallop to Westminster to be crowned three days later. Henry I's inherited love of hunting may have been the reason that in 1103, three years into a long reign, he was signing official papers at the now-royal castle of Ludgershall. Chute Forest and Savernake were close at hand and, although the early history of the castle is dealt with more fully in the next two chapters it will be appreciated that the regular visits of a monarch and his retinue must have had an enormous effect on the economy of the village. The impact would be comparable to the siting of an industrial estate, or the opening of a hypermarket, on a small community today, and it was most likely accompanied by at least a doubling of the population.

A mediaeval king was accompanied on his travels by clerks, who dealt with the paperwork, and priests who said prayers for his soul. There were cooks and scullions, brewers and washerwomen. Robemakers and cobblers, smiths and grooms, huntsmen and body servants, courtiers and place-seekers. Stables and barns would be needed, firewood and forges, stacks of hay and straw, barrels of strong drink and joints of meat, Men-at-arms would stand sentry, and ladies' maids put out gowns for their mistresses. Local supplies of grain, beans, mutton and ale would soon prove inadequate, and merchants travelled to Ludgershall from as far afield as Southampton to sell luxury goods and necessities. A royal castle created demand for many kinds of labour and, as we shall see, the men-at-arms and administrators, servants and maids, tended to settle just beyond the castle walls and eventually became part of the community.

The Domesday enquiry dealt separately with Biddesden (Bedesdene), which was recorded in the Exeter Book under the Amesbury (Ambresbury) Hundred rather than as part of the parish of Ludgershall. Bedesdene was a poor hamlet of seven householders—one villan, two bordars and four serfs, and it was held by Robert Fitz-Girold, who was also the principal landowner in South Tidworth. Bedesdene was worth a mere thirty shillings. The first Rector of Ludgershall was called William de Budesden, and the diocesan authorities were still calling the combined benefice Ludgershall and Biddesden in the fourteenth century. The reason for this apparent case of the tail wagging the dog is that the church or chapel at Biddesden had been originally set up and financed by the powerful and wealthy Benedictine monks at Amesbury, and the notion that this was *the* mother-church for Ludgershall survived a long time. Spiritual life may have had two centres, but economic life now had a single focus. The new castle at the end of the High Street and built alongside the road to Winchester was to be at the heart of things for at least two centuries.

SOURCES FOR CHAPTER TWO

CARDIGAN, Earl of	*The Wardens of Savernake Forest*. (Routledge and Kegan Paul, London), 1949.
ELLIS, Henry	*A general Introduction to Domesday Book*. 2 Vols. (Frederick Muller, London), 1971 edition.
FINN, R. P. A. Welldon	*The Liber Exoniensis* (Longman, London), 1964.
GARMONSWAY, G. N. (ed.)	*The Anglo-Saxon Chronicle*. (Dent, London), 1972.
HOARE, Richard Colt	*The History of Modern Wiltshire; Hundreds of Everley, Ambresbury and Underditch*, London, 1826.
JAMES, H.	*Domesday Book of the Great Survey of England of William the Conqueror A.D. MDCCCLXV; facsimile of the part relating to Wiltshire*. (Ordnance Survey, Southampton), 1862.
JOHNSON, C and CRONNE, H. A. (eds.)	*Regesta Regum Anglo-Normannorum*, Vol. 2 (Oxford 1956), 630–1.
JONES, W. H.	*Domesday for Wiltshire*, Bath, 1865.
KITE, Edward	'Amesbury Monastery, with an account of some discoveries on the site in 1860'. *Wiltshire Notes and Queries*, volume 3, 1899–1901, 265.
POOLE, A. L.	*From Domesday Book to Magna Carta, 1087–1216*. Vol. 3 of Oxford History of England series, 1955.
PUGH, R. B. and CRITTALL, Elizabeth (eds.)	*A History of Wiltshire, VCH*, Volume V, (IHR, London), 1957.
STEVENSON, Janet H.	'The Castles of Marlborough and Ludgershall in the Middle Ages.' *WAM*, vol. 85, 1992, 70.

CHAPTER THREE

The Castle and John The Marshal

King Henry I came into formal possession of the castle at Ludgershall between the years 1100 and 1103, but the man who held it for him in the last years of the monarch's life and during the bitter civil war that followed his death was of the Fitz-Gilbert family, but known to the world as John the Marshal. He came from a Wiltshire family of the middling kind, and the office of Marshal was a perquisite inherited, with lands, from his father. The office-holder acted as second-in-command to the Constable of the royal household, and his routine duties at Winchester, Marlborough and Ludgershall would have been the maintaining of order, checking accounts and overseeing the stable. A large, active and cruel individual, he had an eye always to the main chance, and by marriage, judicious changes of allegiance, personal bravery and clear thinking he turned a minor office into a major power base, leaving it in the undisputed possession of descendants.

The estates at Clyffe Pypard and North Tidworth were probably among the possessions of the Marshal's family; his first wife was the daughter of William Pipard who was a minor landholder in the area. John held property on the corner of Jewry Street in Winchester not far from the royal castle and palace where his duties lay. He also had control of lands in Somerset and Berkshire, and at Hamstead Marshall in the valley of the Kennet he owned a hall and other houses within a large enclosure which he fortified into an earth and timber castle during the reign of Stephen. His position in society was improved by an advantageous marriage with Sibyl, the sister of Patrick, Constable of Salisbury Castle, with whom he had, initially, clashed. Peace was restored between them when John discarded his first wife in order to marry Patrick's sister, but he did not disown his first family and it was his eldest son, Walter, who followed his father as Marshal. Walter was succeeded by John, first son of the second marriage, and then by William the fourth son. William the Marshal, Earl of Pembroke, served five monarchs and at the end of his life was virtual ruler of England as the protector of the young Henry III.

John the Marshal was careful not to commit himself too strongly to one side or the other on the death of his master, and the commenator John of Worcester wrote that he backed the male heir while the *Gesta Stephani (The Deeds of Stephen)* recorded him as a supporter of the empress. In the event, he supported Stephen from 1136 to 1139, was indecisive for two years and then switched to Matilda. Stephen was the nephew of Henry I and had been brought up in the royal household. There he was well liked for his gaiety and charm, and his uncle endowed him with estates both in England and on the Continent. Stephen made a successful marriage to Matilda, the rich heiress of the Count of Boulogne, who proved to be a capable and loyal wife.

The Empress, also called Matilda, was the only surviving legitimate child of Henry I and her father, being anxious to secure the throne for her after his death, had exacted an oath of loyalty to her from his barons in 1127. She had been brought up in Germany and had gained her title from her first marriage to the

German Emperor Henry V who died in 1128. Subsequently, Matilda married Geoffrey Plantagenet of Anjou, and the succession to the throne of England should have passed through her to her infant son, Henry Plantagenet. But the barons, not relishing the idea of a female ruler and one who had not endeared herself to the people on her short visits to England, broke their oaths of homage and offered the crown to Stephen. Stephen was quick to respond to the offer and entered the City of London where he was welcomed by the citizens who elected him king by a special prerogative they claimed to possess, and swayed by a substantial grant of privileges. Stephen hurried on to Winchester where his brother, Henry of Blois, who was a powerful bishop, persuaded the Church to support his cause and with the treasury and the castle at Winchester in his hands, Stephen returned to London to attend his coronation which took place on 22 December 1135, a mere three weeks after the death of Henry I.

Matilda counter-attacked with an appeal to the Pope in Rome, and then began to enlist supporters. Her half-brother, Robert of Gloucester, who was a bastard son of Henry I, declared for her, and his Constable, Milo of Gloucester, was entrusted with her personal safety. With hostilities imminent, the castellans in southern England began to fortify for the fray, and an account of 1138 shows that John the Marshal was one of those taking due precautions.

> 'This year Bishop Henry caused to be built a very strong tower in Winchester also the castles of Merdon, Farnham, Witham, Dunton and Taunton; Roger Bishop of Salisbury, the castles of Salisbury, Sherborne, Devizes and Malmesbury; the Earl of Gloucester strengthened Gloucester, Bath, Bristol, Dorchester, Exeter, Wimborne, Corfe and Wareham; Brian Fitz-Count, Wallingford and Oxford; Bishop Alexander, Lincoln; John Marshal, Marlborough and Ludgershall; Geoffrey de Mandeville, the Towers of London and Rochester. There was no one of any position in England who did not make or strengthen his stronghold.'

The capture of Stephen at Lincoln in 1141 persuaded John the Marshal to plump for Matilda, and in September of that year when she was blockaded at Winchester he took part in her dramatic escape to Ludgershall. The episode has been variously described, and of the four versions that follow only one gives him a direct role. Let us start with Agnes Strickland's account of events:

> 'Matilda . . . prevailed on her gallant brother, Gloucester, to provide for her retreat. He opened a passage for her through the besiegers at sword's point. She and her uncle David, King of Scotland, by dint of hard riding escaped to Ludgershall; while Gloucester, battling by the way, arrested the pursuit, till, all his followers being slain, he was taken prisoner September 14th, 1141.
>
> The empress, whose safe retreat to Ludgershall had been thus dearly purchased by the loss of her great general's liberty, being surrounded . . . at Devizes, only escaped their vigilance by personating a corpse, wrapped in grave clothes and placed in a coffin, she was borne . . . to the city of Gloucester . . . where she arrived faint and weary with long fasting and mortal terror.

No mention at all of John the Marshal although, of course, it is hardly likely that she would have been accommodated at his castle without either his presence or approval. When David Crouch published a biography of William the Marshal in 1990 he based his account of events in 1141 on the romance poem *Histoire de Guillaume le Mareschal*, a near-contemporary eulogy of John's son. This version says that John the Marshal planned the escape and obliged Matilda to ride astride during the retreat to Ludgershall so that she could spur her horse rather than go side-saddle as a lady should. When the opposing forces closed in on the little convoy he led them off and took refuge in Wherwell Abbey. They set fire to the building, and the molten lead splashing down from the roof caused severe burns and the loss of an eye. He was supposed to be a charred corpse, but after his pursuers moved on he got to his feet and walked twenty-five miles to Marlborough. One part of the story has corroboration elsewhere. The monk who wrote the Worcester chronicle gleefully repeats the story of the great empress riding astride in an unladylike fashion. Marjorie Chibnall, writing in 1991, pours scorn on the *Histoire*, and her account says:

> *'The besieging armies were able to bar the roads leading to Winchester and cut off food supplies. William of Ypres captured and burnt the town of Andover and prevented the empress establishing a 'castle' at Wherwell where the nunnery was burnt in the fighting. By that time it had become apparent that the empress must at all costs be got away from Winchester. While her supporters fought a delaying action, she slipped out of the city under the escort of Reginald of Cornwall and Brian Fitz-Count with the aim of escaping to Ludgershall and from there to Devizes. They travelled along the Stockbridge Road, riding at full speed. This was the occasion when the empress was forced by the urgency of the pursuit to ride astride like a man. The highly dramatised account later given in the poetic life of John's son, William the Marshal, cannot be taken at its face value; she could not have gone with John the Marshal by way of Wherwell occupied by the Flemish mercenaries of William of Ypres, and though John the Marshal fought indomitably and lost an eye in the battle, he was not with the party that accompanied her along the Stockbridge Road. Robert of Gloucester fought the rearguard action at the ford at Stockbridge and delayed pursuit long enough for her to disappear into the folds of the Danebury Downs and put the waterlogged marshes of the Test between her and her pursuers before he was captured along with a number of knights including William of Salisbury and Humphrey de Bohun.'*

Yet another account of the retreat from Winchester is given in R.H.C. Davis's biography of King Stephen printed in 1990. His version is close to that given by Agnes Strickland, but has two new features. Davis says that King David was captured three times in the fighting, and three times purchased his release. Milo of Gloucester discarded his armour and accoutrements and was *'glad to escape with his life.'* Confirmation of the latter episode came in the eighteenth-century when a silver seal belonging to Milo of Gloucester was found by a ploughman near Ludgershall. The centre has a knight on horseback in chain mail and helmet with a shield in one hand and a lance in the other. The inscription round the rim reads:

'Sigillum Milonia de Gloecestria'

and a drawing appears overleaf.

John the Marshal's influence increased after the death of Milo (sometimes called Miles) in 1143 in a hunting accident, while Hervey Brito, Earl of Wiltshire, abandoned Devizes and fled to Brittany leaving a power vacuum in the county. The high point of his popular fame came in 1152 when John besieged Newbury. King Stephen had demanded John's son William as a hostage during a truce, and threatened to hang him at the gates when negotiations went sour. John made a famous reply. The boy's life, he said, meant nothing to him because he still had the hammer and anvils to make more and better sons. Other threats were made on the life of young William but the king, who had found the boy a charming and artless companion, refused to carry them out.

Thereafter, John's position slowly weakened. He was quick to align himself with Henry II, but the new king only kept him with him in 1155 and 1156. He did not go to court after the second date, and in 1158 Henry II took Marlborough Castle from him. He retained the post of marshal with its allowances of twenty-four deniers a day, one loaf, a septier of wine and twenty-four candle ends, and property that included the manor of Wexcombe. In 1163 he was under a cloud for attempting to relate the Merlin prophecies to current events, and even though he tried to regain the king's favour in 1164 by joining in harassing Thomas Becket there was no way back. When he died in 1165 Ludgershall Castle passed effectively into royal hands and its affairs were conducted by a series of royal governors and keepers for the next fifty years.

'Seal of Milo of Gloucester'

SOURCES FOR CHAPTER THREE

AWDRY, W. H.	'Ludgershall Castle and its History'. *WAM*, vol. 21, July 1883, 317–330.
BARLOW, Frank	*The Feudal Kingdom of England, 1042–1216*. (Longman, London), 1961
CHIBNALL, Marjorie	*The Empress Matilda: Queen Consort, Queen Mother and Lady of the English*. (Blackwell, Oxford and Cambridge Mass.), 1991.
COLVIN, A. M. (ed.)	*History of the King's Works*. (HMSO, London), 1963. Volume 2, 729–731.
CROUCH, David	*William Marshal: Court, Career and Chivalry in the Angevin Empire, 1147–1219*. (Longman, London and New York), 1990.
DAVIS, R. H. C.	*King Stephen, 1135–1154*. (Longman, London and New York). Third edition, 1990.
DUBY, Georges	*William Marshal; The Flower of Chivalry*. (Faber and Faber, London and Boston), 1986.
MUIR, Richard	*Castles and Strongholds*. (MacMillan, London), 1990
POTTER, K. R. (ed.)	*Gesta Stephani*. (Oxford Mediaeval Texts), 1976.
STRICKLAND, Agnes	*Lives of the Queens of England*, London, 1867.
WEAVER, J. R. H. (ed.)	*Chronicle of John of Worcester, 1118–40*, Oxford, 1908

CHAPTER FOUR

Castle and Forest, 1165–1216

The first date signals the loosening of the iron grip of John the Marshal on Ludgershall, and the second the death of King John from a combination of dysentery and over-eating and bad temper at hearing that his treasure had been lost during the crossing of a tidal river in the Wash. In the years between there were momentous developments nationwide in the fields of justice and finance, while the character and function of Ludgershall Castle underwent a total change. Let us start with the larger canvas and then move on to local developments.

One of the results of practically two decades of civil war had been gross debasement of the coinage, with some barons minting their own and much clipped money in circulation. A mutilated halfpenny of Stephen's reign has been found on the castle site at Ludgershall while Henry II had to introduce a silver penny of the proper weight in 1180, and John called in the bad coins in circulation and made a new issue stamped with an outer circle to frustrate the clipping of coins. A legal precedent was set at the coronation of Richard I in 1189, for the date was chosen to mark 'time immemorial' so that any institution or practice that existed then was subsequently deemed to have existed since time began, and Common Law decisions today continue to honour the principle. Magna Carta, of course, is held out as the supreme achievement of early democracy, but it marked something else as well. John is named as *rex Angliae*: the Great Charter says nothing about Normans or Frenchmen; it is the English who benefit from the concessions made in it. Many of the castles built during the reign of Stephen were pulled down; the elective principle that had governed Stephen's acquisition of the throne gave way slowly to Henry II's desire that primogeniture be the basis of kingship. The peace was now the king's peace; the fragmentary civil service was composed, literally in some cases, of his servants, while judges went round on circuit much as they do today hearing cases, at first with the king present and then on their own. The landowners began to behave less like bandit chiefs and more like local administrators and tax collectors; castles changed from being draughty strongholds for the housing of men, weapons and horses to something resembling a residence where king and court could rest from constant travel in all weathers.

The Pipe Rolls for the period—the accounts for royal castles—show some expenditure at Ludgershall during the reign of Henry II but a great deal more under King John. In 1184–85 the expenses involved in carrying fifty softwood boards from Wallingford are noted, and we can speculate that this timber was flooring for an upper storey. Five years later Richard I gave Ludgershall Castle to his brother John, then Earl of Monteyne but King in turn from 1199. Richard spent very little time in England during his reign, but John rarely went overseas and was a frequent visitor to Ludgershall, both before and after his coronation. His appetite was prodigious, and when he ordered a new kitchen built in 1205 it was specified that the ovens be large enough to contain two or three complete carcasses of oxen.

In the early part of his reign he caused the area around Ludgershall Castle to be designated a royal park, and in 1210–11 spent the then enormous sum of thirty-seven pounds, sixteen shillings on a tower and repairing the walls. These walls were guarded by mounted knights, sergeants and foot soldiers, for whom provision was duly made in the Pipe Rolls.

At this period there was a governor and a keeper of the castle. Hugh de Nevill was keeper in 1194 as well as being in charge of Chute Forest and had to send to Southampton for a:

good and strong carriage to convey thence such wines as Daniel should deliver, two casks of white wine and four alnet to Ludgershall . . .

while King John's appetite had a plus side insofar as the poor were concerned. Church rules were framed to forbid the consumption of meat on Fridays, and when the King broke them the punishment was fixed at a tariff corresponding to his high position in society. The accounts show that he:

Spent in alms for dinner given to one hundred poor persons . . . because he had eaten meat twice on Friday next after the Feast of St. James at Ludgershall, nine pounds and twenty pence delivered to Brother Thomas the Almoner.

Hugh de Nevill was still in post in 1227 after John had been replaced by Henry III, and he received a curious instruction from the criminal court. A man called John Blund of Ludgershall had been executed for murder, and de Nevill was charged with restoring his goods to Gunhilda, the widow. He was to soften the blow somewhat by telling her that she was to keep her husband's house in the village to hold it thereafter at the King's pleasure. Another member of the de Nevill family was Jollan de Nevill who eventually became governor of the castle when the Fitz-Peter family, who had nominally held the post since 1164, were displaced. Jollan de Nevill was also principal warden of the royal forests, with a duty to ensure a supply of game during the winter months when shortage of feed cut down the number of cattle available. Venison was consumed in large amounts, and red and fallow deer were conserved under game laws that operated separately from the main stream of Common Law. It will do no harm to run ahead of events a little so as to cover the rise in importance of local woodlands to the economy of the castle, and then chart the decline.

The Forest of Ludgershall, created in 1203, was part of the greater Forest of Chute and lay partly in Wiltshire and partly in Hampshire. It was said in a report of 1228 to be '*ancient forest*' that had never known the plough, and is briefly described as

Ellis Croc's bailiwick in Wiltshire

so that we may fairly assume that it was managed by a descendant of Croc the huntsman who held land in Tidworth and Collingbourne at the time of the Domesday survey in 1089. The forest was an area of land rather than a mass of trees, and the nearest equivalent nowadays would be an African game reserve where some hunting takes place under strict supervision but from which most local people are excluded. We know that at a later date the Forst of Chute encompassed roughly ninety-eight square miles, with the northern boundary being the edge of Savernake Forest, and the southern the old Roman road from Salisbury to Winchester. With the western boundary being formed by the Avon it will be appreciated that Jollan de Nevill, principal warden of royal forests, had a large area to supervise, and we must first look at the structure of control that was employed.

The early provincial courts defined what counted as 'game' in a royal forest, and the protected animals were in three groups. The *'beasts of the forest'* were hart, hind, hare, boar and wolf. Next came the *'beasts of chase'* which were buck, doe, fox, marten and roe. Lastly, *'beasts and fowls of warren'* embracing rabbit, pigeon and partridge. The Justices in Eyre (from the Norman-French word *erre*, meaning a journey) dealt with pleas of the forest during the twelfth-century, and evolved into Justices of the Forest in the thirteenth-century to enforce the Forest Law. Their special courts became known as Eyres, and decisions were made on boundary disputes and quarrels between neighbours as well as the most common offences of *'trespasses of vert and venison'*. This kind of wrongdoing usually took the form of chopping down trees, or taking away firewood, and poaching the deer.

One complication in administering forest law was that many manors existed within the forest boundaries and the lordly families found it difficult to resist temptation. At a Forest Eyre held in 1257 in Savernake the case of Geoffrey, son of Walter of Oare, came before the court. Geoffrey had been caught red-handed in possession of a fawn and was fined ten shillings. The verderers who caught him presented an imperfect indictment which failed to include the date and year of the offence and were themselves fined for negligence. Other court records show that the townships in Chute Forest required to send a representative to inquisitions about forest matters included:

    Collingbourne Abbatis (Collingbourne Ducis)
    Tidworth of Alan la Zuche (South Tidworth)
    Tidworth Hose (North Tidworth)
    Chute
    Farnham (Vernham Dean)
    Biddesden
    Conholt
    Harrowdean

and that trespasses of vert and venison had been noted at:

    'Collingbourne Wood'
    'in the hay of Chute'
    'at the king's chase of Hippenscombe'
    'on Ludgershall moor'
    'Widgerly'
    'Shoddesden between Coalridge and Woodcroft'
    'in the woods belonging to Hurstbourne Tarrant'
    'in the manor of Standen'

The centre of Ludgershall Moor would be where Wood Park stands today, and in the nineteenth-century it was described as:

> *'a long flat common sprinkled with gorse and scrub . . . on which many people have grazing and other rights.'*

Towards the end of the thirteenth century the boundaries of Chute Forest contracted and the Forest of Ludgershall formally ceased to exist. An inspection in 1300 found that the former forest was reduced to consist principally of the *'king's demesne wood of Chute'*, and the area it covered is practically identical with the modern boundaries of the parish of Chute Forest. The Manor of Ludgershall and its adjacent woods remained subject to forest law as part of the ancient demesne of the Crown, and the dismantling of Chute Forest went on. In 1330 the *'Prioress of Amesbury's Wood'*, which was also called *'Woodcroft'* and stood between Biddesden and Great Shoddesden, was declared disafforested. Richard I's gift to his brother, John, of *'Ludgershall with the Forest;'* was now diminished by the loss of much of the second element, and there are few reminders of its importance. The red deer have gone, but when St. James' Church was being refurbished in 1873 a souvenir of past times was unearthed. The holes in the walls that received rafter ends were lined with chunks of red deer antlers to take the thrust of the timbers, and must have been performing the task since they were inserted six hundred years before by the workmen who constructed the building and who, presumably, roamed the forest at night to take a king's beast when the verderers and wardens weren't looking.

SOURCES FOR CHAPTER FOUR

AWDRY, W. H.	'Ludgershall Castle and its History'. *WAM*, volume 21, July 1883, 317–330
CARDIGAN, Earl of	*The Wardens of Savernake Forest.* (Routledge and Kegan Paul, London), 1949.
COLVIN, H. M. (ed.)	*The History of the King's Works*, (HMSO, London) 1963, volume 2, 729–731.
COX, J. Charles	*How to Write the History of a Parish*, London 1886.
HEANLEY, R. M.	*The History of Weyhill and it's Ancient Fair* (Warren and Son, Winchester), 1922.
MUIR, Richard	*Castles and Strongholds.* (MacMillan, London), 1990.
POOLE, A. L.	*From Domesday Book to Magna Carta; 1087–1216.* (Oxford History of England series, Clarendon Press), 1966.
STEVENSON, Janet H.	'The Castles of Marlborough and Ludgershall in the Middle Ages'. *WAM*, volume 85, 1992, 90.
WANHS	Excavation report in *WAM* volume 61, 1966, 104.

CHAPTER FIVE

The Archaeological Record

Two nineteenth-century scholars and one twentieth-century antiquarian believed that the castle at Ludgershall stood either on the site of a prehistoric fortress or a Roman marching camp, and their mistake was a natural one when all that could be seen on the site was a flinty crag on a grassy mound. It was not appreciated that Norman castles began as *'motte-and-bailey'* structures thrown up in a few weeks by gangs of coerced peasants, and then enlarged and improved over time. The *'motte'* was a cone of earth with a flattened top and wooden palisade, and the pattern can still be seen at Totnes in Devon where the shape has been retained although a stone wall has replaced the wooden one. *'Baileys'* were even simpler, being level areas surrounded by an earth wall and ditch or ditches and, as at Ludgershall where the earthworks have a figure-of-eight shape, often linked to form an inner and an outer bailey. A stone keep or tower in or on the inner bailey, or on the *'motte'* itself, would be constructed later to form a centre of resistance, a store for arms and provisions, and somewhere to rest between forays. They were defensive structures, and fighting would begin outside the castle walls and, when they were breached, continue at the outer bailey crowded with stores and animals, carry on into the inner bailey and end with a siege of the keep or donjon.

So little was known about the six-acre site of Ludgershall Castle that excavations were begun in 1964 by Dr. Peter Addyman, on behalf of the Ministry of Public Buildings and Works, with the help of teams of students from Belfast and Southampton Universities and many local volunteers organised by the Ludgershall Local History Society. The aim was to get answers to specific questions; to date construction, plot the defences, note the building phases and come to a conclusion as to its uses over time. In the first season work was begun in the northern ringwork in an area which lay inside the double bank and to the east of the standing ruins. The dig revealed that there had once stood at this point a simple late mediaeval flint and mortar building which measured thirty-six feet by fifteen-and-a-half feet internally. In it was an oven and a hearth at one end. There was fifteenth-century pottery on the clay floor, and a coin was found in the layers beneath which dated the building to the years between 1344–1391. This building was completely excavated and the standing remains were consolidated for display. In other areas of the ringwork, a complex range of buildings were exposed. Built in flint and mortar and with greensand dressings, the walls were faced with plaster. Fourteenth-century levels were reached.

Work was carried out in the southern ringwork, and here trial trenches were dug in the eastern half of the site. No traces of stone buildings were unearthed, but possible remains of timber buildings and scatters of twelfth-century pottery were found. A deep rectangular-shaped latrine was dug down into, and from it much early twelfth-century pottery was recovered and a clipped halfpenny dating from the reign of King Stephen. Still in the southern ringwork, sections were cut

Ludgershall Castle in 1994

through the inner bank and ditch, which proved to be V (vee) shaped and measured a vertical height of thirty-five feet from the bottom to the present top of the bank. Pottery sherds found in the silt at the bottom of the ditch and material found in the layers under the bank gave a probable date of the early twelfth-century for the building of the defences in the southern ringwork.

Excavations at the castle continue in the following season, and the range of thirteenth to fourteenth-century buildings which had been located in the northern ringwork in the previous year was found to include what was probably the undercroft, or vault, of a first-floor hall. There were various ante-rooms and a substantial latrine tower. The standing building had an entrance at ground floor level and a latrine shaft; the first floor room may well have been a solar, which was an upper room for the private use of the lord of the castle and his family. This standing building was also thought to date from the thirteenth to fourteenth-century.

The defences of both the northern and southern ringworks were investigated at this time using a method which is called *'resistivity surveying'*. Using this method, it is possible to detect features that are hidden under the earth without actually digging them up and so destroying the evidence of the later levels of occupation on the site. Based upon geophysical principles, the technique consists of measuring the electrical resistivity of the earth, and chalk and gravel are the most suitable soils for the method as they are both well-drained and ditches and pits can be easily detected. Ludgershall Castle was, therefore, an ideal site on which to use this method and it helped to indicate the most promising areas to be dug. In the northern ringwork it helped to reveal a flight of massive stone steps and a balustrade, or line of pillars, in well-dressed stone and a thick destruction layer of ashlar, or dressed surface stone. This was thought to be the remains of a demolished fore-building, perhaps for a keep or a hall. Still excavating in the northern ringwork, a trench was dug through the defences to the north of the standing bulding which revealed that there had originally been an inner bank into which the thirteenth and fourteenth-century domestic structures had been inserted. The trench was continued through the inner ditch, and the outer bank and ditch, which were found to have steep outer faces but less steep inner faces and were seventeen feet and fifteen-and-a-half feet deep respectively. Building debris and materials from the destruction deposits filled the inner ditch with thirteenth to fourteenth-century pottery, and below that there was a considerable depth of weather-silted material, mostly from the outer lip of the bank. In the top of this were substantial slabs of masonry from the nearby thirteenth to fourteenth-century buildings which must have fallen in during or after the late sixteenth-century when the castle was reported to be *'clene down'* by the antiquary, John Leland.

In the southern ringwork, excavation uncovered a deep narrow trench inside a large section of the bank; this was probably used originally to bed in the timbers supporting a massive superstructure and was an integral part of the defences of the castle. The banks in the northern ringwork were found to contain post-holes and emplacements for horizontal timbers on the outside which would have held the timber revetment necessary to strengthen the banks. The resistivity survey of the southern ringwork revealed that the banks and ditches were continuous, indicating that perhaps this ringwork was the earlier of the two.

Excavation of the castle continued in the season of 1967. In the north-east corner of the northern ringwork there was uncovered the end of the undercroft that had been located in the previous season. It was seen that it had been a three-bay bulding measuring forty-two by eighteen feet with a centrally placed doorway at its eastern end which had been blocked late in the Middle Ages. There was another doorway in the south-west corner of the undercroft which had been exposed by the previous season's dig. A variety of buildings lay to the east and south of the undercroft; some of them had clearly extended over the filled-in inner ditch. There was other evidence to suggest that the castle had been extended in a piecemeal manner during the thirteenth and fourteenth-centuries. These additions had included a massively-constructed building lying near the centre of both ringworks. This was left to be excavated in the following season. In the southern ringwork the inner bank had also been partly levelled in the thirteenth to fourteenth-centuries so that domestic buildings could be constructed. These were timber-framed with low flint and chalk foundation walls, but they were much flimsier in construction. Inside the walls was found an oval-shaped latrine pit with a small room adjacent to it and an oven with part of its superstructure and a base of a chimney. These clearly indicated that the buildings were for domestic use.

In the fifth season of excavation at Ludgershall work continued in three separate areas of the castle. In the northern ringwork the later mediaeval stone buldings were cleared for conservation and display, and selected areas of eleventh and twelfth-century buildings were revealed. In the southern ringwork the three-bay timber buildings located in 1967 were removed and earlier twelfth-century timber buildings were investigated. A length of adjacent rampart was also looked at in order to clarify conclusions drawn from the section dug in 1965. The bank was found to be revetted internally with vertical timbers and struts of the type employed to support a rampart walk. At a later stage, when the posts decayed, a dry-stone wall replaced it. The south side of the southern ringwork was dug to reveal many pits in a rectangular group—suggesting post-holes for a massive timber structure, and within the pits much twelfth-century pottery, probably contemporary with the raising of the ringwork and tossed into the pits created by the removal of timbers as the earthwork rose.

At this stage Dr. Addyman felt able to suggest a sequence of building. At the bottom was the old plough soil in which worn pieces of Roman pot had been found. Narrow trenches had been dug in it—presumably foundation trenches for huts. Then followed four phases of timber buildings, with the last of them still standing in the twelfth-century and having aisles, a porch and a mortar floor. Sometime in the same century the timber buildings were replaced by a large stone structure with ashlar green-sand dressings. This building was perhaps the original *'keep'* and the building which contained a door and a wide flight of stairs was the *'fore-building'* belonging to the keep. From the occupation material taken from the mortar floors, it appeared that it had been in use from the middle of the twelfth-century onwards. The earthworks and the timber defences of the ringwork might also have been constructed at this time. The large stone structure had been demolished shortly after this period, and the tower which today constitutes the main standing building was constructed. Architectural details of the tower suggest that it too was made before the end of the twelfth-century. It has a deep ground-floor room which suggests that it may have been a *'mural'* tower, that is a tower built on a wall, and it is partly embedded in the earth. The timber defences and large post-holes behind it may have been connected with a wall walk, or have given access to the stairs.

This mural tower was embodied into the later thirteenth-century layout of the castle which radically altered the character of the buildings. On the eastern end of the tower was added a large building measuring forty by eighteen feet; it had a latrine at the north-west corner, doorways in the south-west corner and at the eastern end and, in the centre of the building, there were central wooden columns standing on stone bases. To the east of this large building were one or more smaller buildings. In the thirteenth-century, or perhaps later, the mural tower seems to have been altered and windows, doors, a fireplace and a latrine were added. These additions would indicate that the tower was then in use as a solar or private room, perhaps leading to a first-floor hall above the undercroft to the east. Similarly, in the thirteenth-century, a large building was added in the middle of the ringwork. From its size and the high quality of its architectural decoration it was thought to be the new hall that was built in 1244–46 at the order of Henry III, and which is described in the next chapter.

During the later thirteenth and fourteenth-centuries further domestic accommodation was added. It appears that the undercroft had been sub-divided into at least four rooms with two latrines. Some of the new accommodation was built over the completely filled inner ditch confirming that, by this time, greater comfort was considered more important than strong defences at the castle at Ludgershall. Henry III's hall was found to have been dug out and re-floored in mediaeval times, and later still, a vast hearth with red tiles set on end had been inserted.

In the southern ringwork excavation was also continued and showed that, unlike the buildings in the northern ringwork, there was a range of flimsy twelfth-century buildings set in parallel division behind the rampart. On the south side of the ringwork a possible gateway was exposed, and there appeared to have been a massive timber structure with a substantial underground chamber. As a rule, there was only one large gateway to a castle, but some had two and many had a small postern-gate for a quick foray outside the defences or a frantic dash to escape when the building was overwhelmed. This never happened at Ludgershall; the castle did not stand a single siege in its long history.

The excavations make it possible to sketch out the history of the site. There are no prehistoric or Roman marching camps under the earthworks, and the earliest timber structures are pre-Norman Conquest. The ringwork and early substantial buldings are Norman, with a keep replaced by a tower and a walled fortress turning slowly into a comfortable residence. The comfort can be confirmed by the finds on the site. They include a casket lid decorated with three central strips pierced and backed with silver, fragments of fine glass goblets and glass urinals in the latrines. The standard of living was high. Remains were found of oyster shells, lobsters, game, fish, venison and fruit. The games played were draughts and dice; there were three chapels for spiritual consolation. Hunting arrowheads, whistles and horse harness including a gilded fourteenth-century spur testify that hunting parties went out into Ludgershall and Chute Forests for sport, while a great deal of wine was brought in for guests. When the castle became ruinous in the sixteenth-century some stonework must have been embodied in local buildings, and the magnificent

Tudor fireplace in the *Queen's Head* public house in the High Street is probably from the site. John Britton, writing in 1801, gave the castle its epitaph.

> It *'was reduced'*, he said, *'to its present state by the operations of time who neither bestows mercy on man nor his works but involves both the beggar and the king, the palace and the cottage, in one common fate of irretrievable ruin.'*

SOURCES FOR CHAPTER FIVE

BRITTON, John	*The Beauties of Wiltshire*, Volume II. London, 1801.
COLES, John	*Field Archaeology in Britain*. Methuen 1972.
	Excavation reports in *MA*:

Volume	Year	Page
10	1966	191
11	1967	286–288

MUIR, Richard	*Castles and Strongholds*. (Macmillan, London), 1990.
WAHNS	Excavation reports in *WAM*:

Volume	Year	Page
61	1966	104–105
62	1967	127–128
63	1968	111–112
64	1969	124–126
65	1970/71	205

WARNER, Philip	*The Mediaeval Castle: life in a fortress in peace and war*. (BCA, London), 1973.

CHAPTER SIX

Henry III and the Dowagers

On the death of King John in 1216 his son Henry succeeded to the throne while still a young boy of nine years' of age, but Henry III was fortunate in that he had two great protectors. Pope Honorius II was one, and the now aged William Marshal was the other. William Marshal, born in the middle of the civil war between Stephen and Matilda, was one of the four sons of John the Marshal by his second wife, Sybil of Salisbury, and has already been mentioned in Chapter Three as a child hostage at the siege of Newbury when John the Marshal coined his celebrated rejoinder to threats from King Stephen. A younger son, William had little patrimony, but was a faithful servant to three kings and married the second richest heiress in England. As Earl of Pembroke and the greatest soldier of the age it was natural that he was a prime candidate to be *de facto* Regent to the young Henry III. On his deathbed King John had committed the heir and kingdom to William Marshal's care, with the result that Ludgershall Castle was held once again by the family and the young king formed an attachment for the building and the locality.

Henry was a frequent visitor to Ludgershall, and the royal apartments in the castle were greatly improved at his command. In 1234–35 the king's chamber was whitewashed, the plaster painted with lines to look like masonry, and panelled. He had a stained glass window with a crucifix depicted on it installed at the head of his bed, and in 1244–45 built a new hall measuring sixty by forty feet for meals and conducting state business. It had a buttery and pantry attached, and was lit by four large windows. The wooden posts were coloured to look like marble; there was a dais at one end and a painting of the story of Dives and Lazarus in the opposite gable. A covered passage led from the hall to the queen's chamber so that she would not get wet coming and going. The queen was Eleanor of Provence, daughter of Raymond Berengar, Count of Provence, and her sister was married to the French king so that although the marriage of Henry and Eleanor was a happy one it also had a sound political basis. Eleanor was beautiful, extravagant and strong-willed, and spent the last eleven years of her life at the nunnery at Amesbury from where she distributed weekly, every Friday, the vast sum of five pounds in silver to the poor.

We know from the surviving accounts that royal patronage and presence brought benefits to Ludgershall. In 1242, for example, payments were made for *'digging white stone called chalk at Shudebury (Sidbury Hill) for making the walls of the chapel and chamber'*, and that the village women collected moss for the bedding of tiles, brought in the bracken for thatching the temporary lodges used by the carpenters and masons and cleaned the state apartments in preparation for the king's arrival. In the 1250's the castle was probably looking its best, for the walls were repaired and newly-furnished with battlements and loopholes all the way round, the kitchen and sausery had been rebuilt and a new chamber added for the use of Edward, the heir to the throne. The new room had two fireplaces and two privy chambers—the height of luxury in the thirteenth-century. There were three chapels dedicated to St. Leonard, St. Katherine and St. Nicholas. In 1250 the king ordered that an expensive crucifix and an image of the Virgin Mary be sent to Ludgershall; it has been estimated that Henry III spent ten per cent of his income throughout his reign on royal castles, with Ludgershall one of many beneficiaries. The stables were rebuilt in 1261 and repairs continued during the last ten years of his reign.

In December 1302 Edward I spent nearly a fortnight in Wiltshire on his way from Windsor to spend Christmas at Odiham in Hampshire. His route can be traced from the writs that he issued; it was the custom for the King to live on the country as he passed through but if his requirements were considerable he would issue writs in advance to the sheriff of the county asking for specific quantities of goods to be purveyed and delivered at a given time and place.

It would appear that he spent two nights at Ludgershall and that the supply of fodder was a lucrative business. Philip Westprei and Peter Eleyn provided hay for the King's horses. The total amount for a few day's supply of hay, straw, oats and vetches consumed at Ludgershall came to £1–1s–4d. Peter Eleyn was the royal reeve or magistrate for the borough, but probably not its most important inhabitant for Richard de Lutergarshale was mayor of Salisbury in 1291 and again in 1303–04 and with his son John had significant landholdings at Harnham across the water meadows from the newly-built cathedral.

On the death of Henry III in 1272 Ludgershall Castle became part of the dower of Queen Eleanor—a dower being the widow's share for her life only from a husband's estate. The flow of royal income slowed, and in 1285 she was grateful to receive a gift of twenty-four oak trees to re-build one of the chapels and a chamber. The building is now being described in official documents as the *'manor'* of Ludgershall, and it seems that around the year 1280 there occurred the crucial change in status from military and administrative centre to private residence. Additionally, for the next one hundred and fifty years the castle took on its new role as retirement home for the queens of England and unmarried ladies of the royal family.

Queen Eleanor remained based at Ludgershall for eight years after the coronation of her son, Edward I, and did not vacate the castle until she had made absolutely sure that the Pope would ratify the dower arrangements that made her a rich woman. She had a strong business sense, and as a young queen had imprisoned the sheriffs and lord mayor of London for withholding the dues arising from shipping using her wharf at Queenhithe on the Thames. Day-to-day control of the manor had passed from the descendants of the Earl of Pembroke shortly after his death to a succession of royal servants until 1264 when Henry Esturmy of Savernake assumed control. After the death of Eleanor in 1291 there is no record of maintenance work being done until 1305 when the county sheriff was told to make essential repairs. Edward I seems to have been a rare visitor after he ascended to the throne, and his son, the first Prince of Wales, gave Ludgershall to his sister Mary in 1317.

Mary was the twelfth child of Edward I and Queen Eleanor of Castille, and had been sent away from court at the age of five to live at Amesbury, where she took the veil in 1285. The nunnery belonged to the order of Fontevrault at this time and, as in France, the nuns were recruited from the highest social strata. The abbess at

Fontevrault in the Loire valley was always a member of the royal family, and the same pattern obtained in England so that Mary soon became the Abbess Mary and presided over an establishment that grew to be the second wealthiest and fifth largest of its kind in England in the fifteenth-century. Mary's position as abbess did not prevent her from attending court regularly with a large entourage, and her extravagance, flirting and gambling suggests, according to one eminent historian, that she did not take her vocation too seriously. She seems to have used Ludgershall Castle regularly on her travels, and on her death in 1332 the custody of the building passed to Phillipa of Hainault, wife of Edward III and mother of the Black Prince.

Phillipa was an energetic and practical person; she invested in coal mines and encouraged a countryman, John Kempe, to open a woollen works in Norwich. She spent two hundred and forty-four pounds on repairing the roof of the tower of Ludgershall Castle, and re-built a chapel. The east window of this chapel embodied leaded glass panels with the arms of her husband and a representation of the Passion of Christ, and the work was done by John le Glasiere of Calne at a cost of six pounds. After twenty years or so the manor of Ludgershall was granted to Isobella, Countess of Bedford, and Phillipa's eldest daughter, so that Isobella stayed regularly at Ludgershall until her death in 1379. Possession then passed to Anne of Bohemia, wife of Richard II, but she died of the plague at the early age of twenty-seven and is now chiefly remembered for her support of John Wyclif who made the first translation of the Bible into English.

The next royal occupant was Joan of Navarre, widow of John V, Duke of Brittany, who received the manor on her marriage to Henry IV in 1402. She was a little old, thirty-three, and was not popular with the English people because she was French in outlook and reputed to be avaricious. She nursed her husband through an attack of what was thought to be leprosy which rendered this formerly handsome man hideous to look at. Henry IV died in 1413, and at first Joan received attention and respect from her step-son, Henry V, until in 1419 she was suddenly arrested at her dower-palace of Havering-atte-Bower and accused of witchcraft. Committed to the custody of Sir John Pelham at Pevensey Castle, she was deprived at Henry's order of all her rich dower-lands, money and personal possessions, even her fine clothes, and placed in solitary confinement. There she remained for almost four years until Henry, seized with remorse, gave orders for her release and restoration of her dower and property. He furthermore stipulated that she might have four or five new gowns of any colour and material she might prefer, and provided transport for the removal to a place of her choice. The death of Henry V took place exactly five days after her release.

Joan chose to go first to Leeds Castle in Kent, which was also one of her dower castles. It is not known exactly when she gave orders for the repairs to her *'manor'* in Ludgershall, but minor repairs were carried out to the tower gate-house and other buildings at the castle during her time. Joan was treated with proper consideration by the young King Henry VI: she died at Havering-atte-Bower in 1437 and was interred in Canterbury cathedral in the superb altar-tomb which she had commissioned for her husband Henry IV, and their effigies reside there today, side by side.

Joan was the last queen to inherit the dower of Ludgershall. The *'manor'* passed into the possession of the Earl of Richmond who held it from 1453–56, and then to

George, Duke of Clarence. George was the brother of King Edward IV who had come to the throne after defeating the Lancastrian forces at Mortimer's Cross in 1461, and the king had rewarded his brother with a command in Ireland. George was said to be a *'paranoiac young man, easily swayed'* and he allowed himself to be used as the obvious figurehead for Warwick the Kingmaker's machinations against Edward so that his plotting was soon detected. The king, to his credit, shrank from putting his brother in the Tower, and would not sign the death warrant, but on the 18th February 1487 George, Duke of Clarence, was drowned in his bath. The subsequent tale of his being drowned in a butt of Malmsey wine is probably the invention of a contemporary chronicler who could not resist embroidering a good story to match George's known preference for the beverage. His lands were forfeit, and the manor of Ludgershall was placed under Exchequer supervision.

There ensues a blank page or two in the record, for the next certain knowledge we have is that when John Leland, the antiquary, made a visit in 1546 he reported that Ludgershall Castle was *'clene down'* although *'there is a pratie lodge made by the ruins of it, and longgithe to the Kyng.'* In the interim the manor had been owned by the Earl of Bedford, while in 1518 Henry Brydges was noted as having custody of the manor, town and park of Ludgershall. The Brydges family were to evolve into the Dukes of Chandos and live at Biddesden, but the first step was taken by Richard Brydges, son of Henry. He was knighted by Queen Mary, represented Ludgershall as a Member of Parliament in 1553, and has his family tomb in St. James' Church. The castle had become of no military value when the turmoil of the Middle Ages ceased, and little use as a hunting lodge as the forests declined in economic importance. As a minor royal palace for the use of lesser members of the royal family it had now become too distant from the centre of power in London, and too decrepit to restore. In five hundred years it had gone from a simple Saxon residence to Norman motte-and-bailey stronghold to a castle complex of solid stone buildings, to grassy ruin and solitude. There is one royal connection remaining. The choir in St. James' Church retain the red robes, once the exclusive mark of royal patronage, as a symbol of past glories.

SOURCES FOR CHAPTER SIX

AWDRY, W. H.	'Ludgershall Castle and its History'. *WAM* volume 21. July 1883, 317–330.
CANNON, John and GRIFFITHS, Ralph	*The Oxford Illustrated History of the British Monarchy*. (Guild Publishing, London), 1988.
COLVIN, H. M. (gen. ed.)	*The History of the King's Works*. (HMSO, London), 1963. Volume 2, 729–731.
DUBY Georges	*William Marshal: The Flower of Chivalry*. (Faber and Faber, London and Boston), 1986.
FINES, John	*Who's Who in the Middle Ages*. (Blond, London), 1970.
FRYDE, E. B. and MILLER, Edward (Eds.)	*Historical Studies of the English Parliament: Origins to 1399*. (Cambridge University Press, 1970), volume 1.
GARAMOND PUBLISHERS LIMITED	*Mediaeval Queens*. (Garamond, London), 1990.
ORMROD, W. M.	*The Reign of Edward III*. (Guild Publishing, London,) 1990
PELHAM, R. A.	'The Provisioning of Edward I's Journey through Wiltshire in 1302'. *WAM*, volume 54, June 1952, 350–360.
POWICKE, Maurice	*The Thirteenth Century, 1216–1307*. (Oxford History of England Series, Clarendon Press, 1962), second edition.
PRESTWICH, Michael	*Edward I*. (Guild Publishing, London), 1988
STEVENSON, Janet H.	'The Castles of Marlborough and Ludgershall in the Middle Ages'. *WAM* volume 85, 1992, 90. The article gives a complete list of the owners of Ludgershall Castle.
STRICKLAND, Agnes	*Lives of the Queens of England*, London, 1867.
WANHS	Tropenell Memoranda. *WAM*, volume 37, June 1913, 550.

CHAPTER SEVEN

The Church of St. James

Ludgershall's church was probably founded in the eleventh-century, but early documentary evidence is sparse and for the first three hundred and fifty years or so it was subordinate to the church at Biddesden. The presentations, or appointments, to the Rectory of Ludgershall in the Sarum Registers are in the name of Budesden (Biddesden) from 1306 to 1446. They then appear in the joint names of Ludgershall and Biddesden until 1465, and after that date Ludgershall appears on its own. Biddesden belonged to the priory or monastery of Amesbury, and this major religious foundation in south-east Wiltshire was first a Benedictine abbey and then re-founded by Henry II as a priory of the Order of Fontevrault with the first Prioress and twenty-four nuns brought over from France. The first Rector of Ludgershall was William de Budesden appointed in 1300, and his name may be seen heading the list of Rectors on a triptych on the north wall of the nave in the church. The Prioress at Amesbury had the right of presentation, or gift of the living, down to 1540 when Amesbury was surrendered to the Crown as part of the dissolution of religious houses brought about by Henry VIII. Amesbury was initially given to Edward, Earl of Hertford, and the right of presentation at Ludgershall passed to Jane, the widow of Sir Richard Brydges, in 1566 and thence through the hands of a string of local families including the Selwyns and the Grahams until, in this century, it became vested in the Lord Chancellor.

The fabric of St. James is, in the words of Sir Nicholaus Pevsner,

'A large spreading church of flint and rubble.'

There is a Norman window and a blocked Norman doorway in the north wall of the nave. The base of the bell-tower is late Mediaeval, and the rather plain Norman font is octagonal and lead-lined. Embedded in the south wall of the nave to the right of the main entrance is a fragment of a crucifixion carving which is thought to be Anglo-Saxon; it came from an early restoration and suggests that there was a church on the site which pre-dated the Norman building. The church is in the form of a simple cross; the nave measures seventy-one feet in length and the chancel twenty-nine feet. The unbroken expanse of timbered roof above creates a feeling of space and freedom. It did not always appear so, for when Sir Richard Colt Hoare, the wealthy patron, artist and antiquarian, visited St. James' Church in 1826 he recorded that,

'a wooden screen separates the nave and the chancel between a pointed arch.'

It is still possible to see the remains of a stone staircase immediately behind the pulpit which once led up to the rood-loft above and down to the crypt below.

The other arm of the cross is formed by the North and South Chapels which are in the Perpendicular style of architecture which dates them to the latter part of the fourteenth-century. The exterior of the South Chapel is probably Elizabethan, having been remodelled in the sixteenth-century. Inserted into the opening of the

St. James' Church

South Chapel is the fine Tudor tomb of Sir Richard Brydges and his wife, Jane. Pevsner, the noted authority on English buildings and monuments, describes it as,

> *'one of the most important of its date in England. A date representing in terms of style, no longer early Renaissance and not yet Elizabethan.'*

This large monument is in the form of a tomb-chest, on its northern face it has an array of four blank shields and on the south face; in what is now the vestry, five kneeling children looking demure in Tudor dress. On top of the tomb-chest lie the effigies of their parents, Sir Richard and Lady Jane Brydges. Above them four baluster columns support an arch beneath which hovers an angel and the top achievement of this beautiful tomb shows cherubs riding sea-monsters. John Aubrey, a social historian, said in 1671 that

> *'The effigies having received some injury in their horizontal position, were for some time placed erect in the chancel,'*

and they were reported in 1855 as *'falling into decay;.* The Rector in 1969, the Rev. Peter Chesters, was a keen local historian and determined to save them. He sought the assistance of the Pilgrim Trust and obtained grants of £1,400. The tomb was restored under the auspices of the Council for the Care of Churches by Miss Inger Norholt who finished the task in 1971. The present very attractive appearance of the monument arises through the blending of rich colour—gold, red and blue-green—and fine stone carving. When repair was undertaken to the scantling flow of the South Chapel in 1972 several graves were unearthed in the vault below the monument apparently belonging to the Brydges family. The inscription on the tomb itself reads:

> *'Heare lyeth the body of Sir Rychard Brydges Knyght whose soule Jehu take to his mercy. He decessed the fyrst day of August anno 1558. Heare lyeth the Lady Jane wife to Sir Rychard Brydges Knyght and dowghter to Sir Wylyam Spencer Knyight.'*

Richard Brydges was the brother of the first Baron Chandos; he was elected Member of Parliament for Ludgershall in 1533 and was knighted at the Coronation of Mary Tudor in the same year. Jane, his wife, was the daughter of Sir William Spencer, an ancestor of the present Princess of Wales. A manor house was built for the couple from the ruins of Ludgershall Castle, and when Richard died Lady Jane stayed on in the village with her son, Edmond. When she re-married it was to Sir Simon Harcourt. She was appointed the executrix of the will of Sir Richard Brydges; his heir was their son Anthony, but he made proper provision for Edmond leaving him his manor of Bradley in Somerset and to his daughters Jane and Francis he left five-hundred marks apiece. He obviously trusted Lady Jane to carry out his wishes which he laid out in detail;

> *'Executrix to yearly receive rents and profits of following, viz. of my manor of Bradley, co. Somerset, manor of Leybrooke in Ringwood, co. Hants, my manor of Falley, c. Berks. my manor of Asshton Gyfforde, and of my lands in Penarde, Bottisboroughe and Stratton St. Margarets, co. Wilts, until sufficient be received to pay detts, and to accomplish legacies to two daughters . . . if both die said legacies to be divided between Jane my wife and Anthony Brydges my son and heir, so that said Anthony do attain 21, if he die under age, to Edmond my son.'*

There follows a detailed list of his bequests to Anthony, and also the gift of his best gelding to William Hutton, clerk, parson of Letcome Bassett. The residue was to go to his wife Jane with the instruction that

> *'She to find Edmond, Jane and Francis, in meat etc.'*

The supervisors named in the will were Sir Anthony Hungerford and Sir Richard Pecksall, who were to receive £4 apiece for their trouble.

Sir Richard Brydges had thought of all possible contingencies, and the will continues,

> *'If it shall happen my said wife, being my said executrix, to be in mind to marry again, that then I will that he that shall so marry he be bound with good and sufficient sureties unto my said supervisors for the performance and fulfilling of this my present testament.'*

'Witness, Sir William Deakin, priest, parson of Ludgershall, Robert Knight, Henry Monday, Bartholomew Downe, and other. Proved 1 Sept. 1558.'

Lady Jane carried out the instructions embodied in her husband's will; she continued to live in Ludgershall and is buried in the Church of St. James. She also left a will from which the Church and the poor people of Ludgershall benefitted. It reads;

> *'I Jane Harcort, of Ludgershall, co. Wilts; late wife to Simon Harcort, esq. deceased, otherwise called the Lady Jane Brydges, sometime wife to Sir Richard Brydges knt; deceased; Mother Church of Sarum 2s. parish church and chapel of Iland of Ludgershall, where I doe commonly use to sit, £10 to be paid to the wardens and parrishioners there at the discretion of my executors, so that they will become bound to my said executors to joyne or annex the said Chappell or Lland to the church aforesaid, and to keep the same in continual reparacions, as usually they do and ought to keep the said church. Poor there 20s. Church of Newbery 40s.*

Parish church of Argaston 40s. poor of said parish 40s. Parish church of West Shifford 10s. poor there 10s.'

There then follows a list of bequests to Edmond Brydges and his heirs, and the will is dated 10 March 1589.

The most distinguished man buried in the church is John Richmond Webb. General Webb was at the height of his fame in 1712 when he was Commander of the Land Forces in Great Britain, but his Ludgershall connection goes further back because he was the Member of Parliament for the ancient borough in 1690. His hatchment, a diamond-shaped panel of wood and canvas bearing his arms, hangs on the north wall of the nave, and is interesting for being heraldically incorrect. The all-black background should mean that he outlived both wives and died a widower, but the general's second wife survived him and married again. The motto he adopted is peculiarly apt for a soldier, for *Moriendo Vivo* (in death I live) echoes the toast so often heard in the officer's messes of the period—

'hot work, and a sickly season'

—signifying that promotion came easiest when casualties were highest. Webb commanded a brigade at the battle of Oudenarde in 1708, and a later victory at Wynendael earned him a chapter in Thackeray's *History of Henry Esmond* which, although fiction, is strongly based on fact.

General Webb died in 1724 and was buried on the south side of the chancel beneath the choir stalls. A coat of arms and the shape of a sword in the stone indicate the spot; the brass inlay has disappeared. His first wife, Henrietta, daughter of a fellow Member of Parliament, William Borlase, died in 1711 in London but was buried in Ludgershall. The parish registers show that his daughter, Catherine, was buried *'in the Isle of this Church'* in 1730, as was his second wife. She was Anne Skeate, the grand-daughter of Thomas Villett of Swindon, and her arms appear with his on the hatchment. After his death in 1724 she married Captain Henry Fookes and was interred at Ludgershall in 1737.

The other hatchment is on the south wall of the nave and is in memory of the Everett family, although we cannot be certain which member it commemorates. The most likely candidate is Thomas Everett, a London banker who bought Biddesden House and sat as member of Parliament for Ludgershall from 1776 to 1810. His son Joseph represented the borough from 1810 to 1812, and the family was prominent for about a century and active in village affairs throughout. Another Thomas Everett, for example, was the Rector in the 1860s, and when the church tower was heightened in 1870 and four pinnacles placed on the corners it was paid for in memory of Richard Thomas Everett by his widow. They gave the land and built the school in Butt Street, in 1856, and the building still stands as a private house. The motto on the hatchment is *Resurgam* (I shall rise again), and while the family left Ludgershall in the nineteenth-century the family tomb remains surrounded by railings in the church yard close to the north chapel which has stained glass windows in memory of Thomas and Joseph Everett.

Having dealt with three leading families and sketched out the early history of the building it is only right to split the rest of the church story into two parts. The next chapter will deal with the artifacts and some of the clergy and laymen that have served the parish over so many centuries.

SOURCES FOR CHAPTER SEVEN

BRITTON, John	'Historical, Topographical and Antiquarian Sketches of Wiltshire' in vol. XV of *The Beauties of England and Wales*, London, 1814.
CALENDAR OF STATE PAPERS (DOMESTIC)	On open shelves in British Library, London.
CHANDLER, John (comp.)	Collection of photocopies in Ludgershall Public Library, 1977.
CHESTER, Peter	*A brief History of Ludgershall—Church and Castle*. 1983 pamphlet in possession of author.
DIXON, Winifred	*A short guide to the Parish Church of St. James Ludgershall and Faberstown*. 1987 pamphlet—copy in WRO.
HATCHER, Henry	*An Historical and Descriptive Account of Old and New Sarum, or Salisbury*, 1834.
HOARE, Richard Colt	*The history of Modern Wiltshire; Hundreds of Everley, Ambresbury and Underditch*, London, 1826.
JACKSON, J. E. (ed.)	*The Topographical Collections of John Aubrey*, 1862.
	Parish Registers and triptych in St. James' Church.
PEVSNER, Nicholaus (ed.)	*The Buildings of England; Wilts*, (Penguin, Harmondsworth), 1963.
THOYTS, E. E.	*How to Decipher and Study Old Documents*, London, 1909.
WALTERS, H. B.	*Church Bells of Wilts*, (WANHS, Devizes), 1928.

CHAPTER EIGHT

Church and People

A village church often serves as a collective memorial to those who built, extended or modernised the fabric, and the present appearance of the Church of St. James owes much to the skill and good taste of John Loughborough Pearson, a famous nineteenth-century architect who built Truro Cathedral and restored Westminster Abbey. Pearson's principal contribution to Ludgershall's church was at the east end of the building. He saw that the chancel was Early English in style and had originally been lit by a triple lancet window, although this had been replaced by a single Gothic perpendicular window in the fourteenth-century. He advised the restitution of the triple window and supervised the re-seating in the nave so that the interior we see today is largely as he left it in 1874. The roof, lectern and pulpit date from that year, and the only major addition is the reredos, or screen, at the back of the altar put up in 1900 in memory of the Rev. William Henry Awdry, who was Rector from 1872 to 1899 and who had brought in John Pearson to re-shape the interior of the church. Pearson also designed St. Mary's Church in Chute Forest and St. Nicholas' Church in Upper Chute during the 1870's; he is buried in the nave of Westminster Abbey where he had been Surveyor in succession to Sir George Gilbert Scott, designer of the Albert Memorial in London and the Martyrs Memorial at Oxford.

The north chapel is the oldest of the two, and was dedicated to St. Mary as a chantry in 1365. Originally, it was a place where prayers were said for the repose of the souls of the dead, but it later became known as the Biddesden Chapel because the members of the family occupying Biddesden House habitually sat there. The stained glass windows and a memorial tablet in it commemorate the Everett family mentioned in the last chapter, but today the north chapel is difficult of access because a fine Walker organ takes up most of the space. This organ came from a private house in Berkeley Square, London; it was built in 1867 and installed at Ludgershall in 1947 when Richard Miller was Rector. The south, or Brydges, chapel has a distinctive Tudor appearance and is chiefly used as a vestry and for early morning and evening services when there are a small number of worshippers. It has a pre-reformation piscina, or stone basin, bricked-over for centuries before being re-discovered, and a panel displaying the arms of Queen Victoria. The parish registers are kept here: they date from 1609, and were written in Latin until 1620. Ludgershall is one of only four parishes in Wiltshire to retain possession of its original records, and this is largely due to the foresight of the Rev. Peter Chesters, Rector from 1966 to 1983, who saw the importance of retaining a record of christenings, marriages and burials in the village for posterity.

At the west end of the church stands the rather squat bell-tower, which was reported as *'long since fallen down'* by the church-wardens in 1668. In their Presentment to be made to the Cathedral on the visitation of the Bishop of Salisbury, they complained,

> *'Imprimis, we present the Church windows be not well glazed and the tower is long since fallen down and the font hath not a cover, nor a book of canons, nor a printed table of the degrees of marriage nor noe common hearse cloth'*

Whether all these matters received proper attention we do not know, but it would appear that the tower at least was repaired. There is an inscription on the south side of it which reads F E P M C N T M and is dated 1675 A.D. These letters were interpreted by a parish clerk in the nineteenth-century to be FE (Francis Evans), PM (Peter Mundy, CN (Charles Newman) and TM (Thomas Mackarell), the re-builders of the tower in 1675. Other inscriptions on the eastern and western sides of the tower commemorate the additions made in 1870 by the Everetts and read

> *'In gloriam Dei et in piam memoriam'* and *'Thomas Everett Anno Salutis 1870. Evi Crook Evan Williams Church Wardens.'*

The churchwardens were leading farmers, and will appear again in this history when the nineteenth-century economy of the village is dealt with.

The belfry is reached nowadays by climbing a rough wooden ladder, and it contains six bells. In 1553 there were only three; in 1786 there were five, and a sixth was added in 1908. At the time of adding the last bell the others were re-hung at a cost of £200, and the service of dedication was led by Bishop John Wordsworth, founder of Bishop Wordsworth's School in Salisbury. This last bell is the smallest and is inscribed

> *'Henry Charles Waller Byrde B.A. Rector, William Piper, Herbert Holdrich Williamson, Church Wardens.'*

Williamson was a long-serving village doctor, and the field to the west of the church where he kept his horse is still known as Doctor's Meadow. The second bell in size is twenty-seven and a half inches; on the rim is inscribed,

> *'Jacob Crook & Daniel Dobbs, Churchwardens. James Wells Aldbourne Wilts. Fecit 1818.'*

The third bell is twenty-eight and three-quarters inches, and on its waist it has the Royal Arms and a patent and the name of its maker—J. Warner & Sons Ltd, London, 1859. Jacob Crook was a prominent local farmer, and will be mentioned again in this history. The next bell in size is the oldest; it measures twenty-nine and three-quarters inches and bears the inscription

> *'O Prayse the Lord I.D. 1631.'*

The fifth bell in size is thirty-three inches, and is the second oldest, bearing the simple inscription,

> *'ANNO DOMINI 1638.'*

The sixth and largest bell is elaborately inscribed

> *'ON EARTH BELLS DO RING IN HEAVEN ANGELS SING HALLELUJAH'*

and around the waist are the names

> *'Henry Cave Browne M.A. Curate Evi Crook & Evan Williams Churchwardens. Cast by John Warner & Sons Ltd. 1859',*

and the Royal Arms and Patent. It measures thirty-five and one half inches. It would seem that only the 1631 and 1638 bells survive from the five bells in the tower in 1786, with one added in 1818, two in 1859 and one more in 1908. Most of the glass in the church is Victorian, or later, but two small pieces of stained glass are of special interest. On the south wall of the chancel is a window showing St. Stephen, and inset at the foot is a section of mediaeval glass. It bears the arms of Henry Chichele, Archdeacon of Salisbury and Bishop of St. Davids in 1408 and Archbishop of Canterbury from 1414 to 1443. A possible explanation is that Chichele, a wordly cleric who was often employed by Henry V is an ambassadorial role, might have visited Ludgershall in connection with the affairs of Queen Joan, step-mother of the king, during the years 1413–19 when she was on good terms with the sovereign and at liberty. We know also from the correspondence of Henry III that he owned land at Penton Grafton a few miles away. Henry Chichele is remembered as the founder of All Souls at Oxford where the forty fellows are still enjoined to pray for the soul of Henry V, Thomas, Duke of Clarence and the English captains who had fallen in the French wars. The other item of glass is in a small lancet window on the north wall of the nave at the west end of the church. It shows Jacobus Major (James the Greater), the saint for whom the church is named, and it includes the scallop or cockle shell which was widely employed as a badge by pilgrims making the long and difficult journey to Santiago de Compostela in northern Spain where the body of St. James was reputed to be buried.

Humble folk are also remembered in the church. On the north wall of the nave in a blocked Norman doorway hangs a wooden triptych, or three-panel board, that bears the names of all the Rectors of Ludgershall from 1300. It was made by A. S. Sturgis, a member of an old village family, while a tomb in the churchyard recalls an earlier generation. After naming Selwyn, Elizabeth, Emma and James Sturges, the inscription says:

> *'They were ancient and respectable inhabitants of this place, and brought up, by constant example and honest industry and uprightness, a numerous family of children. As a tribute of respect to their memory this stone is erected by a friend to the family.'*

These burials took place between 1813 and 1818, and in another place lie William Sturges and Elizabeth his wife, who died in 1717, and Sarah and Ephraim Sturgess who died in 1784 and 1794 respectively. At least one descendant still lives in Ludgershall and is a regular attender at St. James' Church. Members of the Piper family are buried in the eastern section of the churchyard, and William is buried beside the path leading to the church door. Several of them served as church organists through the generations. William Piper was the organist for fifty years down to 1913, as a brass plate in the chancel records, and he was also churchwarden for twenty-six years. The current generation of Pipers now live a few miles away, but return to worship from time to time. An almost grassed-over stone beside the same path marks the grave of John Capps, who was a servant at Biddesden House and kept a remarkable diary in the eighteenth-century that casts a great deal of light on local history in the period. At the entrance to the churchyard is a lych-gate where brides often stand to be photographed, but its original use was quite different because it was the place where a coffin would be set down to await the arrival of the clergyman who was to conduct the funeral. The substantial lych-gate at St. James' was put up in 1925 as a memorial to Dr. James E. Jones, a much-loved physician, by Douglas Hatcher, carpenter and joiner in the village, who charged £65 for his work.

A list of the Rectors of St. James' Church appears in Appendix Two, and the longest-serving clergyman appears to have been Richard Yalden Yaldwyn who was appointed in 1707 and held the post for fifty-six years. There is an inscription to this effect in the chancel. The one that we know most about is the Rev. John Selwyn, who was Rector from 1777 to 1823 and who left ample written material concerning his ministry. He was conscientious and well-connected at a time when many clergy fell into neither category, and his family had been established in Ludgershall since 1733 when an ancestor, Colonel John Selwyn, purchased the manor of Ludgershall to obtain control of the parliamentary seat. Thus it was that the Rev. John Selwyn gained the preferment through the influence of his uncle, George Augustus Selwyn, who was a noted politician and wit and who sat for the borough in Parliament for a number of years. Another nephew of George Augustus Selwyn was Thomas Townsend, Baron Sydney, who owned the building now called the Old Rectory or Erskine House, and here the Rev. John Selwyn lived as, in his words, there was

'neither parsonage house nor glebe in the village.'

Church attendance figures for 1783 show that Ludgershall was not a particularly godly village in the reign of George III, for the population was about 470 persons and Selwyn noted that he had:

'kept an exact account of the communicants since my residence which commenced at Christmas 1777 A.D. in which time I find the greatest number of communicants on Easter Day 1779 A.D viz twenty-three and the least number on the last Easter was fifteen.'

From the questionnaire sent to the Rev. Selwyn prior to the Bishop's visit in 1783, and the very full answers that he gave, it can be seen that he was a man who took his duties as the parish priest very seriously. Divine service was performed twice every Lord's day, prayers and a sermon in the morning and prayers at three in the afternoon. The holy sacrament was administered four times every year at Easter, Whit Sunday, the Sunday nearest the feast of St. Michael, (the Feast of St. Michael and all Angels is held on 29th September) and on Christmas Day. His account of his duties continued;

'I catechise the children and the younger part of my parishioners and expound the catechism to them in the English language after the 2nd. Lesson on Sunday afternoons in the summer . . . The churchwardens in my parish are chosen every year in the Easter week, one by the minister and the other by the parishioners.'

John Selwyn had other posts apart from his cure at Ludgershall. He was rector at East Coulston in Wiltshire, Master of the Wigston Hospital at Leicester and Succentor, or deputy to the Precentor, in Salisbury Cathedral choir. He died on 28th October 1823, aged seventy-one, and his remains, with those of his *'excellent wife Bridget'*, lie directly under the spire of Salisbury Cathedral. A memorial stone in the south transept of that building is in the shape of a shield with hands holding a torch above it, and his epitaph is *'Ce que Dieu garde est bien garde*—that which God guards is well guarded. John Selwyn's nephew, also called George Augustus Selwyn like his own uncle, became the first Archbishop of New Zealand, and Selwyn College at Cambridge is named in his memory. We will be looking again at the writings of John Selwyn when examining tithes and the enclosure of land in the nineteenth-century.

SOURCES FOR CHAPTER EIGHT

ATTWATER, Donald	*The Penguin Dictionary of Saints*, Harmondsworth, 1965.
CHESTERS, Peter	*A brief History of Ludgershall—Church and Castle.* 1983 pamphlet in possession of author.
CHESTER, Peter	Letter dated 27th April 1982.
CLUTTERBUCK, R. H.	*Notes on the Parishes of Fyfield, Kimpton, Penton Mewsey, Weyhill and Wherwell.* (Bennett Brothers, Salisbury), 1848.
	DNB
DIXON, Winifred	*A short guide to the Parish Church of St. James Ludgershall and Faberstown.* 1987 pamphlet—copy in WRO.
HOARE, Richard Colt	*The history of Modern Wiltshire; Hundreds of Everley, Ambresbury and Underditch*, London, 1826.
	Parish Registers and triptych in St. James' Church.
JACOB, E. F.	*The fifteenth Century, 1399–1485.* (Oxford History of England series, Clarendon Press), 1961.
	Receipt for the erection of the lych gate dated 6th March 1925 in possession of author.
PUGH, R. B. (ed.)	*A History of Wiltshire. VCH*, volume IV, 1959.
RAMSOME, Mary (ed.)	*Wiltshire Returns to the Bishop's Visitation Queries 1783*, (WRS, volume XXVII, Devizes), 1972, 143–145.
RIBA	*RIBAJ*, volume 5, 1897–98, 113.
WALTERS, H. B.	*Church Bells of Wilts*, (WANHS, Devizes), 1928.

CHAPTER NINE

Biddesden House

The land on which Biddesden House stands once belonged to Amesbury Abbey, and in the reign of Edward VI it passed, with the manor of Ludgershall, to Sir Richard Brydges. There seems to have been a dwelling on the site of the present house, and after the widow of Sir George Browne sold the nucleus of the Biddesden Estate to John Richmond Webb in 1692 the latter determined to re-build it as a suitable residence for his descendants. John Richmond Webb was a younger son; his father was Colonel Edmund Webb of Rodbourne Cheney, the Member of Parliament for Cricklade who had commanded a regiment for James II against the Duke of Monmouth in 1685, but with no patrimony John Richmond Webb had to make his own way in the world and chose an army career. Rising from Cornet to Colonel in eight years, he served under the Duke of Marlborough in Flanders from 1703 onwards. He was present at the battles of Blenheim and Ramilles and, as a Major-General, won a decisive victory over the French at Wynendael in 1708. Promoted Lieutenant-General in 1709 and granted a pension of £1,000 a year, he was severely wounded at Malplaquet and made governor of the Isle of Wight a year later. His active soldiering was over, but he was promoted to be a full General in 1712 and made commander of United Kingdom land forces. In 1711 he began to re-build Biddesden House.

A Queen Anne facade was put up facing the road, and what remained of the earlier house was incorporated into the kitchen area. A round tower arose on the north-east corner of the building to house a bell captured at Lille after the Wynendael victory, and in the entrance hall there hangs to this day a life-sized equestrian portrait of General Webb, proud and assured. When the novelist William Makepeace Thackeray wanted to illustrate this pride he put a telling phrase in *The History of Henry Esmond*. At the first meeting between the hero of the book and his commanding officer the general produces a splendid put-down of John Churchill, the Duke of Marlborough.

> '*We were gentlemen, Esmond, when the Churchills were horse-boys.*'

Pride may have dictated some features of the design of Biddesden House because its leading architectural characteristics are the hall that projects from the body of the house and the roundels adorning the facade which invite comparison with Hampton Court or Kensington Palace. The corner pilasters are crowned with classical trophies, and heraldic carvings embellish the curved pediment. The frontage of the house has altered little in almost three hundred years.

General Webb was buried in the village church in 1724 and was succeeded by his son, Borlase, who died without issue in 1738. The property passed to the general's children by a second marriage. His first wife, Henrietta, died while the house was being built, and in 1720 John Richmond Webb married a '*comely widow*' called Anne Skeate who bore him a son who, confusingly, was also called John Richmond. The latter seems to have had extensive interests away from Ludgershall because he was a

Fellow of Lincoln's Inn, Member of Parliament for Bossiney between 1761 and 1766, and a Justice of the Peace for the counties of Glamorgan, Brecon and Radnor, and it seems probable that the house was either let for some years, or sold in the 1740s, because when the window tax assessment for the Amesbury Hundred was compiled in 1748 the Duke of Chandos paid for the 98 windows at *'Bisdon'*. Confirmation comes from the diary of John Capps which shows that in August 1754 there was a scandal involving the husband of one of Anne Skeate's daughters, who no longer lived at Biddesden House. The extract reads

> *'Mr Thomas Humphries that married Mr Webbs sister, and now lives in a farm in Chute Forest, (When his wife layin after they had been married upwards of twenty years) Committed rape upon the body of his Maidservant, the daughter of William Lewes of Chute, but was put to reference and agreed without the maid swearing to the fact, the referees was Mr John Earles, & Wm Hutchings of Penton they awarded the maid £20 for her abuse.'*

James Brydges, the first Duke of Chandos, was a lineal descendant of Sir Richard Brydges who is buried in St. James' Church and whose brother was the first Baron Chandos who held the post of lieutenant of the Tower of London when Lady Jane Grey was imprisoned there. The first Duke of Chandos had been paymaster-general during the War of the Spanish Succession and had become immensely rich, but it was his son, Henry, the second Duke, and his grandson, James, the third Duke, who lived at Biddesden House, and the family was based there until the latter's death in 1789. The third Duke had only one daughter, Anna Elizabeth, and she married Richard Grenville who became the first Duke of Buckingham and Chandos. Biddesden House was sold in 1790, but at least one local family was founded as a result of the Chandos association. John Cook, christened in St. James' Church in 1776 but born a year earlier, was the son of Thomas Cook and his wife Mary, and the register shows the father to have been *'Coachman to the Duke and Duchess of Chandos many years.'*

Biddesden House was purchased by Thomas Everett, a London banker, in 1790. Everett obtained a number of burgages in Ludgershall that conferred voting rights in Parliamentary elections although the majority of them were owned by Lord Sydney and the voting interest in the borough became divided. Thomas Everett sat for the borough from 1796 until his death in 1810; his son Joseph Hague Everett represented Ludgershall from 1810 until 1812 with one short break. Joseph's eldest surviving son, called Henry, was the patron of Theddingworth as well as Biddesden, while his younger son, called John became a magistrate at Colbury near Southampton. From Henry Everett, Biddesden House passed down to Charles Everett in 1895 but it appears to have been sold or rented at this time to Mr. T. J. E. Metcalfe. By 1897 Alfred Henry Huth was living at Biddesden House, and he is remembered in Ludgershall for the design he made for the iron railings around the ancient market cross which were installed to mark the Jubilee of Queen Victoria in that year.

Biddesden House next became the residence of George J. Gribble who also took an interest in the village of Ludgershall, and he gave the Scout's Hall to the community in 1912. The hall is situated in Chapel Lane on what was the site of the Baptist Chapel built in 1815. The small grave-yard next to the hall is all that remains of the Baptist presence in Ludgershall. The Hon. Guy Victor Baring bought Biddesden House in 1914. Educated at Eton and Sandhurst, he joined the

Coldstream Guards in 1893 and served with the Second Battalion in South Africa in 1899–1900. He married Olive, the younger daughter of Hugh C. Smith of Roehampton, and they had four sons and a daughter. Lieutenant-Colonel Baring was the Conservative Member of Parliament for Winchester from 1906. Recalled to active service in the First World War, he died 16th September 1916. His name heads the list of the fallen on the north wall of the church of St. James' and on the west face of the village war memorial at the Triangle, Ludgershall. His widow continued to live at Biddesden until 1930, being active on the Parish Council, and in 1931 a Mrs. Fothergill bought the estate. From her the Biddesden Estate was purchased by the Hon Bryan Walter Guinness in 1935.

Bryan Guinness, poet, novelist and barrister at law, attracted men and women of culture and distinction to come and share his quiet country retreat at Biddesden and an account survives of a gathering that took place there in April 1935. Julia Strachey writing in her diary recorded:

> *'Easter at Biddesden. Randolph Churchill and Stanley Spencer are staying here with Bryan Guinness. In the library after dinner Stanley perched himself on a high chair in the centre of the hearth and held the floor, talking all evening without stopping, while we all lolled around him on sofas and armchairs. He told us how his Academy picture of the crucifix and the weeping Magdelen came to be painted. He had heard or read a phrase 'women wept on the high roads and strong men broke down in the side streets' and it was this phrase that inspired him'*

The new owner of Biddesden House married Elizabeth Nelson in 1936 after his first marriage to Diana Mitford had been dissolved the previous year, and they had four sons, one of whom died, and five daughters. He served in the Royal Sussex Regiment in World War Two, and became the second Baron Moyne in 1944. A director of the famous brewing company founded by Arthur Guinness in the eighteenth-century, he served as vice-chairman from 1949 to 1979 and was also a trustee of the two housing associations bearing the family name that provided low-cost accommodation in London and Dublin. His benefactions in the village of Ludgershall included the preservation of Perry's Cottage and the Memorial Hall which serves as the community centre. A contemporary of John Betjeman, he valued literature above all things, and published seven collections of poems, two plays, nine novels, three volumes of autobiography and many charming children's stories. Lord Moyne died on 6 July 1992, and at his memorial service in St. James' church on 9 July his poem *'What are they thinking'* was read in requiem. Two lines were particularly apt:

> *'Is he cast down at the thought of his brevity?*
> *Or does he look forward to fond immortality?'*

SOURCES FOR CHAPTER NINE

Andover Advertiser	10 July 1992
BRITTON, John	*The Beauties of Wiltshire*, volume II, London, 1801
CAPPS, John	Diary, Copy in possession of author.
CLARK, George	*The Later Stuarts, 1660–1714*. (Oxford History of England series, Clarendon Press, 1991 reprint).
CLUTTERBUCK, R. H.	*Notes on the Parishes of Fyfield, Kimpton, Penton Mewsey, Weyhill and Wherwell.* (Bennett Brothers, Salisbury), 1898.
	DNB.
	Encyclopaedia Britannica.
The *Independent*	21 April 1992 and 8 July 1992
LEVELL, Eric	Recollections of things past: verbal input.
	Parish registers.
PUGH, R. B. and CRITTAL, Elizabeth (eds.)	A History of Wiltshire, *VCH*, volume V. (IHR, London), 1957.
THACKERAY, W. M.	*The History of Henry Esmond, Esq.* (Nelson, London), 1906, 282.
TIPPING, H. Avray	'Country Homes and Gardens Old and New: Biddesden House, Wiltshire, the seat of the Hon. Mrs. Guy Baring'. *Country Life*, 28 June 1919.

Biddesden House

CHAPTER TEN

Ludgershall's Members of Parliament, 1295–1791

Ludgershall was an ancient borough by prescription—it was so old that although it had no charter or corporation it was accepted as a self-governing borough with a bailiff and two constables appointed by the steward of the manor at the annual court leet. As in the case of other boroughs, Ludgershall had to send two burgesses to Parliament when the king sent out his summons, and the full list of those who represented Ludgershall from 1295–1831 appears at Appendix Three. In the beginning, it was not a summons that property-owners particularly welcomed, because kings tended only to send for burgesses and knights of the shire when they wanted money, and the representatives often came back with news of new taxes. Between 1294 and 1336, for example, a tax was levied on movables in the Wiltshire towns, and in 1294 only Marlborough was taxed at the higher rate as a borough. Between 1296 and 1307 Salisbury, Calne, Cricklade, Downton, Marlborough, Old Salisbury and Wilton were rated as boroughs on eight occasions. Bedwyn, Chippenham, Devizes and Malmesbury were so rated seven times; Ludgershall was rated as a borough on six occasions. The assumption must be that in mediaeval times Ludgershall was one of the top dozen towns in the county in economic terms.

Becoming a burgess was not just a matter of money; you had to enjoy a form of tenure of property 'in burgage', which was a kind of lease with a low quit rent, and transferable. A document in the Button-Walker-Heneage collection in the Somerset Record Office at Taunton contains this entry for the grant of a burgage:

> *'Robert Attewater perpetual chaplain of the Chantry of St Mary of Ludgershall by consent of John Mervyle (or Morvyle) and William atte More seneschals (or stewards) of the chantry have granted to John and Margery North two burgages in Ludgershall in the street called Wynchesterstret between the tenement of John Morvyle on the west and the tenement of the said John North on the south, for 101 years paying 8d. a year. Witness John Pille, Wm. Bushap, Walter South and John Sabbe then Beiliff of the vill.'*

The date is 1 November 1405, and William atte Moure had been the member summoned to attend the Parliaments of 1384 and 1385 besides being a church official. Winchester Street, mentioned in the document, is now the Andover Road, and the parchment has the seal of the town of Ludgershall attached to it, although it is too indistinct to reproduce. John North was already a burgess with a vote, but in the years to come the purchase of property to obtain a vote or stand for Parliament became commonplace. By the middle of the fifteenth-century it had become a privilege to go to Westminster, and outsiders and men of importance sought election. The process may be noted in Ludgershall from 1422.

There were two members of the gentry representing Ludgershall in 1422, Johannes Sturmy and Johannes Saymour. The Sturmy or Esturmy family had owned land in Wiltshire since the Domesday survey, and the position of the King's

Warden of Savernake Forest was held by successive heads of the family. John Sturmy, who sat for Ludgershall, subsequently represented Marlborough and Bedwyn. John Saymour may have been a member of the illustrious and rich Seymour family which was linked to the Esturmy family by the marriage of Roger Seymour to Matilda Esturmy. Their son, John, inherited wealth; he became Warden of Savernake Forest, Sheriff of Wiltshire, and was knighted. A Sturmy was elected in 1467, but from 1510 the Brydges family came to dominate the borough and represent it in parliament. In November of that year Henry Brydges, A gentleman usher of the chamber, was granted custody of the manor, town and park of Ludgershall which had previously been held by Sir John Langford. It was granted to him for thirty years at an annual rent of £15, and after his death his only son Richard Brydges received a further grant in November 1539 for forty years at the same rent. Father and son were the two members in 1529, and Richard held the seat again twice in the 1550s.

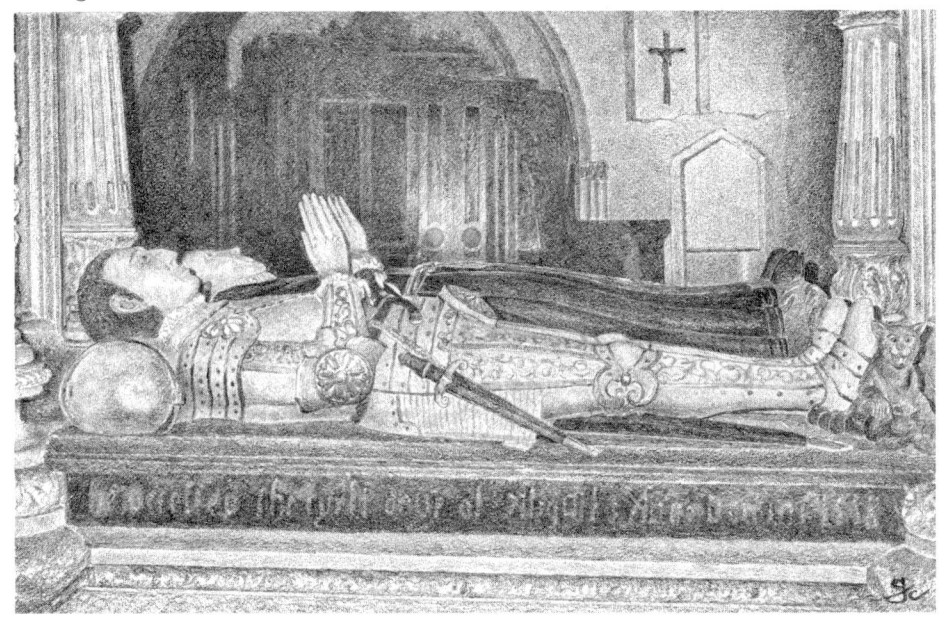

Tomb of Sir Richard and Lady Jane Brydges

At the beginning of the reign of Elizabeth I the widowed Lady Jane Brydges still lived in the borough and the MP's elected in 1563 owed their places to her. They were Griffin Curtis, who was a servant of the Seymours, and George Cope, who had married her niece. In the later part of the sixteenth-century none of the members elected had a direct link with the borough; five were returned for their family's local standing and three had connections with the Earls of Pembroke. At the end of the reign of Elizabeth I, Edward Seymour, now the Earl of Hertford, was responsible for the return of his servant, James Kyrton, in 1601 and probably for the two other members; Henry Hynde elected in 1589 and Richard Leake elected in 1597, while Richard Kingsmill who owned property near the borough was instrumental in obtaining the seat for his younger brother, John Kingsmill, and for Christopher Wray and Chidiack Wardour. Christopher Wray is the only serving

Ludgershall member who was Speaker of the House of Commons, although John Smith of Tedworth House, who was Speaker from 1705 to 1708, represented the borough from 1678–89. In the year 1640 one of the two members for Ludgershall was Sir John Evelyn. He was the nephew of another Sir John Evelyn of Godstone, Surrey and Lord of the Manor of Everleigh, whose family had established their fortune by the grant of a monopoly for making gunpowder under the Tudors. The Ludgershall member was also a cousin of the famous diarist Sir John Evelyn and he had succeeded to a property which his father had bought at West Dean, nine miles from Stockbridge in Hampshire.

Sir John Evelyn was Presbyterian and he opposed King Charles I on religious grounds. Charles' wife Henrietta Maria was a Catholic and his household was run on Roman Catholic principles. The other member for Ludgershall at this time was William Ashburnham, personal treasurer to Charles I and owner of the South Tedworth estate, in the Parliament which was called on November 3 1640. This session was not finally dissolved until 16 March 1660 and so was known as 'The Long Parliament'. During those twenty years there was civil war and internal strife with family members taking opposite sides. Sir John opposed Charles and was proclaimed a traitor: John Evelyn, the diarist, was a royalist and although he did not fight for Charles I he was in the good graces of Charles II and was given appointments that kept him in the public eye.

The next family to control the seat had local connections through their ownership of the Tedworth Estates. A London merchant called Thomas Smith bought the South Tidworth property in 1650 and his grandson, John Smith, represented Ludgershall in 1678–79, 1680–81 and 1688–89. His initial election in 1678 owed itself to two factors: the ruling court party in Wiltshire was split and complaints were subsequently made that the result arose from 'briberies or unbounded drinking'. When John Smith was defeated in the following year his side put out a pamphlet saying that the electors

'made a worse choice sober than perhaps they has ever done, stark mad.'

John Smith had embarked upon his political life at the age of twenty-three; he firmly supported the Whigs and was a confirmed Protestant. In appearance, he was of medium height and had a fair complexion. He was described as an agreeable companion in conversation and, despite his own allegiance, remained on good terms with the Tories. He was a bold speaker, with keen views which he expressed with clearness and he gained a number of important posts which he filled with great ability. He took an active part in debates and acted as the leading whip for the Whigs in the 1693–94 Parliamentary session.

He continued to prosper, and from May 1694 to November 1699 John Smith was Lord of the Treasury. At that time he represented Andover, which he continued to represent until 1713. From 1699 until March 1701 he was again Lord of the Treasury; he was twice elected Speaker of the House of Commons and he stood well with Queen Anne who made him the handsome gift of the Snowdonian estate of Vaenol. The estate covered some forty-seven thousand acres and included an elegant country house on the banks of the Menai Straits and a huge tract of country around Mount Snowdon. The estate provided subsequent members of the family with a substantial income from the Llanberris slate mines. The slate was shipped from Dinorvic to the rapidly expanding capital; there is still a Dinorvic Wharf in Westminster.

Being a famous political figure, John Smith entertained rich and powerful men at his country seat in Tidworth. He married Anne, the daughter of Sir Thomas Strickland, about the year 1684 and they had at least five children including three sons and his son, William, eventually inherited the estate. On retirement, John, who had powerful friends such as the Earl of Godolphin and the Duke of Marlborough, was given the lucrative post of one of four Principal Tellers of the Exchequer. John Smith died at Tedworth House on 30 September 1723 and was buried at the old South Tidworth church near his father. Lady Anne continued to manage the estate until her death at Tidworth in 1727. Ornate marble tablets were put up in their honour in South Tidworth Church and these were subsequently moved to the small Burial Chapel in Church Lane.

We saw in the last chapter that John Richmond Webb bought the Biddesden Estate in 1692, and two years after that he gained one of the Ludgershall seats when John Deane, a local squire, died. Webb and Thomas Neale represented Ludgershall in Parliament for three years, but they were daggers drawn because Neale was a Catholic adhering to Sir Anthony Browne's faction that had briefly controlled the seat in the 1660s. In the 1698 election Thomas Neale was initially returned, but by a petition and order of the House of Commons the result was set aside and John Richmond Webb declared elected. For thirty years thereafter the Webbs held the field; at least one Webb and a nominee, and sometimes two of them, sat for the borough. In the 1705 election they paid three guineas for each vote, while the Bruce family, whose power base was at Marlborough, countered with *'two hogsheads of drink on Easter Monday'* in 1707. Tampering with the returning officers, however, proved in the end to be the most effective way of wrestling control of the Ludgershall seats. The end of Webb domination of the Ludgershall seats is summed-up concisely in John Capps diary entry for 1734. He wrote:

> *'Mr. Richard Earle of Chute dyed in the month of April, and on the 27 of the same month, and year, came on at Ludgershall an election of members to serve in Parliament for that Borough. The candidates were my master Barlow (Borlase) Webb Esq. and John Dalston Esq. Peter Delme Esq. Daniel Boone Esq. and a great struggle it was at the polling. But as there happened to be two returning officers by name William Crouch. John Sturgess, the later which was in the interest of Mr Delme, and M. Boone, and by means of art, and power, obtained the writ and so returned them as duly elected to the Sheriff of Wilts. Who was also of the same side of the question, and likewise absolutely refused William Crouch' return, tho' carried by Mr. Webb himself in person to Westbury Leigh, the place where the sheriff lived, whose name was Thomas Webb Phipps Esq. I likewise attended Mr. Webb in this journey. But the principle person interested in this affair was John Selwyn, Esq. commonly called Col. Selwyn, who had at this time purchased a considerable number of valuable tenaments, so that Mr. Delme Mr. Boone was nominated candidates, by him, (at least Mr. Delme was), and both sat in that parliament.'*

Colonel John Selwyn had purchased the manor of Ludgershall from the Treasury in 1733, and that gave him the right to name the returning officer or officers. John Sturgess was manifestly in his pocket, and we can assume that William Crouch was a Webb supporter from his conduct. Returning officers could decide which votes were valid, and which not, and with a comparatively small number of electors every single vote counted. In the 1713 election, for example, John Richmond Webb got fifty-eight votes, Robert Ferne fifty-seven and Henry Skylling, the Bruce candidate, forty-four. With fourteen votes between top and bottom of the poll it can be seen that while Ludgershall was not, as in the case of Old Sarum, a completely 'rotten' borough, it had a narrowly-based electorate with much potential for corruption. Additionally, voting tended to be confined to property-holders belonging to established families, and Appendix Four lists the principal voters in 1772 and 1791–98. Common surnames in both lists are Cook, Hutchins, Selwyn and Sturgess. Joseph Munday seems to be a descendant of Peter Mundy who re-built the church tower in 1675, and William Mundy who owned property near the High Street in 1670, and Robert Horne a descendant of a man of the same name who bought pasture land south of the Ludgershall-Tidworth road in 1677. John Baiden is the ancestor of a family of local teachers who are still well-remembered in the village.

The Selwyns consolidated their hold on Ludgershall in 1741 when Major Charles Selwyn, brother to Colonel John Selwyn, was elected, and six years later George Augustus Selwyn, youngest son of John Selwyn, took over. In 1754 he was elected to fill his father's former seat at Gloucester; the Ludgershall seats he used to augment his income by placing them at the disposal of the Crown. In 1766 George Selwyn got no less than £9,000 for the double seat. He professed direct adherence to the person of the King, whom he called *'my royal master'* and he told Lord Holland,

> *'I will have nothing to do with any persons who mean to act independently of the King for let my circumstances be what they may, I will belong to nobody else.'*

His loyalty to the Court party was amply rewarded by a number of sinecures; the first he obtained while a very young man through the good offices of his father was that of Clerk of the Irons and Surveyor of the Meltings of the Mint. The work was, in fact, carried out by a deputy and Selwyn's part was to dine weekly at public expense. In 1753 he was appointed Registrar of the Court of Chancery in Barbados; from 1775–1782 he was Paymaster for the Board of Works and in 1784 he became the Surveyor-general of Crown Lands.

By 1780 Selwyn was so unpopular in Gloucester that, as he recorded,

> *'I was yesterday burned and today hung in effigy upon a signpost.'*

This unpopularity was acquired by his staunch support of the prime minister who persisted in opposing the Americans in their War of Independence. When Selwyn saw his interest in Gloucester collapsing, he took refuge in Ludgershall and writing to Lord North at this time he said,

> *'It is my intention to resign all thoughts of being a candidate at the next election of the city of Gloucester. I have given directions for the election at Luggershall to be of Lord Melbourne and myself.'*

He occupied one seat there for the rest of his life, and although conspicuously silent in the House of Commons was a noted wit, clubman and gambler. He feared the loss of his Ludgershall seat in 1790 because:

> *'my hopes of any emolument to be derived from it will be frustrated because, although I have done the utmost in my power to assist his Majesty's ministers for three and forty years, I am become quite useless to them.'*

He preferred to have his time pass *'with as little disquiet as possible'* but he was known to have exerted himself in his friends' interests, and spent many hours advising Lord

Carlisle on his finances. After suffering for years with dropsy and gout he died in 1791. The various placemen who stood for Ludgershall during the last thirty years of his life are mostly unmemorable, with one exception. Lord George Gordon, a fervent anti-Catholic who was probably a little deranged, was one of the Ludgershall representatives from 1774 to 1780, and in 1779 presented a petition to Parliament on behalf of the Protestant Association. A crowd of six thousand supporters gathered to accompany him to Westminster; they came into the lobby of the House of Commons and refused to leave so that rioting broke out. The so-called Gordon Riots went on for six days with many lives lost and much property damage. Lord George Gordon was arrested for high treason, but he was found not guilty. Later arrested for publishing a libel, he got five years at Newgate and died there in 1793. With the deaths of Selwyn and Gordon the last, and slightly more respectable, phase of the Ludgershall Members of Parliament may be said to begin.

SOURCES FOR CHAPTER TEN

AWDRY, W. H.	'Ludgershall Castle and its History', *WAM*, volume 21, July 1883, 317–330.
CAPPS, John	Diary. Copy in possession of author.
CRONAN, David J.	*A History of Tidworth and Tedworth House*, (Phillimore, Chichester), 1991.
	DNB.
DOBSON, Austin (ed.)	*The Diary of John Evelyn*, (Macmillan, London). 1908.
EVELYN, Helen	*History of the Evelyn Family*, London, 1915.
HISTORY OF PARLIAMENT TRUST	*The House of Commons*. Published in dated sections by HMSO and Secker and Warburg between 1964 and 1983.
JESSE, J. H.	*George Selwyn and His Contemporaries*, London, 1844.
LUDGERSHALL HISTORY SOCIETY	List of freeholders for 1772. Copy in possession of the author.
	Ms. of conveyance and lease in names of Euan Muspratt and Stephen Penton dated 1677 and 1670 in possession of author.
PIGOT and Co.	*Directory of Wilts, 1826–30*
PUGH, R. B. and CRITTALL, Elizabeth (eds.)	*A History of Wiltshire*, *VCH*, volume V, (IHR, London), 1957.
RATHBONE, M. G. (ed.)	*Wilts Borough History before 1836.* (WRS, Devizes), 1928.
STALKER, C. (comp.)	*Universal British Directory of Trade, Commerce and Manufacture*, London, 1791–98.
STUCKEY, Robert G.	'An analysis of the Parliamentary Representation of Wiltshire 1688–1714', *WAM*, volume LIV, June 1952, 289.
	Who Did What, (BCA, London), 1985

CHAPTER ELEVEN

Ludgershall MPs: The last thirty years

George Augustus Selwyn managed to leave his seat as well as the settled property to his nephew and heir, Thomas Townshend, Lord Sydney, although at first the electors of Ludgershall rebelled and petitioned Parliament to have the 1790 result set aside because the franchise had been too narrow. In the event, the election of Selwyn and William Assheton Harboard in 1790 was deemed valid, and for the election of April 1791 the Sydney faction put up Samuel Smith of Putney as their man. The odds were on their side because the returning officer was the Rev. John Selwyn, a kinsman, who obliged by disallowing a large number of votes for the opposition. As we have seen earlier, Thomas Everett, the banker, had bought Biddesden House at about this time and *his* candidate was Nathaniel Newnham, a City of London alderman. When Samuel Smith was returned, a petition of familiar tendency was presented to the House of Commons, but the result of the enquiry was not made known and when Smith died in 1793 Nathaniel Newnham became a member for Ludgershall. In the meantime, Lord Sydney had been making his mark in the national sphere. As Secretary of State he initiated the policy of sending convicts to Australia, and the city of Sydney is named for him. He owned the Old Rectory, otherwise known as Erskine House, where John Selwyn lived, and the land in St. James' Street where the elementary school (now the Seawell workshop) stands, appears on old maps as 'Lord Sydney's Garden'.

Erskine House

Thomas Everett had manifestly made a close study of the rules governing eligiblity for election at Ludgershall, and they had two components. First, the right of choosing a candidate and the returning officer was vested in:

> *'such persons who have any estate or inheritance and freehold or leasehold determinable upon life or lives within the borough not confined to entire ancient houses or the sites of ancient houses within the said borough'*

and that meant, in practical terms, ownership of either the manor of Ludgershall or Biddesden House. Second, the votes depended on property qualifications, and some of the owners of property lived elsewhere and had to be persuaded to attend. The expression used was that they had to be:

> *'kind enough to come here at the time of election to perform the ceremonial part of delegating a representative for the borough to the legislative assembly of the British Nation.'*

Thomas Everett saw that a new, and more scientific approach was needed to gain and hold control of the borough, with the old methods of outright bribery and plentiful free drink as too uncertain for his purpose. He was a rich banker, and bought both Biddesden House and a number of the burgages or tenements—particularly those with absentee owners. He had the priceless advantage of being on the spot and able to obtain by benevolence and good works the trust of the inhabitants, and by patronage the attachment of local tradesmen. George Augustus Selwyn, on the other hand, had treated the borough in a contemptuous way, and Lord Sydney was often busy elsewhere. The result was that Thomas Everett held a seat from 1796 until his death in 1810, with Magens Dorrien Magens, also a London banker, joining him from 1804 to 1807. When Thomas Everett died in 1810 his son, Joseph Hague Everett, took over, but in 1811 Joseph accepted the Chiltern Hundreds—an office of profit under the Crown that disqualified holders from being members of Parliament—to let Lord Headley have the seat. This was going back to the bad old practices that had flourished under the Selwyns, and although Joseph and Magens Dorrien Magens won both seats in 1812 they then gave way to a family that purchased the manor of Ludgershall in that year and who were to retain political control until the Parliamentary seats ceased to exist.

The Dukes of Montrose had been a power in Scotland and England since the death of Queen Anne when the first Duke was created a regent pending the coronation of George I, and he subsequently took the principal part in suppressing the Jacobite rising of 1715. James Graham, the third Duke, sat for Great Bedwyn in the 1780's and 1790's, and he is chiefly remembered for restoring the kilt and plaid to highlanders after many years of prohibition. It was a relative, Sir James Graham of Kirkstall, Yorkshire, who purchased the manor of Ludgershall from Lord Sydney's heirs in 1812, and his son, Sandford Graham, who took the seat vacated by Magens Dorrien Magens in December 1812. Sir Sandford Graham, as he became, stepped down at intervals to allow other opposition spokesmen to appear at Westminster, but he represented Ludgershall in person from 1812–15, 1818–25 and 1830–31. The Grahams retained the manor of Ludgershall until the 1849s when it passed to Mr. W. H. Maund, and he sold it to Nathaniel Young who died in 1894. Young was the last private lord of the manor, for his heir sold Castle Farm, otherwise known as Manor Farm, and the lordship to the War Office in 1898, and its successor, the Ministry of Defence, is lord of the manor today. The Everetts may have lost political control in 1812, but the family remained in the area for another eighty years. Charles Everett was still the principal landowner in 1895 although Biddesden House was in the possession of Mr. T. J. E. Metcalfe. The widow of Richard Thomas Everett went to live at Ramridge Cottage, a substantial house between Appleshaw and Weyhill, while Henry Everett was a Justice of the Peace in Ludgershall in 1881. By the beginning of the twentieth-century the Everetts seem to have moved on.

We are fortunate to have a cross-section of the voters who lived in Ludgershall during the last years of Sir Sandford Graham's lordship, and they are listed in *Pigot and Co's Directory for 1826–30* in three groups. First come the gentry, who are Mrs. Ruth Blackmore, Jacob Crook, Joseph Hague Everett and the Rev. Allen Boardman Hutchins, curate at St. James' Church who lived at Weyhill. The proprietors or tenants of the two public houses come next, and they are George Lansley of the *Crown* and Jane Piper of the *Queen's Head*—both are from long-established local families. George Lansley is also listed as a veterinary surgeon, with Elizabeth Lansley as a shopkeeper and baker and Thomas Lansley, blacksmith. Three members of the Hutchins family are given as Sarah, a straw hat maker, Joseph, a painter and plumber, and William Hutchins, butcher. The two men called James Baden (probably father and son) are boot and shoe makers, while Daniel Dobbs is parish clerk and runs the boys' day school. James, Thomas and John Sturges are bricklayers, although John is also a shopkeeper. There are four members of the Hunt family; George, a miller, Henry a carpenter and wheelwright. James is a baker and William a boot and shoe maker. John Cook is a blacksmith, while Thomas is a bricklayer. Caroline Gibbs is a milliner and dressmaker, while Eliza Whitmarch and Charlotte Philemore are both straw hat makers, as is Sarah Hutchins, previously mentioned. To have so many makers of straw hats seems odd, but a possible explanation is that the navy had contracted for a regular supply of straw hats as part of the sailors' summer uniform, while men and women wore hats as a matter of course in all seasons of the year and in all sections of society.

The fullest job description goes to John Walcot, grocer, draper and representative of the Norwich fire office, while Samuel Walcot is a baker. Other bakers in the village were Elizabeth Sollis and Joseph Purdue, and there were two tailors— William Spicer and Richard Lever. Richard Sleat, carpenter, and Joseph Reeves, bricklayer, complete the list, but Joseph Purdue, who has been mentioned as a baker, also doubled as a carrier. He went to Andover every Saturday morning, and to Devizes every Wednesday evening. The directory also gives an indication of coach services. The *Plough* from Southampton to Cheltenham called at the *Queen's Head* on Tuesday, Thursday and Saturday at noon. The return journey to Southampton was by way of Andover and Winchester, and the *Plough* stopped at the *Queen's Head* at four in the afternoon on Monday, Wednesday and Friday.

These leading inhabitants of Ludgershall appeared to live in a stable, safe and prosperous world, but beneath the veneer there was poverty, misery and want. Trade had fallen off after 1815 and the end of the Napoleonic Wars; wages were down and there was a succession of poor harvests. Unrest found many outlets, and the return of the Whigs to power in 1830 meant that reform of the Parliamentary system was inevitable if discontent was to be checked. The Whigs wanted ordered

The Crown *and the* Queen's Head

change, and the northern manufacturing interests wanted better representation. In the background, as we shall see in the next chapter, lay the recent violent protests of village working men, and in the latter end of 1831 the mob broke the Duke of Wellington's windows, jeered the Archbishop of Canterbury and sacked the city centre of Bristol. The Reform Act was long-debated, but the upshot was that fifty-six ancient boroughs, including Ludgershall, lost their representation, while twenty-six new boroughs were created—mostly in the Midlands, northern England and London. The balance between north and south, which had so long been tilted in favour of southern agricultural areas like Wiltshire, was now somewhat adjusted, although the £10 property tests for a vote—somewhat akin to the burgage test that had applied at Ludgershall since 1295—remained so there were still more qualified householders in the south than in the north. It was to be another forty years before the property qualification went, and nearly fifty more after that before women received the vote.

Local reaction to the Reform Bill was mixed. Thomas Assheton Smith III, owner of Tedworth House, Member of Parliament for Andover and said to be *'the richest commoner in England'*, was bitterly opposed to reform, and he lost his seat shortly afterwards. Sir Sandford Graham was more philosophical and probably made the most effective speech of his life in 1832 when he contributed to the debate in the House of Commons that ended the borough's Parliamentary status. His objectivity is praised by Walter Bagehot, the distinguished constitutional commentator, for the member for Ludgershall put the point succinctly to the House:

> *'I am the owner of the borough of Ludgershall. I am the constituency of the borough of Ludgershall, and I am the member for the borough of Ludgershall; and in all three capacities I assent to the disfranchisement of Ludgershall'*

and rarely can a politician have bowed out with a finer sense of style.

SOURCES FOR CHAPTER ELEVEN

BAGEHOT, Walter	*The English Constitution.* London, 1867.
BRIGGS, Asa	*The Age of Improvements, 1783–1867.* (Longman, London), 1975.
BUTLER, J. R. M. and CASS, Frank	*The passing of the Great Reform Bill.* London, 1964.
	Commons Journals (In OPL in British Library).
CRONAN, David J.	*A History of Tidworth and Tedworth House.* (Phillimore, Chichester), 1991.
	DNB.
EVANS, R. J.	*The Victorian Age, 1815–1914.* (Western Printing, Bristol), 1968.
HISTORY OF PARLIAMENT TRUST	*The House of Commons.* Published in dated sections by HMSO and Secker and Warburg between 1964 and 1983.
	Kelly's Directory (various dates).
KERR, S. Parnell	*George Selwyn and the Wits.* (Methuen, London), 1909.
	Morning Chronicle 28 June 1791.
PIGOT and CO.	*Directory of Wilts, 1826–30.*
PUGH, R. B. and CRITTALL, Elizabeth (eds.)	*A history of Wiltshire, VCH,* volume V. (IHR London), 1957.
ROSCOE, E. S. and CLERGUE, Helen (eds.)	*George Selwyn: His letters and His Life.* London, 1899.
STALKER, C. (comp.)	*Universal British Directory of Trade, Commerce and Manufacture.* London, 1791–98.

CHAPTER TWELVE

Crime and Public Order

In the twelfth and thirteenth-centuries public order was the responsibility of the sheriff of the county and it was one of the duties of the sheriff, among many others, to commit persons suspected of serious offences to the county jail pending trial. At this period the principal jail was at Old Sarum, but at times other castles were used; Ludgershall between 1259–60 and 1268; Marlborough between 1238 and 1305. Devizes castle was used between 1219 and 1242 and in 1283, and again in 1288 when poachers were imprisoned there. From the later thirteenth-century onwards the sheriff regularly visited all the hundreds at Hocktide (April and May) and Martinmas (October and November) when minor misdemeanours and nuisances, and cases such as cattle-theft, were heard. Much of the sheriff's work centred round the County Court where small personal actions were decided in cases where the value of the property was less than forty shillings. Pleas of trespass and for the legal enforcement of debt were heard, and fugitive villeins could be claimed there. Cases of beating and wounding which were not alleged to have broken the King's peace, and with which the Lord's court had not dealt, could be tried in the County Court. From the end of the thirteenth-century until the sixteenth-century there were two Wiltshire gaols in regular use; these were at Old and New Salisbury. Devizes Castle was sometimes used to house state prisoners, venison trespassers and, on occasion, suspect felons. From 1421 onwards the jail at Fisherton Anger is mentioned; it stood just beyond the Avon which formed the city of Salisbury boundary, but the gaol at Old Sarum also continued in use until 1508. Policing in Ludgershall was the responsibility of the bailiff and his constables, who were chosen at the Court Leet held by the lord of the manor. The parish constables were a very ancient institution—far older than Parliament itself. In later years constables were appointed by the Justices of the Peace at Quarter Sessions.

From the foregoing it is easy to appreciate that the administration of justice was a ramshackle affair, run by part-time and unlettered personnel and notably unable to deal with the well-placed, and a determined mob that was well-armed. The system could not deal with Lady Jane Brydges when she hid the weights that were going to be used at the annual St. James' Day fair, nor with mass trespass in search of game. The steward in charge during the Somerset Protectorate wrote plaintively to his immediate superior:

> 'Certyn of these lewd people of Hamshyre entryd my Lord's Grace parke at Ludgershall on Fryday last at nyght, brake the parke and toke theyr pleasure in huntyng and byllyng the dere. But although Mr. Richard Brydges who hathe the custody and profytts thereof, dyd not resyst them, I thought it not ryght to be suffred begyng my Lord's Grace and desyred them to remove in the mornyng erly, that happy was he that could runne fastyst nevertheless takyng many of them dyd show no manner of cueltie uppon theyr further promyse that they wyll do no more so: and hath bownd them to answer when they shal be commandyd.'

When the legal system was prodded into action by someone in authority it often created injustice. Immediately after the Civil War many discharged soldiers became, in effect, licensed beggars with passes to beg their way home, and in March 1661 a militia officer called John Mompesson was in Ludgershall when he heard the beat of a drum. He asked the bailiff, in whose house he then was, what the noise meant and was told that an *'idle drummer'* had been asking for money by virtue of a pass and warrant. John Mompesson, who lived at Tidworth and was a scion of the prominent Salisbury family, sent for the drummer and looked at his papers. He decided they were counterfeit, seized the drum and ordered the parish constable to bring the drummer before the local Justice of the Peace. There were several versions of what followed, but all agree that Mompesson retained the drum and the constable let the drummer go. One month later the phenomenon known as *'The Daemon of Tidworth'* or *'The Tidworth Drummer'* was experienced at Mompesson's house, with thumping, drumming and objects being thrown about. The drum was destroyed, but the drumming went on. Joseph Addison, the famous essayist, wrote a play about it in 1715, and the incident became part of popular folklore.

Finding the truth after so many years is difficult, but there is some firm ground. It seems likely that Zouch Manor in North Tidworth was the venue for these events, although it was claimed that people at Tedworth House heard drumming around 1900. The drummer's real name was probably William Drury, and he was twice tried, once as a witch, and sentenced to transportation. King Charles II sent Lord Falmouth down to investigate, and the Queen asked Lord Chesterfield to make enquiries, but neither nobleman could get to the heart of the matter. Many years later John Wesley, the famous preacher, spoke to John Mompesson's son to get an opinion. The reply was that whatever John Mompesson really thought he was obliged to treat the whole thing as a hoax. Had he behaved otherwise so many would come to visit as to eat him out of house and home. Present-day investigators believe that as children were present during many manifestations of drumming and moving articles the whole affair can be classified as a poltergeist experience, with the drummer having nothing to do with it. His treatment by the legal system would excite a great deal of media attention nowadays.

By and large, the eighteenth-century was peaceful in Ludgershall, with only two capital crimes recorded. In 1730 Edmund Munday, a groom, shot a girl he was courting in the castle grounds and afterwards re-loaded and killed himself. The victim was Martha Gold, who was employed as *'farmer Noyes maid'* and the killer was denied churchyard burial. The parish registers show that he was buried:

> *'at the end of Widmill Hill whose grave is in line with y chalk pit and Lower Collingbourn Church.'*

In 1757 the daughter of Roger Newman killed her bastard child shortly after its birth, and was sent to the Salisbury Assizes for trial. Elizabeth Newman had been servant to Matthew Hutchins, the butcher at Collingbourne. The girl was condemned, and John Capps records that she was:

> *'Executed at Sarum in this present month of July and the Surgeon Anatomised the body.'*

The delivery of the body for dissection was not part of the punishment; it merely reflected the growing scientific approach of the medical profession to their work where a knowledge of anatomy was deemed essential. To prove the point that Elizabeth Newman was not singled out in this way it is only necessary to refer to the near-contemporary case of Laurence Shirley, the 4th Earl of Ferrers, who murdered a servant in 1760. Earl Ferrers, the last nobleman executed in England, was hanged with a silken rope, but his body was nevertheless delivered to the surgeons for dissection.

An increase in crime and disorder in the early nineteenth-century in rural districts owed much to economic changes, for with the collapse of the Continental System in 1813 the Baltic ports had sent large quantities of wheat to Britain. This brought down the price of home-produced wheat and posed a threat to the prosperity of landowners and farmers. Parliament, which was largely made up from those with landed interests, dealt with the threat by passing The Corn Law of 1815 which forbade the import of wheat until the home price had reached 80 shillings (£4) a quarter. This measure in turn, forced up the price of bread from ten pence for a four-pound loaf to one shilling and two pence, (fourteen pence). The farmers were well-pleased, but the mass of people were driven near to starvation. All over the country men took to petty crime and violence; poaching became one way to supplement the family diet and so the government passed the Game Law of 1816. Under this law, a man could be sentenced to seven years' transportation to Australia simply for being found in possession of a net for catching rabbits. When the law was enforced in Hampshire and Wiltshire there were two cases involving famous men who were considered model landlords. Lord Palmerston at Broadlands and Sir Thomas Assheton Smith at Tedworth House were responsible for sending to the gallows-tree two young poachers who resisted arrest. William Cobbett, the radical journalist, rode into Tidworth in October 1822 and wrote that he would have called to recollection with pleasure a fine coursing he once saw there if he could have forgotten the hanging of the men at Winchester. Four years later, when riding from Marlborough to Salisbury, Cobbett, who would often stop on his journeys and ask labourers what they were paid and what there was to eat, noted that the people he spoke to were:

> *'the worst used labouring people upon the face of the earth. Dogs and horses are treated with more civility.'*

Manifestly, the growing despair was bound to lead to disorder, and when it came, the first target was the labour-saving machinery that seemed to put men out of work.

The 'Swing' riots of 1830 got their name because an imaginary Captain Swing was supposed to be issuing the orders, and the associated offences were grouped under arson, machine-breaking and riotous assembly by the authorities. Cases were recorded at Weyhill, Thruxton, East Woodhay, Quarley, Barton Stacey, Vernham Dean, Micheldever, Upper Clatford, St. Mary Bourne, and Burghclere. One of the most serious was the destruction of the foundry belonging to Messrs. Tasker of Anna Valley, and a rate was later levied on all the parishes in the hundred in compensation for the damages sustained, with most contributing about £100. At Penton Grafton on 22 November 1830, two hundred persons *'riotously assembled'* together and destroyed a threshing machine and a chaff-cutting machine; their leader was sentenced to seven year's transportation.

At Ludgershall in the following year, Henry Wilkins was charged with arson. He was indicted for having riotously assembled together in the company of several other persons, to feloniously set fire to and burn down a cottage or dwelling house, the property of William Peachey of Ludgershall. From the evidence given, it appears that a fire broke out at South Park Farm at nine o'clock on the evening of the 20 November and the prisoner was seen attemtping to set fire to a cottage about twenty-five yards from the farm. Two witnesses gave evidence that he had confessed to the crime, saying that having flung firebrand upon firebrand onto the thatch without success, he entered the cottage and bored a hole through the ceiling when *'it burnt away a good one'*. Despite his employer giving him very good references and his protestations of innocence, Henry Wilkins was found guilty and was hanged on the drop erected for that purpose over the entrance to Fisherton Jail in Salisbury.

The economic position of the agricultural labourer remained precarious for many years despite electoral reform and an upturn around the mid-1850s. Working on the land was still the largest source of employment, but the workers had to accept low wages. Frederick Engels, the German Marxist, explained that they:

'cannot combine to raise wages because they are scattered, and if one alone refuses to work for low wages there are dozens out of work . . . and thankful for the most trifling offer'

Attempts to form strong agricultural unions mostly failed, as in 1874 when a Labourers Meeting was called and the local land-workers paraded Ludgershall streets singing the *'Song of the Warwickshire Labourers'* and carrying banners. The delegates from the National Agricultural Labourers Union and Enos Howell, a farmworker from Netheravon, were arrested and appeared at Everleigh Petty Sessions and then for sentence at Devizes. The arrests were made by officers of Wiltshire Constabulary, founded in 1839, with the parish constables losing their positions in 1844. The union men were taken initially to Ludgershall's first police station at Stable Cottage in Butt Street where the foundations of a small court-room may still be seen in the back-yard, while the stable at the foot of the garden housed the pony that pulled the light cart driven by the area Superintendent.

We know the names of some of the policemen posted to Ludgershall in the early days. James Clark married a local girl in 1847, and Thomas Johnson did the same in 1851. Constables called on 'flock masters' to check that sheep had not been stolen and kept an eye on gypsies and tramps. The coming of the railway enabled criminals to extend their activities, and policemen had to meet morning and evening trains each day to look out for suspicious strangers. In January 1871, 1st Class Constable Smith was commended for displaying great zeal, intelligence and activity in tracing and arresting in London a fowl thief who stole poultry from the Collingbourne/Tidworth area and took them by train from Andover to London. Constable Smith was promoted to 2nd. Class Sergeant and was awarded £3 at Quarter Sessions.

In due course, Ludgershall became an Inspector's station, and the best-remembered officer is Inspector Mark Elkins, who was appointed in 1911. On his retirement he continued to live in Ludgershall where he opened a garage with his son, at first in the High Street and afterwards in the Andover Road. Mr. Elkins took a very active part in village affairs, becoming a Parish Councillor and a village representative on the Pewsey District Council. He was also a steadfast supporter of the Ludgershall Mission. His successor was Inspector Harry Shaw and later Inspector George James Crouch held the post. In Mark Elkins time, Ludgershall was in the Pewsey petty sessional division, and the court registers for 1920–23 show the pattern of local offences. On 25 May 1923, for example, there were seven cases. One was remanded elsewhere, and the six cases heard related to unlicensed firearms, road traffic offences, arrears under a bastardy order and non-payment of the poor rate. It was this last offence that drew the strongest punishment. The defaulter was convicted and sentenced to one months' imprisonment. Another offender, summoned for riding his bicycle without a light, was dismissed with no penalty imposed.

SOURCES FOR CHAPTER TWELVE

	Andover Advertiser 6 March 1874.
BELLAMY, John	*Crime and Public Order in England in the Later Middle Ages.* (Routledge, Kegan and Paul, London), 1973.
CAPPS, John	Diary. In possession of author.
COBBETT, William	*Rural Rides.* (Penguin, Harmondsworth) 1973.
CRONAN, David J.	*A history of Tidworth and Tedworth House.* (Phillimore, Chichester), 1991.
ENGELS, Frederick	*The Condition of the Working Class in England.* (Panther, St. Albans), 1974.
	DNB
HOARE, Richard Colt	*The History of Modern Wiltshire: Hundreds of Everley, Ambresbury and Underditch.* London, 1826
HOBSBAWM, E. J. and RUDE, G.	*Captain Swing: The Agricultural Labourers' Rising of 1830.* London, 1968.
JACKSON, J. E.	'Notes on the Border of Wilts and Hants'. *WAM*, volume XXI, July 1883, 330.
	Parish Records in the Chuch of St. James.
	Pewsey Court Register for 1920–23 in WRO.
PUGH, R. B. and CRITTALL, Elizabeth (eds.)	*A history of Wiltshire. VCH*, volume V, (IHR, London), 1957.
SAMPLE, Paul	*The Oldest and the Best; The History of the Wiltshire Constabulary, 1839–1989.* Salisbury 1989.
WANHS	Letter to Sir John Thynne published in *WAM*, volume XV, 299.

CHAPTER THIRTEEN

Everyday Life and the Poor Law

William Cobbett, radical journalist and traveller, was greatly bothered with flies on a windless day as he rode into Ludgershall on 27 August 1826, and his bad temper was only partly relieved by a meal and the politeness of Jane Piper, landlady of the *Queen's Head*. He wrote down his impressions in a passage that has been quoted ever since.

> '. . . we entered the rotten-borough together. It contained some rashers of bacon and a very civil landlady; but, it is one of the most mean and beggarly places that man ever set his eyes on. The look of the place would make one swear that there was never a clean shirt in it since the first stone of it was laid. It must have been a large place once, though it now contains only 479 persons, men women and children.'

Was it really that bad? We know that the cottages were mostly of cob and thatch, with the walls painted pink, and that there was little in the way of (modern at that date) Georgian architecture. Laurel House in Winchester Street (Andover Road) on a site now occupied by Gateways supermarket, and Highfield House in the Tidworth Road had Georgian frontages, while the Old Rectory (Erskine House) possessed a handsome Queen Anne facade. There were brick and flint cottages in the High Street, Castle Street and Deweys Lane; brick at 28 St. James Street, with an older timber-framed house now called Merle Cottage opposite. The meaner cob and thatch cottages were on Winchester Street and on the site of the present Kennet car park behind the *Crown*. The surviving chalk houses such as Perry's Cottage, Lynton Cottage and the house now called Dallas in Butt Street are larger than most labourer's cottages of the period, which often had two small rooms up and two down, with a scullery at the rear of the ground floor. The people who lived in these tiny dwellings were, in the words of a Board of Agriculture report of 1816,

> 'unhappy men . . . living in tied cottages and bound to work at certain low wages all the year'.

The parish registers confirm that life was hard for the rural poor, and that old age was probably the most difficult time to obtain enough to keep body and soul together. In 1727, for example, the funeral took place of:

> *Jane Hunt widow near a hundred years of age was buried April 4 Day. Kept by the parish many years.'*

while the village was an unhealthy place in the last quarter of the eighteenth century, with typhus a regular cause of death. This disease, often recorded as putrid or jail fever, killed two people in 1779, and four persons including twenty-six year old Sarah Reeves in 1780. Henry Reeves, Elizabeth Cooke and Mary Bendal died in the next year from this cause, and the reasons are not hard to establish. Typhus is carried by lice and flourishes in conditions of overcrowding and poverty—such as obtain in small thatched cottages with many inhabitants. It would be likely that village women were more prone to the disease because of the time they spent

Lynton Cottage and Perry's Cottage.

indoors tending to their large families, while field workers had a better chance of escaping infection. In another serious epidemic in 1818–19 there were thirteen deaths from typhus.

Accidents at work were commonplace. In 1783 Joseph Mundy was killed by the overturning of a cart at Weyhill and Richard Smith, aged four, was scalded by falling into a tub of boiling wort. (Wort is an infusion of malt or other grain which, after fermentation, becomes beer.) James Horne aged forty-three died in consequence of a fall from his horse in 1791. Some accidents hardly deserved the description. John Beal, aged thirty-six, died in 1792 after *'an astmah and consumption occasioned by drinking great quantities of spirits'*. Other causes of death were

Merle Cottage and the Doctor's House in St. James' Street.

suicide and poor health care. In 1789 Jane Cooke, *'in a fit of insanity'*, drowned herself in the pond at the bottom of Castle Street. Mary Reeves aged twenty-four died after child-birth in 1788, as did Mary Sturgis in 1793.

Church and parish records also tell us a great deal about the care of the sick, orphans, the unemployed and the old, because from the days of Elizabeth I the parish had been responsible under the Poor Laws for its own disadvantaged inhabitants. In theory, people were not encouraged to leave the parish where they were born and wander about the country seeking work or alms, and the parish was supposed to provide work for everyone. A system of outdoor relief provided sufficient to maintain a bare minimum standard of living to tide families over until they were able to provide for themselves. In Ludgershall a local rate was set by the Overseers of the Poor, who in 1796 were Joseph Hawkins and Thomas Batt. The rate they set in 1797 was two shillings in the pound, which was levied on all the major house and land-holders in the village, some twenty-two in all. The Rev. John Selwyn headed the list, being rated at £210 for the house he lived in. James Wilkins of Biddesden Farm was rated at £193 and Joseph Hawkins of Castle Farm at £166. Thomas Everett was rated to pay £80 for Biddesden House and £76 for Crawbush Farm. James Black, who farmed at South Park and Kingsfield to the south of the village, was rated at £78. The figure set by the churchwardens and Overseers of the Poor varied annually. It was as low as ninepence in the pound in September 1812 and as high as three shillings in December 1816, reflecting the degree of distress in the parish.

Hard times brought more property-owners into the system. In 1807 James Hunt was rated at £40 as he owned the windmill close to where Astor Crescent now stands, and William Lansley had to pay £78 because he ran the brick kiln. Two years later, in 1809, The Rev. John Selwyn found his annual rate had gone up to £260—a rise of £50 on the 1797 levy, while the Everetts were only paying £50 for Biddesden House—a drop of £30 from the 1797 figure. These changes reflect, we can be sure, the loss of control by the Selwyn family and the rise of the Everetts to local political prominence. Castle Farm, now rented to Joseph Crook, was rated at £282.19s—about 70% up on the valuation of 1797, and James Wilkins, still at Biddesden Farm, was paying 25% more at £245.8s. Thomas Smith paid on a rating of £103.5s. for Crawbush Farm, and the name was changed to Crawlboys around 1814 with the most likely explanation being that the new name derived from the French with croix (cross) and bois (wood) being amalgamated to make Crawlboys as the local dialect version. There seems to have been a certain amount of creative accounting at work because James Hunt was only paying £4 for his windmill in 1812—a tenth of the 1807 figure—and Henry Reeves, who had taken over the brick kiln from William Lansley, paid only £2 for it in 1812. At this latter date there is a payment of £10 in respect of the *Crown*, now in the hands of Richard Skeate, but nothing for the *Queen's Head*, the largest inn in the village.

The distribution of outdoor relief, as the payments to the poor who had their own homes was called, had originally served to bind the families of labourers to the parish, for they could get nothing elsewhere, but after 1816 it became modified to be a wage support system named for Speenhamland in Berkshire where it began. Labourers who earned less than a basic minimum calculated by reference to the size of family and the price of bread, had their wages made up from the parish poor rate, and farmers both welcomed the development because it kept wages down and complained that the poor rate was always rising. The scheme was ultimately doomed because it treated the industrious and the thrifty in the same way as the lazy and feckless, and because there were no price controls. At Weyhill in 1830 the scale of relief was halved because of the rising price of bread, and the labourer's diet was reduced to a quarter of a loaf a day.

Parliament tried a new approach based on levelling out the differences between parish incomes and distinguishing between the deserving and the undeserving poor.

The Poor Law Act of 1834 was designed to rationalise the administration of relief and the new scheme created unions of parishes to level out expenditure and income. The 328 Wiltshire parishes were formed into twenty-six Unions, although sometimes parishes joined Unions centred on adjacent counties. A Relieving Officer paid out the deserving poor, and for Ludgershall it was the job of Robert Cooke who lived at Penton Grafton. He has left a record of his duties, so that on Wednesday his round went as follows:

> *'Kimpton, Snoddington and to a public house at Shipton where the paupers are paid and receive their bread from a contractor's cart on to South Tedworth where paupers are paid at the pauper's house and bread is delivered . . . to North Tedworth and Ludgershall where the papers are paid at the house of the person who supplied bread for the contractor . . . to Fifield to pay paupers at the pauper's house and bread supplied there also'.*

Long-term pauperism was a growing problem nationally and so it was considered better dealt with in workhouses where food and shelter was exchanged for labour. The Andover Union was formed following a meeting at the Town Hall in 1835, and Jacob Crook of Castle Farm was elected Guardian of the Poor for Ludgershall. The Andover Workhouse was built in 1836 in what is now Junction Road, and the idea was that it would contain about four hundred indigent paupers and be cheaper than outdoor relief of the kind dispensed by Mr. Cooke. The Union workhouse would provide a level of care above starvation limits, but would be sufficiently austere so that no-one would want to remain there if slightly better conditions obtained outside. Vagrants and tramps would be accommodated in a Casual Ward on a nightly basis and then sent on their way.

The Andover Workhouse was found to be about 20% less expensive to ratepayers than outdoor relief, and at first the middle-class visitors found much good in the regime. Industry, order and cleanliness was enforced and prayers were read twice a day. Female paupers did the indoor work; the men and boys ground bones and corn by hand, with eighty pounds a day being the quota. The institution was run by a Master and Matron, a former Sergeant-Major McDougal and his wife, and things began to go wrong when these officials proved to be dishonest and cruel. They sold the food provided for the inmates, diverted the milk destined for the children and even made away with the small quantities of beer and gin supplied for the old people. The inmates were seen to be thin and hungry, and visitors saw them chewing the rotten bones given to them to crush. Complaints reached the Home Secretary, and an investigation proved them correct. Cartoons appeared in the national press, it was called a 'National Scandal' and the Board of Guardians was strongly admonished but the system was not dismantled, and the poor of Ludgershall were sent to Andover from 1835 to 1879, and then to Pewsey Workhouse from 1879 to 1930.

After 1846 the practice developed of sending deceased paupers back to their native parishes for burial, and these tended to be either very young or very old inmates. John Shore, buried on 2 May 1853, was eighty-two years old, and James Sturges of the well-known Ludgershall family who was returned for burial in 1878 was as old as the century. At the other extreme there was John Coombes, buried in 1857 and just two years old, and Annie Annals, buried on 17 November 1869 and three months old. One of the oldest paupers in Pewsey Workhouse who came back to be buried was Jane Cook, aged ninety-three, and interred on 1 December 1903. The last inhabitant of Ludgershall known to have been sent back to the parish for burial seems to have been Rebecca Amelia Cocker who died on 14 January 1914. The workhouse changed its character after the old age pension was brought in by Lloyd George's administration just before the First World War, and housed the incompetent rather than the poverty-stricken, but it lingered on until the 1940s. It was still possible to see grey-suited paupers walking about in Amesbury in 1944, but after the twin institutions of National Assistance and National Insurance were created in 1948 the workhouses closed or were converted into National Health Service hospitals. The Elizabethan Poor Law, and its Victorian successor, had lasted just about three hundred years.

SOURCES FOR CHAPTER THIRTEEN

ANSTRUTHER, I.	*The Scandal of the Andover Workhouse.* (Geoffrey Bles, London), 1973.
CHILD, Melville T. H.	*Farms, Fairs and Felonies.* (Holmes, Andover), 1967.
COBBETT, William	*Rural Rides.* (Penguin, Harmondsworth), 1967.
ENGELS, Frederick	*The Condition of the Working Class in England.* (Panther, St. Albans), 1969.
HUMPHREY, Barbara	*Ludgershall Then and Now.* (Homes, Andover), 1991.
	Parish registers in St. James' Church.
RANSOME, Mary (ed.)	*Wiltshire Returns to the Bishop's Visitation Queries 1783.* (WRS, volume XXVII, Devizes), 1972, 143–145.
	Poor Rate-book—original with Ludgershall Parochial Church Council.
THOMPSON, E. P.	*The Making of the English Working Class.* (Pelican, Harmondsworth), 1968.
THOMSON, David	*England in the Nineteenth Century (1815–1914).* (Pelican, Harmondsworth), 1961
	Tithes redemption map of 1841. Original at WRO.
WATTS, Martin	*Wiltshire Windmills.* (Wilts Library and Museum Service), 1980.

CHAPTER FOURTEEN

Tithes and Enclosure

The parish of Ludgershall occupies about 1,789 acres, with some 1,642 acres of agricultural land. It was, and is, primarily arable land, and John Capps tells us that in the eighteenth-century the major crops were wheat and barley. A nineteenth-century survey gave land use as follows:

Type	Acreage	Percentage
Arable	1,272	78%
Pasture	67	4%
Downland	165	10%
Woodland	67	4%
Common	70	4%

and its annual value would have been about £4,270 in 1838–41 when the tithe, or tenth, was fixed at £427 in place of the produce that had formerly made up the annual payments to the Rector. The Whig government was aware that only radical change could pacify the shires after the unrest of the early 1830s, and an Act of 1836 commuted the much-hated payment of tithes in kind to a cash figure based on the corn prices over seven years. Lists of landowners and landholders were drawn up, and they are a valuable source for local historians because they give the leading residents of a village or town and their status in society. Appendix Five has Ludgershall's landowners and occupiers, and we can see at once that the Everetts of Biddesden House are the biggest landowners and that James Steele is his principal tenant. Sir Sandford Graham is second in acreage owned, and Jacob Crook of Castle Farm his leading tenant. Evi Crook, on the other hand, rents land from the Grahams and Thomas Hutchins, while George Lansly has four widely scattered rented plots, none larger than ten acres. Some families are apparently in decline. Mrs. Ruth Blackmore, listed as one of the gentry a decade earlier, now has just three acres, and that is rented out to Thomas Williams. The Muspratts, once a leading village family, have mere handkerchief holdings; George has seven perches which he owns, Joseph rents just four and his holding is shared with 'Another'.

The former tithing system that was thus displaced by cash payments had been recorded by that energetic clergyman, John Selwyn, in 1786. He had a document prepared entitled 'A True note and terrier of all Tythes . . .' and got ten leading inhabitants of Ludgershall to sign it as authentic. The list of produce starts with wheat:

> 'ten sheaves in every Shock out of which the Parson or his Agent chuses one from any part . . .'

and prescribes the same procedure for barley and oats, hay, clover and seeds. The tenth log from felled timber, and the same percentage for apples and pears. Wool,

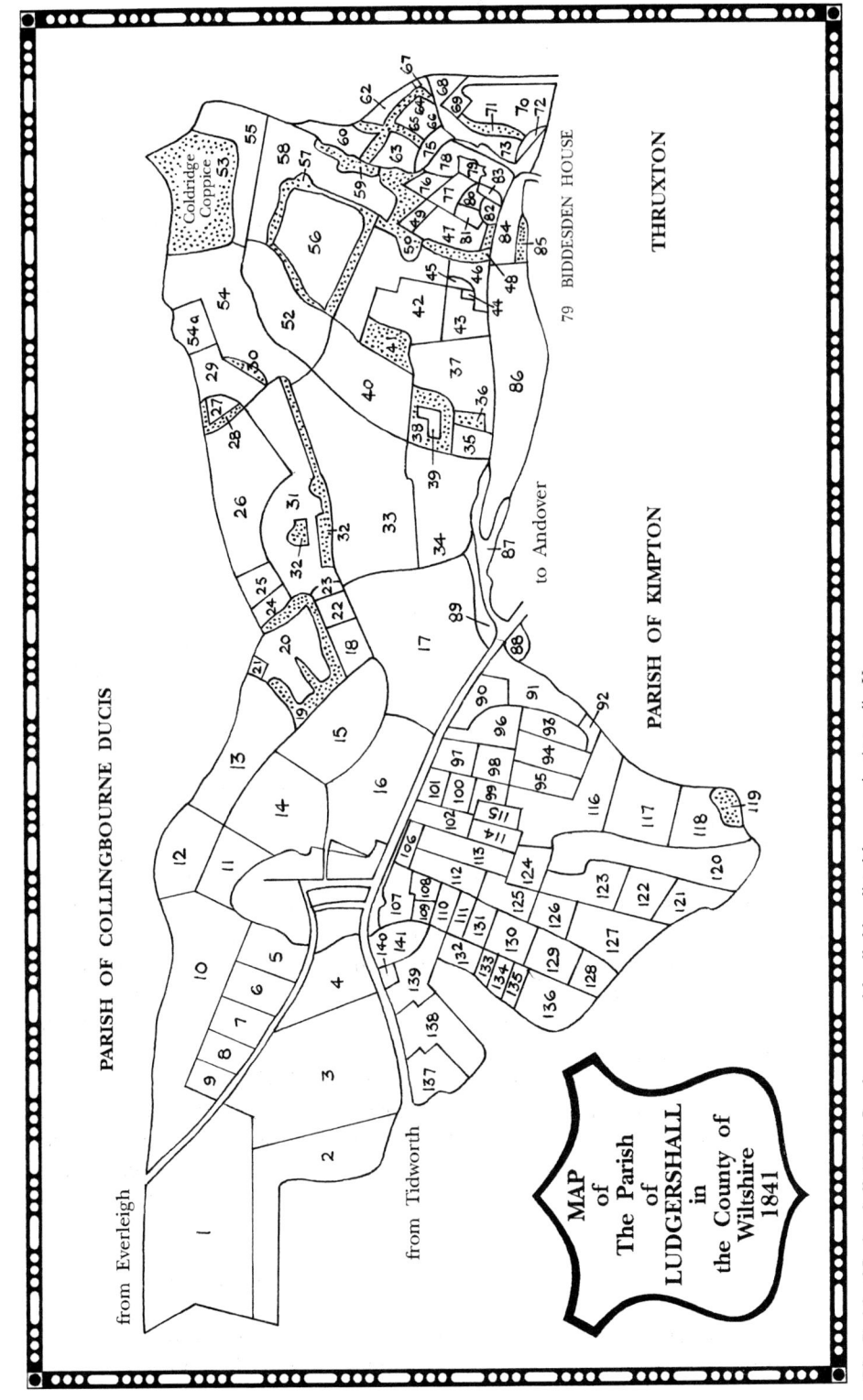

The Parish of Ludgershall 1841. Landowners and landholders listed by name in Appendix V.

milk and the tenth young chicken *'when able to live without the old one.'* The Rector had a special duty in return. The document says that

> *'It is customary for the Parson to find a Bull for the use of the Parish from Whitsunday to St. Thomas's day in every Yeare. which Bull is to be allowed to feed upon the Common called Sprayley (Spray Leaze) and all other commonable places in the said Parish free of all cost whatever to the said Parson.'*

The Parish Clerk and Sexton, who at this date was John Coombs, was entitled to four pence from each family, while from Castle or Manor Farm his entitlement was three shillings and a piece of bacon of about three pounds in weight. A similar fee came from Biddesden, while South Park and Kings Field to the south of the village paid one shilling and a two-pound piece of bacon and 'Croylboys' (Crawbush, later Crawlboys, Farm) paid two shillings.

The rest of his income came from duties performed in and around the church. A shilling for every wedding, and two shillings and sixpence when it was by special licence. Two shillings and sixpence for a funeral, although the fee included digging the grave and tolling the bell. John Coombs also got thirty shillings a year for looking after the clock and tolling the bell at eight o'clock at night from All Saint's Day to Candlemas Day—from 1st November to the 2nd February. It seems likely that this eight o'clock bell was a survival of the curfew-bell rung each night in mediaeval England to warn inhabitants to extinguish their fires and retire to rest, and in an age with few clocks in the home it made sense to signal a general hour for going to bed in the long winter evenings. Coombs is one of the ten witnesses to this interesting document, and these leading inhabitants of Ludgershall in 1786 are listed in Appendix Six (A). They are chiefly elderly men chosen to give *'old evidence and knowledge'* of traditional practices, and the document itself was preserved because it was presented to the Bishop of Salisbury during a visitation, passing eventually into the care of Wiltshire Record Office.

Ludgershall's common land comprised Spray Leaze and No Man's Ball, and these two pieces of land were quite different in shape. No Man's Ball was a lazy 'L' of roadside waste on each side of the Andover Road and Biddesden Lane. The long leg ran from Lavinia Cottage, 32 Andover Road, to the turnpike gate near the latter-day Bungalow Stores, now the Karamand Hair Studio, and the short one from the junction of the Andover Road and Biddesden Lane to the junction of Biddesden Lane and Crawlboys Lane where the last remnant of common land was sold in the 1980s. Spray Leaze was a five-sided piece of rough pasture, chiefly furze and bracken, which ran alongside No Man's Ball and parallel to the Andover Road and Biddesden Lane on two of its five sides, and along Crawlboys Lane as far as the current outbuildings of Marlins Farm on the third. The boundary then ran to the south-east as far as the footpath now bordering the north side of the Wood Park estate, and then on the rough line of Meade Road and Linden Close to the Andover Road. The whole was some 76 acres—a little more than 70 acres estimated in 1838 for tithe purposes and a little less than the total in Appendix Five—and when it was decided to enclose the common land under the 1845 Act the Commissioners gave 71 acres to landowners with a local interest and set aside five acres for allotments and recreation.

Enclosure awards were invariably complicated by mutual exchanges to group holdings together, and after such an exchange the churchwardens and parish

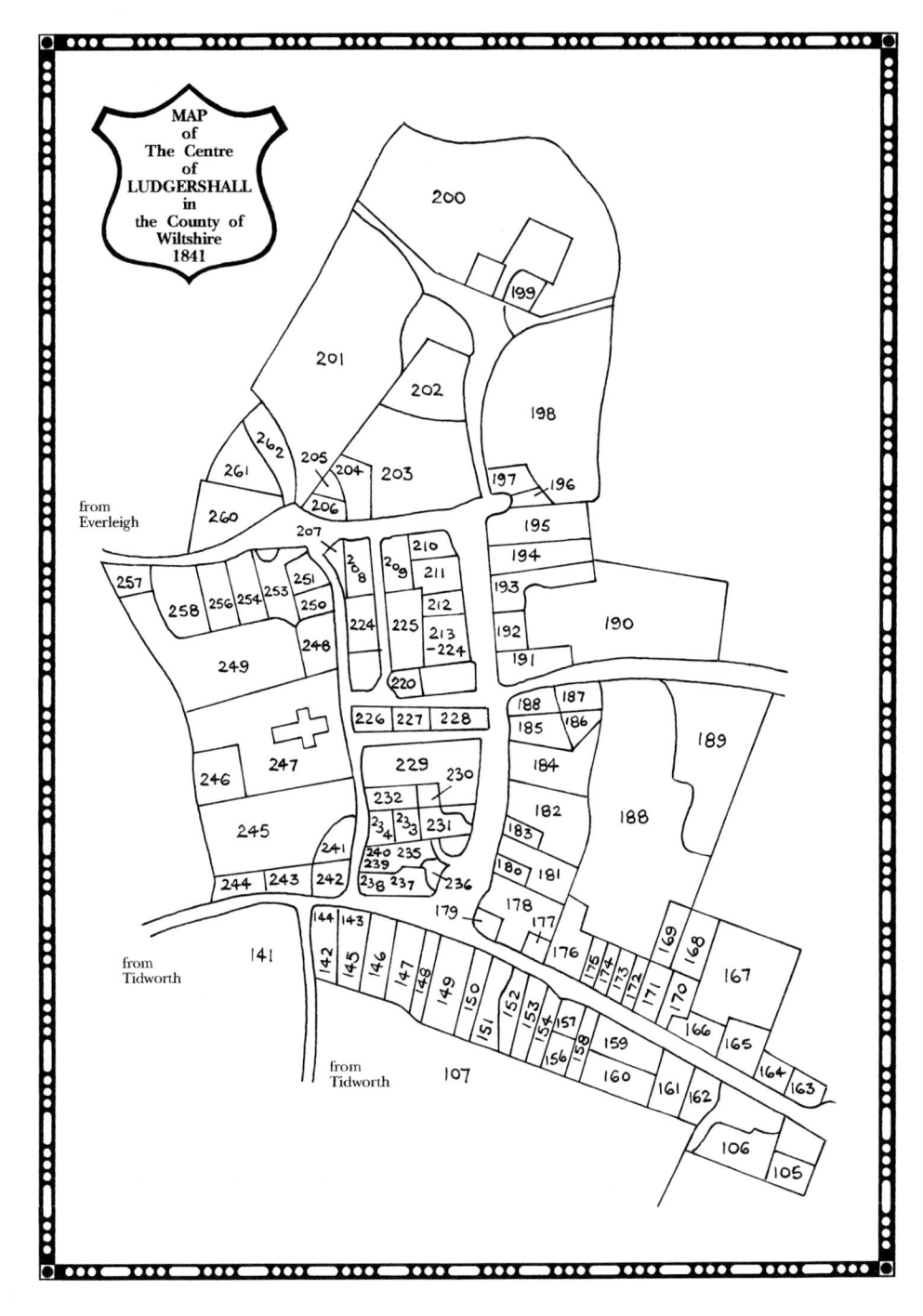

Centre of the village in 1841. Landholders and householders listed by name in Appendix V.

officials obtained two plots on Town Field where the present-day recreation ground is situated. Originally, the top portion on the Deweys Lane boundary was for recreation and the lower part, which at that time joined the Andover Road where the Q8 Garage now stands, was for allotments. Some of the land then considered 'waste' later became valuable building land. The trustee acting for the lord of the manor in 1853 acquired four acres in what became Faberstown and Newton Villas was later built on part of it. The same man also made a bad error of judgment in respect of the north side of Biddesden Lane where numbers 1–9 now stand. He exchanged this award for agricultural land at Kimpton—a decision that descendants might deplore. Some of the enclosed land was not built on until relatively recently, and in the case of No Man's Ball the easternmost tip was not utilised until 1959 when Graylins—number 24 Biddesden Lane and the home of Brian and Tessa Carley—was constructed. The Everetts of Biddesden House obtained land on the eastern fringe of Spray Leaze and adjacent to their existing holdings, and it was sold on when they left the area. In 1951 it became a smallholding where chickens were raised, and in 1968 the first of the estate houses went up on Spray Leaze. Nicholas Close was constructed in a second phase around 1971. Marlins Farm chicken houses now occupy that part of former Spray Leaze common land along Crawlboys Lane, but a substantial proportion remains in agricultural use to the north of the Wood Park Estate.

It is important to appreciate that while the last apportionment of land was taking place in the 1850s the shape and size of the village will hardly change at all in the next thirty years. If we look at the maps printed in those years and at the population statistics it is evident that this was a period of stagnation that was only broken with the coming of the railway and the army at the end of the century. The 1878 survey of Ludgershall reveals that Lavinia Cottage on the Andover Road was still the last dwelling before open country apart from Turnpike House owned by the Everley Turnpike Trust just past the junction with Biddesden Lane. On Deweys Lane the last house was number 5, and opposite was the building that is now the bowling alley behind the *Queens Head*. The road going east towards Biddesden had no houses on it. On the Marlborough road the house called Dallas, which is 13 Butt Street, was the last dwelling, and the land south of it was Bullock's Mead where Hei-Lin Way eventually arose. On the Tidworth Road the last village dwelling on the north side stood where Rusher's Shop, now a private house, is currently situated, although there was a farmhouse owned by James Hunt on the brewery site where Simonds Road joins the main road nowadays. The New Drove from the south passed fields and cottage gardens and came to the village between Highfield House and 29 Tidworth Road where there is now a row of garages. Land had been bought by the Midland and South Western Junction Railway Company for permanent way and a station just south of Ludgershall but work had not yet started. The population, which was 471 in 1801, had risen to 491 in 1881, and fell to 476 in 1891. It did not pass the thousand mark until the first decade of the new century.

Agriculture still dominated the way of life and field names dominated the local geography. Fisher's field was where the Sports Ground now stands, and In-West Field now houses the sidings that serve the D-Med complex and vehicle depot. The railway station was built on a field called Earls, and south of it was another called Late Hutchins—presumably because Thomas Hutchins had died while owning it or had sold it to somebody else. The garden centre is based on Four Acres, and Bowling Alley Park is the name then given to the allotment land on the north side of Deweys Lane. The houses to the south of the railway line at Brydges Road, Lena Close and Princess Mary Gardens stand where labourers once worked on Burgess Piece, Burgess Marl Piece, Reeves Ground, the very long Kings Field and Kesleys and Three Acres. Coneygre, to the north of the castle, was manifestly a good place for rabbits, and Shoulder of Mutton Copse on Everett land to the east seems to have been named for its shape. The industrial revolution had come and gone in northern England, but little had changed in the southern countryside. It was external forces that jolted farmers and villagers, gentry and tradesmen, from the settled ways of five hundred years.

SOURCES FOR CHAPTER FOURTEEN

	Apportionment of the Rent-Charge in lieu of Tithes attached to the Tithe Map of 1841. Original in WRO, and document dated 1839 from a survey taken in 1838.
CAPPS, John	Diary. Copy in possession of author.
CARLEY, Tessa	Personal Communication.
ELLIS, J. R.	'Parliamentary Enclosure in Wiltshire by Public General Acts'. *WAM* volume 72/73, 1980, 155–165.
	Enclosure map of 1852. Original in WRO.
FEILING, Keith	*A History of England*. (BCA, London), 1974.
General Register Office	*Census 1951 England and Wales; County Report, Wiltshire*. (HMSO London) 1955.
	Ordnance Survey map of 1878—original in WRO.
	Ordnance Survey map SU 25 RE of 1978.
	Parish registers in St. James' Church.
PUGH, R. B.	*A History of Wiltshire. VCH*, volume IV, 1959.
	Road repair records held by Ludgershall Parochial Church Council.
SANDELL, R. E.	*Abstracts of Wiltshire Tithe Apportionments*. (WRS, Devizes), 1975.
	'True note and terrier of all Tythes . . .'. Document dated 1786; original in WRO.
TOWNSEND, Peggy	Personal reminiscences.

CHAPTER FIFTEEN

The Railway and the Army

The railway came relatively late to Ludgershall and carried passengers and goods for about eighty years. The parish records show that the first impact on the village was the burial of Robert Matthews on 7 December 1881; he was unfortunately killed when telephone wire fell on him during the building work. In the years that followed the population swelled with men having new occupations associated with railway operations; there were porters, platelayers, signalmen, engine drivers, clerks and station masters. Ludgershall station opened in 1882 and Mr. J. Manning, the first stationmaster, took up his duties in 1883. (Appendix Seven lists the stationmasters at Tidworth and Ludgershall in this period.) The Swindon, Marlborough and Andover Railway (SM&AR) was built as part of a link between southern England and the Midlands: it soon took on a secondary role as a supply and personnel carrier for the Army, and the single track running through the village that survives in the 1990s continues to convey military stores and materials to two Army depots on the western edge of the village. The first proposal for a line to join Manchester and Southampton had been made in 1836, but it was not until 1873 that a private Act of Parliament authorised the construction of a line from Swindon to Andover by way of Marlborough and Ludgershall as part of that great design. The stretch from Swindon to Marlborough was finished by July 1881, and that linking Andover, Weyhill, Ludgershall, Collingbourne and Grafton was ready shortly afterwards. There were problems at Savernake for a year or more so that while Ludgershall and Andover had a service from May 1882, the trains did not start running to Swindon until February 1883.

It was necessary for the up-side of Andover Junction to be re-modelled for the handling of trains from Swindon, and the island platform that is in use today replaced the original platforms for London trains. The north side of this platform was reserved for SM&AR traffic. From Andover, the SM&AR had their own line running parallel with the London and South West Railway (L&SWR) track for 1½ miles to the west. They had bought the strip of land for this track, which was on the north side of the existing track and the L&SRW laid the rails. A temporary junction was made at Abbotts Ann for a few months after the opening in 1882, but a proper connection was made in 1917 and it was called Red Post Junction. This was removed in 1936, but it was reinstated in 1943 and finally taken out in 1963. At Red Post the line to Salisbury parts company with the branch line to Ludgershall. Two miles further on there was the pleasant station at Weyhill where the large goods yard would have been very busy during the annual Weyhill Sheep Fair. Like the rest of the Swindon Line, it lost its passenger service in 1961 and was closed to goods traffic in 1969. The line to Swindon was called *'The Tiddly Dyke'* by the local people who used to go on shopping expeditions to the modern town of Swindon, or to connect with the Great Western Railway (GWR) on trips to the west country.

The Swindon, Marlborough and Andover Railway was not a financial success, and in 1884 a Receiver was appointed. However, just in the nick of time, the line was saved when an amalgamation was arranged with the Swindon and Cheltenham Extension Railway to form the Midland and South Western Junction Railway (MSWJR). The bottleneck at Savernake where it crossed the Great Western line still posed operational problems, but in 1894 the directors of the MSWJR drew up plans to construct a double track skirting Savernake Forest and joining up with the existing track south of the Kennet and Avon Canal. The GWR opposed the plan because it preferred to keep its rival relatively weak, but two new factors came into play. The Marquess of Ailesbury rented land to the MSWJR for the new deviation, and the War Department lent its considerable weight to the passage of the Marlborough and Grafton Railway Act of 1896 which permitted construction. The War Department had been quick to appreciate that the German army had come to rely principally on railways for moving troops and equipment and, as will be seen, was prepared to encourage improved transport links in the vicinity of training grounds. The trend was soon spotted by journalists specialising in transport matters. John Bosham wrote in *The Railway Magazine* in 1900 that:

> *'The Midland and South Western Junction Railway, though but a small, and perhaps little known line, now secures enormous patronage from the War Office since the opening up of Salisbury Plain for military manoeuvres, as it is close to Ludgershall Station on this railway, that the headquarter staff are situated at Tedworth House, and Perham Down Camp is within three-quarters of a mile of the station. Ludgershall has been provided with special loading docks and sidings for the speedy entrainment or detraining of troops and horses, the station yard being lighted by large electric lamps, so that soldiers may be loaded or unloaded at any hour of the night.'*

Salisbury Plain had first been used as a site for large-scale military manoeuvres in 1872 which ended on 12 September with a royal review. This took place at Bulford on the slopes below Beacon Hill when at noon: *'a royal salute announced the arrival of the Prince of Wales who was received by the Duke of Cambridge and a very numerous staff of general officers including the foreign military representatives.'* The march past that followed took one hour and forty minutes as thirty thousand men passed the saluting base and it was followed by a trot past of mounted troops and, finally, a grand parade of the whole army. Further manoeuvres were held on the Plain in 1898 but on that occasion the final review was held at Boscombe Down and fifty thousand men were involved. The Military Lands Act of 1892 gave the Secretary of State the power to purchase and lease land for military purposes and the War Department had decided that the Plain was suitable for their plans. There was some opposition by landowners initially, but as was reported in the local press, sale of the land would help to promote movement and prosperity all round.

> *'The markets will be stimulated, small cultivators of fruit and vegetables and poultry owners will benefit immensely, and the decaying villages and farms on Salisbury Plain will ere long, participate in the general improvement . . . I for one rejoice that Salisbury Plain is likely to realise its manifest destiny as the training ground of the British Army.'* So wrote Sir Henry Malet of Wilbury Park, Newton Tony, and he further pointed out that, *'The greater part of the land in question has long been practically unsalable on any terms.'*

The owner of Tedworth Estates, Sir John Williams Kelk, was willing to sell and his substantial property was purchased by the government on 29 September 1897. It included Tedworth House, which was subsequently used as a headquarters, thirteen farms, eight farm-houses, one hundred and seven cottages and the *Ram*

Hotel, all at a total cost of £95,000. In the summer of 1897 the War Department also acquired Manor Farm, or Castle Farm as it is known locally at Ludgershall, and with it land covering some 666 acres at a cost of £9,350. The purchase was completed on 31 October 1898, but during the latter part of the year further consideration was given to the exchange or purchase of several other small areas of land to the south of Ludgershall which would round off the boundary of the training area.

Sir John William Kelk's estate had included the land which came to be known as Perham Down, and as early as the spring of 1898 it, and an area at Windmill Hill, were classified as official camping sites for the troops. With the coming of the army and the railway on its doorstep, Ludgershall was to see an irreversible change to its former agricultural status. Henceforth, it was to have a service role in both meanings of the term.

From the beginning of the new century, Ludgershall station was a very busy and active place. The railway staff were kept on their toes at the time of the summer manoeuvres, often working a twelve-hour day for six days a week and with no overtime or special Sunday rates of pay but time off in lieu. The station was extended between 1900 and 1902; a turntable and a small engine shed were added, and in 1901 a corrugated iron goods shed costing £400 was built near the turntable. Ancillary to the railway were the services supplied by Messrs. Simonds of Reading who, at the time of the summer camps on the Plain, supplied beer and other refreshment to the thirsty troops at Perham Camp and Windmill Hill and beyond. Local traders, such as E. E. Roy, expanded to meet the requirements for canvas awnings, tents and furniture. With the decision to build a permanent camp at Tidworth, the general manager of the MSWJR, who was quick to spot the possibilities of building a branch line from Ludgershall, obtained an agreement with the War Department to do so. Built on War Department land, it cost £47,905 11s. 9d and it was opened for military traffic on 8 July 1901. Further agreements ensured that the line was open to traffic initiated by traders approved by the War Department and to passengers, including the general public, on 1 October 1902. The traffic department of the MSWJR employed sixteen men each at Ludgershall and Tidworth; the porters, who were the majority of the workforce, looked extremely smart in their uniforms of green corduroy trousers, sleeved waistcoat jackets and pill-box hats.

The Tidworth link line was invaluable for carrying the building materials required to build the extensive barracks which were planned for the garrison. The main building contractor, Henry Lovatt of Wolverhampton, had permission to put a siding on the line at Brimstone Bottom which is situated in a hollow about a mile from Ludgershall on the Tidworth road. This was to enable him to carry his workmen in trains from the temporary work-camp at Brimstone Bottom to Tidworth to build the barracks. The men were carried to Tidworth daily in open goods wagons and the service was known to them as the *'Tin Town Mail'*. The camp at Brimstone Bottom consisted of rows of corrugated-iron huts, and from a contemporary post-card it would appear that several hundred men could have been accommodated there. The site, for obvious reasons, was known humourously as *'Tin Town'*. Two at least of the huts were still on the site and occupied until the 1950's, and one other reminder of these men is the footpath which they made from

Tin Town across the fields to Ludgershall in search of a quiet pint and a game of darts at the end of the day. This route is now Parish Footpath No. 1, and part of it is used daily by the residents of the new housing development which lies south of the railway line as a short-cut to the village shops and school. There was, at the time of the building of the barracks in Tidworth, an isolation hospital at Brimstone Bottom and a tin church. The last inhabitant of Tin Town was George Gamble, who has descendants in Ludgershall.

The railway made it possible for the bricks made at Dodsdown near Bedwyn to be transported direct to the site of building operations at Tidworth. From Grafton station a standard-gauge mineral line was laid running eastwards for about two miles to the brickworks at Dodsdown. The Marquess of Ailesbury, who owned the mineral rights on the land, leased them to A. J. Keeble of Peterborough who built the line from Grafton and worked it with two steam locomotives, paying the Marquess a yearly fee of £50 for wayleaves. The rails were lifted in 1910 when the military construction work on Salisbury Plain had ended. At the same time that the barracks were being built in Tidworth, a rather grand Gothic red-brick hotel was built adjacent to the station at Ludgershall. Called *'The Prince of Wales Hotel'* it had twenty-four bedrooms in anticipation of the many military guests and their wives who would soon be passing through the busy junction. Built on the site of the old *Prince of Wales* Inn which was kept by the Weeks family, the hotel which had been erected with such high hopes never did fulfill the expectations of its promoters, failing to attract sufficient customers for its hotel rooms. Several adaptations were made to it over the years and at the time of the Second World War there were lively parties in its spacious and comfortable bars. In the 1980s it was used by the firm still trading as E. E. Roy as a furniture store, but in the 1990s only the handsome turreted facade was retained when it was converted into luxury flats.

The development of the railway to include a branch line to Tidworth made it necessary to enlarge the station at Ludgershall to accommodate the extra traffic. The original station was planned with a simple layout of two tracks providing crossing facilities and serving two platforms. The new platforms covered a considerable area to cope with the movement of soldiers, with as many as ten train-loads arriving in a day. After the expansion at Ludgershall, the platforms were connected by a lattice work footbridge providing access from the booking office to both platforms with the long downside extending almost to the Tidworth Road. Gates and a ramp were available for milk traffic and parcels. A parcel could be delivered from the station to houses in the village for one *old* penny provided that it weighed less than seven pounds by the local agent, Chaplin and Co., whose office was near to the station. A photograph taken in 1917 shows a Mr. Pollard, who worked for the agents, dressed in cap and jacket with one hand thrust into his breeches pocket. He is wearing boots and leather gaiters—a serviceable outfit for travelling the sometimes muddy and sometimes dusty roads around the village. Further additions and modifications were made to the station at Ludgershall during and after the First World War: an improved signalling system in 1918, and a second signal box beyond the yard, and around the curve of the Tidworth branch. It was known as the Perham Signal Cabin and behind it a garden was created which

The *Prince of Wales Hotel*.

grew not only vegetables but a bright mass of flowers well fertilised by the horse-manure which was one of the chief exports from the cavalry at Tidworth. One load, delivered in 1920, must have been considerable for it cost nine shillings—equivalent to £20 today.

The station at Ludgershall was used in preference to that at Tidworth on the occasion of the visit of King George V on 8 November 1917. The King travelled in the Royal Train, and then rode on his charger to Perham Down to carry out an inspection of troops. His stay lasted three days, and the Royal Train, which was a London and North Western Railway unit, was kept in the bay platform while the King's horses were conveyed in London and South Western Railway standard sixteen and twenty-one feet horse-boxes. Traffic from Ludgershall onto the branch line to the station at Tidworth was very heavy also in the Second World War. Every week three wagon-loads of flour were sent from Avonmouth to be turned into bread at the military bakehouse opposite the barracks named Jellalabad. Once a fortnight a special meat train arrived, and at regular intervals large consignments of coal were delivered which was used in cooking stoves and for heating purposes. Not only the serving soldiers were provided for out of these supplies; families also received a coal ration delivered to married quarters and a food ration. The food ration had to be fetched from the quartermaster's store, and during the Second World War it was often my duty to ride on a bicycle to the cookhouse at Jellalabad barracks with a small ration sack in the basket to collect the weekly ration assigned to us. If the cook was feeling generous, he popped in a few extras including such rare delicacies as dried sultanas and apricots.

Ordnance supplies, horses and men formed the bulk of goods and passengers carried on the railway to Tidworth in both world wars. Sometimes, whole units arrived and departed from the eastern platform which was 828 ft (250 m.) long and

20 ft. (12 m.) wide. Civilian and individual service personnel used the western platform, which was where the station buildings were situated and where the Naafi shop now stands, and was less than half the length of the eastern platform. Altogether the annual receipts from Tidworth were more than the combined total from all other MSWJR stations, and the stationmaster at Tidworth was the highest-ranking on the line. Pride in their status was the mark of all railwaymen in this period, as two photographs taken in 1913 reveal. One shows Ernest Godwin, stationmaster at Tidworth, with his staff. They were smartly dressed; the stationmaster's hat bears gold braid on its peak. In the background is Dick Williams, who began his career as a telegraphist and ended by being the GWR yardmaster at Swindon in World War Two. A picture taken at Ludgershall shows Jim Barlow, Bill Walker and Clayton Cowley at the base of the footbridge. They are similarly smartly dressed, and the message is clear. A young man born in a village is not necessarily destined only for agricultural work. The railway both gives jobs and carries the job-seeker to towns where a wider range of opportunities exists.

SOURCES FOR CHAPTER FIFTEEN

	Andover Advertiser, 22 April 1892.
BARTHOLOMEW, David	*Midland and South Western Junction Railway.* (Wild Swan Publications), 1982.
BOSHAM, John	'How the Railways Assist the War Office'. *The Railway Magazine*, January 1900.
BRIDGEMAN, Brian, BARRETT, David and BIRD, Dennis	*Swindon's Other Railway.* (Red Brick, Swindon), 1985.
BUNCE, Hilda	Personal Reminiscences.
CASEBOURNE, U. W. R.	'The Industrial Archaeology of G.W.R. Secondary Main Lines in Wilts'. *WAM*, volume 74/75, 1981.
FAIRMAN, J. R.	'Andover Junction and Town'—pamphlet in possession of author.
JAMES, N. D. G.	*Plain Soldiering.* (The Hobnob Press, Salisbury), 1986.
	Kelly's Directory (various dates).
MAGGS, Colin G.	*The Midland and South Western Junction Railway.* (David & Charles, Newton Abbott), 1967.
	Parish records in the church of St. James.
SANDS, T. B.	*The Midland and South Western Junction Railway.* (Compfield Press, St. Albans), 1959.
VINES, Sidney	'How the Army came to Salisbury Plain'. *The Hatcher Review*, volume 2, number 20, Autumn 1985.

CHAPTER SIXTEEN

The Railway from 1918 to closure in 1964

A slow contraction of demand for freight and passenger carrying followed the Armistice in November 1918, and as the country returned to a peace-time economy the Midland and South Western Junction Railway experienced financial hardship and sought amalgamation. The Railway Act 1921 prepared the way, and on 1 July 1923 the line passed under Great Western Railway control. One immediate advantage for the people of Ludgershall was that it was now possible to travel to Swindon, change at Swindon Town and Swindon Junction stations, and travel anywhere on the GWR network with a single ticket. Similarly, those seeking to attend the Tidworth Tattoo could make the journey from all parts of the country by rail, changing to the branch line at Ludgershall. Freight carriage began to be specialist in character, and G. Rawlings and Sons, local coal merchants, had their own wagons to bring in domestic fuel to their depot in Tidworth Road. The Navy, Army and Air Force Institute (NAAFI) had a substantial depot and warehouse in Simonds Road that used the railway for bulk shipments, as did George Younger and Sons, brewers, whose office was at Perham House, built in 1898 in the heart of the village, and now the home of Aileen and James Cowen.

The Regular Army lived the year round in barracks, but the Territorials came to Windmill Hill and Hedge End tented camps each summer for annual training. For example, the 144th Gloucester and Worcester Territorial Infantry Brigade came to camp near Ludgershall in 1927, 1930, 1935, 1937 and 1939. The *Andover Advertiser* reported in 1939 that:

> 'The streets of Ludgershall echoed with marching feet on Sunday, when nearly 4,000 Territorials—the largest camp ever to arrive for a local peace-time camp—marched to Windmill Hill and Hedge End from the Railway Station. Coming by special train from all parts of Gloucester and Worcester, they comprised the three Battalions of the 144th. (Gloucester and Worcester) Territorial Infantry Brigade, and these units marched to Windmill Hill, some via the road to Sweet Apple Farm, and others by the road through the village to enter via the Collingbourne Road. The other unit, the 6th. (City of Bristol) Battalion Gloucester Regiment, which on the last occasion was part of the Brigade, is now a mixed Tank Battalion and is stationed at Hedge End for a fortnight.'

In the following year the railway bore the heaviest burdens in its history with seven troop trains passing through to Tidworth at the same time. They carried French soldiers evacuated from Dunkirk and put on trains at Dover, and eye-witnesses confirm that their morale was low. Conrad Dixon, living at the time at Clarendon Terrace in Tidworth, noted that on arrival at Aliwal, Assaye and Candahar barracks they piled their arms in a pyramid on the parade grounds and vowed to fight no more. Few of them joined General de Gaulle and the Free French; most left by train a month or so later and were repatriated by way of North Africa.

Thereafter, although troop trains continued to run regularly until 1946 the numbers involved tended to fall as road transport was increasingly used. The last mass movement of soldiers by rail took place in 1962 when the 51st Ghurka Regiment, complete with auxiliary troops and families, arrived at Tidworth in two trains and was welcomed by a military band. The transport by rail of personnel was in steep decline from 1950, but the movement of military material has not ceased although type and destination has changed much over the years.

The tented camp at Hedge End was on land bought by the War Department in 1897 and adjacent to Simonds Road, and when World War Two was seen to be inevitable the first permanent buildings were constructed. In 1939 they were the basis of a Mobilisation Depot, and then No. 1 Impressed Vehicle Camp was set up on the site. Between 1941 and 1943 it became a Clothing Sub-Depot and a Command Ordnance Depot, and was known to those who worked there as Hedge End Depot. Australian troops camped along Somme Road leading to Perham Down, so that the Junction of Somme Road and the Tidworth Road opposite Tidworth Down School became known as Kangaroo Corner. The Australians are remembered in Ludgershall as robust soldiery with an independent approach to their work. They would block the road with a human chain to get on buses and at weekends, and during an invasion scare, fired at any aircraft overhead. On one occasion they severely frightened an Imperial Airways pilot who flew low over the camp in a type of large biplane they had not seen before, and they ranged their bren guns on local features. When, in 1990, the weathervane of St. James' Church was replaced it was found to be pockmarked with bullet-holes—a souvenir of the Australian presence of fifty years before.

The railway siding running right into the depot was built by the Americans in 1943–44 when sheds 93, 97 and 100 were put up to house vehicles. It is said that crated jeep kits arrived by rail and were unpacked and assembled in these sheds, being finally driven out at the far end. After D-Day in 1944 a prisoner-of-war camp was set up at Kangaroo Corner complete with watch-towers and barbed wire, and the huts that composed it later became temporary accommodation for local families in the post-war period of severe housing shortage, so that at least one Ludgershall man was born in these rounded corrugated-iron huts with a brick chimney at the gable end. The depot on the other side of Somme Road became a Returned Store in 1946 when the army was running down, but was up-graded as the Armoured Fighting Vehicle Depot in 1947. It has retained this latter function to the present day, with the railway link still in operation and access by means of a level crossing over the Tidworth Road. At the time of writing, the vehicle depot is experiencing such demand for storage that a field to the south has been pressed into service with thick barbed wire protecting the massed military vehicles from potential evil-doers.

At the time the armoured vehicle depot was being created the Royal Army Medical Corps store was being transferred from Woolwich to Ludgershall, and the sidings flanking the line to Swindon were enlarged. The buildings that went up off the Marlborough Road were called the Army Medical Equipment Depot originally, and the first commandant was Lieutenant Colonel Herbert Prince. His son, Albert Prince, married Denise Edmonds, daughter of Ludgershall's dentist, and was himself a much respected village dentist. The couple still live in retirement at

Ivy House, having brought up a family in the village and taken a leading part in local affairs over the years. The establishment had a change of name in 1969 when it became the Defence Medical Equipment Depot, or D.Med, and was rebuilt between 1971 and 1982 to supply medical stores to all three armed services. The flow of military stores to and from these depots saved the railway line, but not its civilian role. The Great Western Railway was absorbed into a nationalised grouping in 1948 which began to shed branch lines in the early 1960s. Passenger trains to and from Ludgershall were withdrawn in 1961, and northgoing freight services stopped shortly thereafter. In 1964 all freight services stopped. The line from Ludgershall to Red Post Junction, about a mile and a half from Andover, remains as a single-track military railway serving the two Ludgershall depots.

What was it like to travel on the old Great Western Railway? It was slow, the carriages were grubby and if you leaned out of the window you got smuts in your eye. The good point was that you could get almost anywhere in the country by train, although a journey was a serious event which was normally only undertaken when on business, when taking an annual holiday, or when returning home from a job in the city. It was on the occasion of going home in 1946 that the author last travelled on the GWR line to Ludgershall and Tidworth. It was Christmas Eve and as a young civil servant I had a week's leave. From Watford by the underground railway I had travelled into London and, by changing trains at Bakerloo Station, reached Waterloo. At Waterloo I waited until the train that would take me to Andover arrived at the platform. There was quite a crowd waiting at the barrier, and as the train came in they jostled one-another past the ticket inspector and clambered in. 'Come on gel, I'll give you a hand with that case', said a little soldier holding open the carriage door. Shyly, I thanked him and we settled down to the journey. He also was going to Tidworth, back from leave. The sky was getting very dark and it was cold outside; inside the windows began to steam up. There was loud laughter in the next carriage as the bottle of Christmas cheer passed around. At Andover there was a wait before the train that would take us to Ludgershall was due and I went into the station buffet to get out of the wind. It seemed an age, but eventually it steamed in and we were off again; now it was completely dark outside as we puffed along. Once more we changed trains at Ludgershall and at last were on the fifth train that would take us home. As the steam locomotive chugged around the last bend that twisted around Windmill Hill the lights of the camp came into view and it began to snow. Five trains and five hours, but in the pre-car era the railway was the only sure way of getting home.

What remains of Ludgershall Station that once covered sixteen acres? The bridge carrying the Tidworth Road across the single remaining line to the vehicle depot on the Hedge End site that once was a sea of bell tents, and an old brick lamp room nearby. The houses of Eleanor Court stand on the platform, with only the name of Station Approach to remind the curious that this was once the largest station on the only line to cross Wiltshire from south to north. The Midland and South Western Junction Railway was unique in having a route across the grain of the country to link the industrial Midlands with South Coast Ports, for the other railways are on east-west axis and their focus is London. The surviving line continues to have a north-south function, with one terminus at Ludgershall and the other at Marchwood, a military port on Southampton Water. Its last significant impact on the national consciousness came in the early 1980s when trainloads of white-painted vehicles rumbled south to be embarked for the Falklands War, and watchers noted that it just about eighty years since the line had performed the same service for the vehicles of Queen Victoria's red-coated soldiers when transporting material for that other southern hemisphere war in South Africa.

SOURCES FOR CHAPTER SIXTEEN

	Andover Advertiser, 11 August 1939.
BARTHOLOMEW, David	*Midland and South Western Junction Railway*. (Wild Swan Publications), 1982.
BUNCE, Hilda	Personal reminiscence.
COBBAN, Alfred	*A History of Modern France*, volume 3. (Penguin, Harmondsworth), 1972.
DIXON, Conrad	Personal reminiscence.
HUMPHREY, Barbara	*Ludgershall Then and Now*. (Holmes, Andover), 1991.
JAMES, N. D. G.	*Plain Soldiering*. (The Hobnob Press, Salisbury), 1986.
MacDERMOT, E. T.	*History of the Great Western Railway*. (GWR, 1927).
PRINCE, Denise	Personal reminiscence.
SANDS, T. B.	*The Midlands and South Western Junction Railway*. (Compfield Press, St. Albans), 1959.

CHAPTER SEVENTEEN

Ludgershall's Schools from the beginning to 1920

The Rev. John Selwyn was able to say categorically that there was no school in the village in 1783, but he manifestly decided to set one up early in his long ministry because a return made in 1818 reported that there were:

> *'A Sunday School established in 1786 and supported by the Rector consisting of twenty boys and girls and a day school of industry maintained by the Rector's family for fifteen girls who are clothed once a year and one Sunday School belonging to the Methodists containing about twenty-five children'.*

making two Sunday Schools and a *'day school of industry'* that can be seen as the forerunner of regular daily instruction for children in Ludgershall. This first school seems to have been founded on the initiative of a neighbouring landowner because at the Enquiry into Charitable Benefactions held in 1905 it was said that:

> *'There is a tradition in the parish that Sir William Meadows who died about eighteen years ago and who resided in Conholt Park in the Parish of Chute, left £24 a year for a girl's school at Ludgershall and that this sum was paid to Miss Selwyn, who was the daughter of the late Rector, for schooling and clothing of fifteen or twenty girls and that she represented that this was Sir William Meadows Charity. Miss Selwyn married a Mr. Protheroe and went away to live near Bristol. The Charity was ever since discontinued. No will was found despite a search at Doctor's Commons.'*

(The figure in the first line of this extract should be 'eighty'. Doctor's Commons was a society of ecclesiastical lawyers of great antiquity that obtained a royal charter in 1768 and was dissolved in the mid-nineteenth century. Its records are a valuable source for historians.)

Miss Selwyn's school seems to have been run in imitation of the well-known Bluecoat and Greycoat Schools in London where distinctive clothing was supplied to children yearly as an incentive to attendance, and the Free School founded in 1855–56 in Ludgershall was also on a charitable basis and supported by voluntary contributions. The Old School House in Butt Street was built in memory of Anne Everett, who had died at the early age of thirty-two in 1851, and the building survives as the private home of Catherine and Jack Copping. We know that Lucy Lush was headmistress in 1865, and Blanche Butt, later Mrs. Blanche Crouch, was in charge from 1885, but the early records have not been traced and the first log book with detailed information dates from 1895. There were up to one hundred and seven pupils, with attendance fluctuating in September because the harvest was not in and in October because of the attractions of the Weyhill Fair. Mrs. Crouch was assisted by Kate Hunt, a pupil teacher, and Ellen Baiden, who taught history. Ellen Baiden came back to Ludgershall as infant headmistress in 1914 and did not finally retire until 1937. She lived, with her sister, at The Cedars in Castle Street; a house subsequently occupied by the late Bertha Gale and now the home of Peter and Marguerite Cartledge. The problem with the Butt Street School was that it was never big enough to accommodate the growing number of children in the village, and in 1906 a new elementary school was built in St. James' Street near the church. The land was given by Charles Awdry, a relative of the Rector, and he also paid £600 as half the cost of construction. The junior children and the seniors up to the age of fourteen were taught here; the infants remained at Butt Street. The St. James' Street school is now the Seawell workshop, and its red brick walls are in excellent condition after nearly a century.

We can get the flavour of school life at the end of the nineteenth-century and the beginning of the twentieth by looking at the logbook entries for 1896–97 and 1901. Confirmation candidates were being prepared before Easter, and when the school opened again after the Easter holiday several children were absent *'potato planting'*. Standards IV, V and VI had lessons on *'The African Possessions'* which were still part of the British Empire at that time; also on *'The reign of Henry VIII'*. In June several children were absent because a fire had destroyed their homes, and others were absent haymaking. Four children were sent home, *'on account of their dirty condition'*, while on 15th June it was noted, *'the children had no drill this week on account of the heat'*. July saw another falling off in attendance as children were busy helping with the harvest once again. The new school year brought a half-holiday on 14 September because a circus was due to visit the village and hold an afternoon performance. On 12 October *'attendance being very small'*, the school closed at 3 pm—there being *'a fair for pleasure at Weyhill'*. Several boys were absent in mid-October *'away potato picking'* while Mrs. Huth of Biddesden House visited on the 26th with Miss Heathcote and *'gave sweets on leaving'*. These would have been a rare treat for many of the children; pocket money of a half-penny a week was considered suitable for a child at this time and the smallness of the sum caused great consideration to be given to the choice in spending it.

In November 1896 the Diocesan Inspector examined the children's work in Scripture and found that, *'The children have been carefully taught, their written work is especially good.'* while Her Majesty's Inspector reported, *'The children are well behaved and order is as good as it can be in a crowded room. Work is carried on with energy and with gratifying success.'* The evening class was also considered to be, *very successful. Both teachers and scholars combine to make it go well.'* In December Ellen Baiden was absent all week to attend the scholarship examination; her results must have been good as she passed as a fully-certificated teacher. The school year continued with much the same problems as are coped with today. January 1897 came in a with a heavy fall of snow that blocked the roads and kept pupils at home, and in March some of the children had to be sent home to change their clothes *'on account of a thunderstorm'*. Staffing difficulties were experienced in April 1901. Kate Hunt was ill for some weeks and the Rev. Best, the curate came in to assist. Later in the year Ellen Baiden left to become an assistant teacher in Hertford, and Kate Hunt resigned because of ill health. Miss H. French commenced as an assistant teacher in October, and the numbers of pupils ranged between one hundred and one hundred and twelve. November saw the appointment of Miss Lansley as an assistant teacher, and in December once again it was reported that *'the measles are spreading slowly among the children.'*

The Elementary Education Act of 1870 had converted the original charity school into a state-aided school under the control of a remarkable man called John Wilson who also acted as Head teacher, Assistant Overseer of the Poor and Parish Clerk. John Wilson was, literally, on top of his job because he lived at Wessex House where Crown Lane joins Butt Street, and could see the school from his bedroom window. It was this man who marshalled the facts on the deficiencies of the Old School House and helped to bring about the building of the St. James' Street School. He recorded the rise in attendance in his first year in charge from one hundred and thirty two in April to one hundred and forty in June so that, in his words, it was:

> *'absolutely necessary to use the play ground for reading and slate work; on wet days we crowd the lobby.'*

There was a public meeting to discuss enlarging the school, although nothing was done immediately John Wilson was able to get his message across with the phrase *'Ninety children in a room built for sixty.'* When he did succeed in getting the older children settled into the new school the staff position became acute. The St. James' Street building had one large room divided by two partitions into three smaller ones, but in October 1906 he had just one uncertificated assistant so that Miss Hume had charge of fifty-six children and John Wilson had the remaining seventy. As if this was not bad enough, a further twenty-four children arrived at the end of the month because the temporary school at Brimstone Bottom where the barracks construction workers lived, had closed. The infants school in the Old School House was in better shape, with only twenty-seven children and two teachers.

The numbers of schoolchildren continued to grow. The mixed elementary school in St. James' Street had been designed for one hundred and twenty pupils but it opened, as we have seen, with more than that, and by June 1915 the roll had risen to one hundred and eighty-four. In the previous year the school had been enlarged to take one hundred and sixty-eight children, but there were only one hundred and thirty eight desks and a harassed John Wilson wrote that he *had to borrow forms for the children to sit on.'* The infants school was in no better case; between 1914 and 1916 there were ninety-eight children on the books. The reason is not hard to find. The population was rising fast as the services supporting the army responded to increased demand, and a glance at Appendix Nine will confirm that baptisms and burials in the church were rising sharply around 1916 after a fairly flat pattern in the preceding two centuries. The census statistics tell the same story, with a dramatic rise between 1891 and 1911 when the population more than doubled, and another between 1931 and 1951 when it went up by 50% for roughly similar reasons. The figures are:

Year	1891	1901	1911	1921	1931	1951
Population	476	576	1,117	1,090	1,259	1,906

Staff shortages continued to plague the headmaster. The nominal establishment was himself, two certificated teachers and an assistant, but in 1917 there was just Mrs. Howe to cope with ninety-one children while John Wilson took eighty-seven. The difficulties over staffing were compounded by the extremely low temperature in classrooms in February, which was alleviated by brisk exercise outside, led by the

Old School House in Butt Street and St. James' Street School.

headmaster. March 7 1917 was declared a half-day holiday to celebrate the presentation by 'The Committee of Children's Day August 1916' of three handsomely framed engravings of King George V, Queen Mary and Lord Kitchener. An account of the event in the log says:

> 'The children, after an entertainment at the "Palladium" theatre, witnessed the presentation of the pictures to the school by the School Managers and were addressed by the Rector and Dr. Williamson. Headed by an Australian Band they marched in procession to the school playground and saluted The Flag. Proceedings terminated with the playing and singing of the National Anthem.'

Discipline, truancy and staff shortages were constant problems. In March two boys were absent from school having been sent before the magistrate for cruelty to a pig. They each received six strokes of the birch. Another boy was removed from the school because his mother had been sent to prison for one month for neglect; the children in the family were sent to the workhouse. In September Ernest Clark, who was aged thirteen years and four months, was absent all week and was reported to have followed the Australians to Parkhouse Camp. The year finished with unresolved problems of school cleaning as there was no caretaker. In October the Hon. Mrs. Guy Baring of Biddesden House had visited the school and promised to write to the Director of Education concerning the dirty conditions and the need to keep the fires alight. There were three applicants subsequently for the job of caretaker in November, but with most men away in France it turned out that two were caravan dwellers and one was an ex-schoolgirl, aged fourteen and a half.

The war years did bring some innovations. In 1917 the county school occulist came to the Old School House to hold a clinic and test the children for glasses, while the same year saw the first visit of a dentist. The parish nurse was a frequent visitor after 1916, often calling in company with Dr. Williamson and the Rector visited weekly to instruct the children in Religious Knowledge. The post-war period brought new blood to Ludgershall, for when the Garrison School at Tidworth was *'closed to outsiders'* (to children whose fathers were no longer in the army) they came to Ludgershall, and the first man teacher to be appointed for many years joined the staff. He was Frederick Job who hailed from British Columbia and brought a whiff of the wide open spaces to the schoolroom. The logbook for 1915–31 begins to lose its freshness around 1920, with illnesses and staff changes dominating the narrative so that much less material about individual children appears. This is in stark contrast to its predecessor which was both more informative and personal. Let me end this chapter with a poignant extract from the first logbook about a tragic incident in July 1912.

> 'A sad accident has happened to one of our children, Ena Mead, not yet four years old. She was kept from school by her parents on Wednesday afternoon and, being missed, was found to have fallen into a disused well at the back of their premises. It is supposed that she had gone to look for her kitten there.'

SOURCES FOR CHAPTER SEVENTEEN

	Charity Commission Reports. HMSO, 1906.
	Harrod's Directory. 1865.
	Kelly's Directory for 1855, 1875.
	Parish records in the church of St. James.
PIGOT and Co.	*Directory of Wilts*. 1842.
PUGH, R. B. and CRITTALL, Elizabeth (eds.)	*A History of Wiltshire, VCH*. Volume V, (IHR, London). 1957.
RANSOME, Mary (ed.)	*Wiltshire Returns to the Bishop's Visitation Queries 1783*. (WRS, volume XXVII, Devizes), 1972, 143–145.
	School Log books held at WRO.

CHAPTER EIGHTEEN

Ludgershall Schools after 1920

In the last chapter we saw that from 1906 there were two schools in the village—the mixed elementary school in St. James' Street and the infants school in Butt Street. The overcrowding that had led to a movement away from the Old School House was also a feature with the St. James' Street building, and in 1940 a new secondary school called Tidworth Down (now Castledown) was opened on the parish boundary opposite Kangaroo Corner. The idea was that it would cater for children from Tidworth as well as Ludgershall and surrounding villages, although some were creamed off by examination at the age of eleven to go to Andover Grammar School (John Hanson), Bishop Wordworth's School in Salisbury or Marlborough Grammar School. The overcrowding at St. James' Street resulted in the creation of a number of temporary classrooms, and the Scouts Hall, some temporary buildings off Central Street on the site now occupied by the medical centre and the canteen on Doctor's Meadow attached to the Catholic church, were all pressed into service. Additionally, the Scouts Hall served from time to time as a dining room. It was not until 1978 that education provision settled into its present pattern with the former girl's secondary school in Short Street becoming the primary school and Castledown the principal follow-on secondary school. As related elsewhere, the Old School House is now a private dwelling. The St. James' Street building was sold and is now a workshop; the proceeds went into a trust fund administered jointly by St. James' Church and Salisbury diocese and having a strong educational component.

So much for the buildings; now for the experiences and recollections of children and teachers. The first trip to the seaside seems to have been made in June 1920 when the St. James' Street School closed for a day so that every one could go to Bournemouth, while it was again closed for a day in April 1923 on the occasion of the Duke of York's wedding. (He was subsequently King George VI, and his bride is now Queen Elizabeth, the Queen Mother). The early 1920s saw rolls of about eighty children in the elementary school, and firm methods were used to compel attendance. Frederick Neve was the attendance officer who traced truants, and Win Bourne of Woods Farm tells a story about one visit to her home in the 1920s. She and her brother had seen the attendance officer approaching and hid behind the house. While he was in deep conversation with their mother the two children darted round to the front of the farmhouse and let the air out of his bicycle tyres. Win Bourne, slim and energetic, worked on the farm from four years of age and nowadays walks miles every day collecting for good causes and is a good advertisement for rural living. So, indeed, are Marjorie and Mary Neve, daughters of the former school attendance officer, who live at 10 Short Street and are stalwart supporters of the church and the Memorial Hall.

The largest attendance in the elementary schools history prior to the post-Second World War period was recorded in the log book entry dated 14 October 1932 when the school roll numbered two hundred and five pupils, and in the following month an exciting new development took place. A wireless set enabled the school to hear the Remembrance Service at the Cenotaph in Whitehall, and a dozen of the older boys and girls were taken to the service held at the War Memorial in Ludgershall. In March 1933 cod liver oil was sent from the County Offices to be given to delicate children, and in May Nurse Bayly made her first inspection of the children. The staffing position in September 1933 was, the Headmaster, John Wilson, Ralph James a certificated teacher, Miss Abbott also certificated Miss G. M. Hall and Mrs. G. Lewis both uncertificated at this time. With five teachers for two hundred children, and no electric light, lessons often stopped early on winter afternoons as reading and needlework became impossible. The end of an era came in 1935 when John Wilson, who had supervised the opening of St. James' Street school in 1906, retired. His farewell assembly was addressed by the Rector, the Rev. Alfred Watt, with Dr. Henry Williamson, a governor, and John Piper, the school correspondent who checked the registers, also present. Ralph James, who had been John Wilson's right-hand man, became Headmaster in April 1935, and by the end of the month there were four certificated teachers to help him. They were Mrs. Lewis and Miss Hall, Hazel Humber and Mr. N. H. Cozens. The numbers were down a little in 1935 with one hundred and seventy-six children on the roll.

Ralph James had to contend with all the problems that John Wilson had grappled with: once again the roof was leaking *'in all four rooms'* and he was *'unable to see the lines on this page'* as he wrote in the log book on 18 November 1935 because there still was no artificial lighting in the school. In December many attendances were lost through, *'parties given by the various regiments in Tidworth'* and there was one case of scarlet fever and two contacts among the Lodge family in Faberstown. The New Year saw the first part of the scholarship examination taking place, *'in exact agreement with instructions';* the fortunate few who were selected went on to attend, *'oral examinations, three at Marlborough and one at Salisbury'* in June. The Church choir took part in the Salisbury Cathedral Festival, also held in June, and in the same month H.M.I. G. K. Sutherland inspected the school and noted the difficulties under which the staff carried out their work. One was that there were only four classrooms for five classes; in addition he reported;

> *'Many staff changes which are due in large part to the difficulty experienced by assistants in finding suitable accommodation in the locality. Four new teachers since he (the Head) took charge and of these three at least will have left again by the end of the current year.'*

Because of these staff problems the inspector proposed delaying writing a full report at this time and wisely chose to comment on many of the more positive changes that the new headmaster had introduced. The land adjoining the school had been acquired for a garden, and a start was being made with bee-keeping and aquaria studies. The entry in the log continues, *'The Headmaster deserves to be commended for his keen interest in local history.'*

On 2 November 1936 the school managers, who were the Rev. Alfred Watt, Dr. Herbert Williamson, Mr. P. Berry, Mr. J. Lovell and Mr. H. Rawlings, met together to inspect the classrooms and playgrounds, and their attention was drawn to the dangerous state of the belfry. The children were summoned to school by a bell, and despite the state of the belfry it continued in use until June of the following year when the wire rope broke and it was necessary to summon them by whistle. Lamps were eventually supplied for the use of the evening class and hung by the local firm of Voss and Hatcher. A new device, the telephone, was used in January 1937 to report to Trowbridge that the poor attendance figure of one hundred and sixteen scholars was due to an outbreak of influenza and in May of that year the Headmaster was absent to attend the first meeting of the Pewsey Rural District Council. He, like his predecessor, was an interested member of the Local Parish Council and a representative of the Parish at Pewsey.

Behind the scenes, negotiations had been taking place to transfer the two Church of England schools in Ludgershall to the care of the Wiltshire County Council Education Department. A letter was received to this effect by the Parish Council in September 1937, and they replied that they had no objection. In point of fact, a complete re-organisation of the schools in the area was contemplated; a site for a new Secondary School had been purchased by the County Education Committee at a point east of Brimstone Bottom in 1936 and, despite the objections to the site put forward by Ludgershall Parish Council, it was built there, opening in 1940. Not the least of these objections was that it was situated in close proximity to the training grounds of the Royal Tank Corps and the summer camp-site of Windmill Hill, not to mention the considerable distance to the site from Ludgershall along a dangerous road, which at that time did not even have a footpath alongside it.

St. James' Street school was again said to be overcrowded in December 1938 when the roll reached two hundred, and the raising of the school leaving age to fifteen in July 1939 seemed likely to add to local difficulties. The outbreak of the Second World War a couple of months later led to the school being closed for two weeks for air raid precautions to be taken since Ludgershall was considered to be *'a danger area'*. A shelter trench was dug by volunteers from the Royal Army Service Corps who were stationed at Windmill Hill, and arrangements were made that in the event of an air-raid warning one third of the school-children were to shelter in the church, one third in the school, and one third in the trenches. The first air raid practice took place on 19 August 1940 and it was quickly followed later in the same day by a genuine air-raid warning. Children also went to the shelters on 21 August after a further warning. Evacuees were admitted to the school for the first time during the month of August 1940.

Great changes then took place to the schools in Ludgershall for as the log book records:

> *'After today this school will be reorganised as a Junior Department. The senior children will attend at the new Senior Mixed School at Tidworth Down. Mr. E. S. Smith and Mr. J. E. John and Miss A. Cockburn transfer to the staff of the senior school. Mrs. E. M. Saunders and Mr. R. A. Etherington remain on the staff of the Junior School. By taking up the appointment at the Senior School I am ending seventeen years of service in this school'.*

The above entry is signed *R. J. H. James 30.9.40*. Miss Cubitt became Head of the Junior School and had the assistance of the two teachers from the old school together with two uncertificated teachers, Miss Waters and Miss Burgess. The School reopened with a roll of two hundred and nineteen children; ten of whom were evacuees, in two buildings—the juniors at the mixed school in St. James' Street and the infants at the Old School House in Butt Street. In November the two schools contained two hundred and thirty children; twenty-one being recognised evacuees, and two unofficial evacuees from Leeds, one from Ramsgate in Kent and one from the Channel Islands.

The war brought many beneficial changes. Inoculations against diphtheria began in March 1941 with Nurse Bayley and Mrs. Abbatt, the doctor's wife, marshalling the lines of apprehensive children. A folk-dancing club was started, and a girls' social club. The building in Butt Street was pronounced to be in a dangerous condition in August 1941, and a new wing was added to the Junior School building with the work beginning in September 1942. After many years of complaint that it was impossible to see to carry out writing and sewing in the dark winter afternoons, electricity was at last installed in the St. James' Street Junior School in January 1942. That particular January was a cold and miserable one; attendance in the school fell below 60% and the melting snow caused leaks to the classrooms. Despite the weather, Room 4 was used on January 30 for the distribution of vitamins to the mothers of local babies. Mrs. Mead, a Parish Councillor, organised the distribution, which became a regular weekly event. She was the second woman to be elected to that position, the Hon. Mrs. Guy Baring being the first female councillor. At long last the old coal stoves, which had been a constant source of frustration and totally inadequate at heating the building, were removed when central heating apparatus was installed in February 1942. There were several air-raid warnings in the autumn term, and on 5 November 1942 it was announced that hot dinners were to be provided at school. Money earned by the children by collecting conkers and hips and haws amounted to £2 1s. 0d. and was donated to the Aid to Russia and China Funds. The term ended with great excitement and joy on 2 December when twenty-five children with Mrs. Spargo, wife of the bank-manger, Miss Collier and the headmistress were taken by Americans to Tidworth in jeeps and entertained to lunch. A year later a local American Army unit, 861 Ordnance Company, gave a party for the primary schoolchildren of Ludgershall and I am indebted to the present Deputy-Head of Castle Primary School, John Jenkins, who has kindly loaned me the letters that the children wrote thanking their hosts.

The party was held on Sunday 19 December, and the letters were written the following day. The children were conveyed to the party in lorries and members of the Red Cross assisted with the organisation of the meal, entertainment and film show, and all the children received a present from Father Christmas. More than eighty children went to the party and they all wrote 'thank you' letters to the American Servicemen who had acted as their hosts. The letters were sent on by Miss M. C. Cubitt, the Headmistress, *'quite free and uncorrected'* and some are in ink, others in pencil and with wider or narrower spaced lines according to the child's ability. Brian Sneddon wrote very legibly in ink,

> *'I liked the present you gave me very much it was a Westerland Lysander . . . I think the majician was good tearing paper into a steering-wheel but what a waste of paper it is if he does it many times.'*

Gordon Littlecott, whose handwriting was also neat and regular, appears to have adopted the American vocabulary,

> *'We sure enjoyed the ride in the trucks . . . it was a swell party . . . I am saving some candy for Christmas.'*

He completed his letter with a drawing showing an unmistakably American truck arriving at the barracks. Sheila Lightfoot reported that *'Poor old Father Christmas's beard fell off'* and Clive Blackmore summed up the feelings of all the children saying:

'We enjoyed the party and I hope you enjoyed it too. We were all sorry when we left and wished that Sunday would come again.'

Miss Cubitt left to work at a training centre in 1945, and the redoubtable Irene Ashwell took her place. Her logbook entries leave a graphic description of school conditions at that time. The school was in two separate buildings. One the former Church of England premises in St. James' Street, the other the Scouts Hall. The former building still had four classrooms divided by wooden partitions that were not sound-proof; the lavatories were of the bucket type and the washbasins had only cold-water taps. She had to cope with two hundred and seventy-two children with just three teachers, and her own workload was a class of seventy. In the early 1950s more children came to St. James' Street as the housing estates grew along the Andover Road, and in 1966 the roll reached three hundred. The high point of four hundred and two was reached in 1973, but relief was in sight. The Girls Secondary School in Short Street was new, airy and well-built, having a hall, library, kitchen and dining room as well as ample playground and garden space so that it became entirely logical to move the girls to Castledown School and the juniors and infants to Short Street. It has taken the best part of two hundred years to travel from Miss Selwyn's *'day school of instruction'* to the fine purpose-built village school that serves the community today.

SOURCES FOR CHAPTER EIGHTEEN

BOURNE, Win	Personal reminisences.
	Children's letters lent by John Jenkins.
COLLINS, Wreatha	Personal reminiscences.
NEVE, Marjorie	Personal reminiscences.
	School Logs Books at WRO.

CHAPTER NINETEEN

Utilities

The nearest source of surface water for Ludgershall is the River Bourne, but since Norman times wells had been dug to supply drinking water that was exceptionally pure because it percolated very slowly through layers of chalk into acquifers. Wells still come to light regularly, usually through building work, and are in gardens, as at 25 Tidworth Road, or actually inside houses, as in the case of 28 St. James' Street. Until relatively recently, the other principal source was the three natural ponds in the village where cattle and horses were watered within living memory. The demand for a better class of water supply did not arise until the end of the nineteenth-century, and the impetus for that demand was the existence of a new military reservoir at Perham Down that provided piped water for the tented camps. Ludgershall Parish Council resolved in October 1899 to approach Colonel R. M. Barklie, who had the task of co-ordinating the construction of the barracks, complex at Tidworth, with a view to tapping this source, and the upshot was that he agreed to a meeting. It did not take place until April 1901, and Brigadier Barklie (he had been promoted in the meantime) acted as vice-chairman. There was a full discussion about water supply and drainage, but the matter was eventually shelved and then dropped.

The subject came up again in April 1902 when a letter was received by Ludgershall Parish Council from Pewsey Rural District Council about Captain Faber's water supply. He was Walter Vavasour Faber who lived at Brewery House, Weyhill, and who was a partner in Strong's Brewery based at Romsey and the founder of Faberstown. Strongs of Romsey owned about eight hundred public houses at this time, including all three in Ludgershall, and older readers may recall that the firm ran a very successful advertising campaign all over southern England through signs put up alongside roads and railway tracks and reading—'You are entering the Strong Country'. Walter Faber owned a large tract of land to the east of the village and conceived the notion of planning and erecting a new town bearing his name. (See Appendix Ten for a condensed biography of this almost-forgotten entrepreneur). A road was built running off the Andover Road and building plots were marked out. Anticipating a large community on the site, Faber built a water tower that still stands on the village boundary and had plans for extensive railway sidings and warehousing. The latter plan did not come to fruition, and the erection of houses was a piecemeal process. The Parish Council were aware of the situation, and in January 1903 agreed that Faber could:

> '*construct and maintain a Waterworks and a supply of water in the Parish of Ludgershall.*'

to utilise this space capacity.

Matters went slowly, and in 1908 the waterworks company that Faber had founded asked for more time to develop the project. The final straw came in 1909 when a committee made up of local representatives and waterworks company officials said that a supply of four million gallons of water annually would cost £300.

Councillors declined the offer and inaugurated another scheme. This involved drawing water from a well at the foot of Shaw Hill on the Collingbourne road and distributing water by three branches, but the total cost was £3,500 and in the event the landowner refused to sell the site. A Water Enquiry was held in 1910 at which the chairman and vice-chairman of the Parish Council gave evidence, and William Piper reported the decision of Pewsey Rural District Council to try Faber's scheme again. The Parish Council, fully aware that an outbreak of fever in May 1910 was chiefly due to inhabitants drinking water from the Winchester Street well, tried to hurry a decision by scare tactics. Their resolution read:

Captain Faber's water tower.

> 'In view of the serious consequence to Ludgershall of an epidemic of infectious disease this village being near Barracks and the fact of the village being Out of Bounds (to troops) the Parish Council request the District Council to take the matter into their serious consideration with a view to providing an Isolation Hospital.'

but the move backfired when Pewsey Rural District Council said that any such cases could be provided for at Devizes Hospital while the army authorities subsequently made their own provision of an isolation hospital at Brimstone Bottom. Ludgershall Parish Council had to face up to paying the going rate for water, and in January 1911 sent out a circular letter asking all property owners in the parish for assurance that they would take the new water supply. At the same time, the promoters of the waterworks had dropped their earlier demands and now asked merely for a guarantee of £120 a year for three years.

At a special meeting called in June of that year, a resolution was adopted that the Parish Council accept the two draft agreements with the water syndicate, and they recommended that the District Council do the same. By March 1912 pipes were being laid and the position of fire hydrants was being settled but, meanwhile, the Winchester Street well was still in use. A letter from the Sanitary Inspector in September 1913 called on the Parish Council to repair the well top, but the Council denied liability for the well and expressed the hope that it be closed and pressure be put upon the property owners to connect with the water main. Two months later it was reported that the County Medical Officer of Health had had the water from Winchester Street well analysed with the result that it was declared unfit for drinking purposes. This was followed up by a subsequent declaration that:

> 'the water of the well situated at Lansdowne Terrace and of the well at the top of Butt Street is contaminated and unfit for drinking . . .'

and the guarantee that the water company had sought was given so that mains water be supplied to village houses. The effect was that most dwellings received an indoor tap supply in 1914.

Strange as it may seem to us nowadays the provision of a clean water supply to the village did not embrace facilities for sewage disposal. The need for such a scheme was pointed out in a letter to the Parish Council by a Mr. Ray, who lived in the High Street, as early as November 1914, but with the demands of war any such improvements were put at the bottom of the agenda. There had been earlier complaints to the Parish Council. In 1910, at the time when there was infectious disease in the area, two incidents were reported to the Inspector of Nuisances; one was at Lansdowne Terrace where it was said the contents of a cesspit had been poured into a field by the side of a pond, and the other occurred during the emptying of a cesspit at the Prince of Wales Hotel. Again, in November 1916 a 'nuisance' was reported at the entrance to St. James' Street, and the Parish Clerk was instructed to write to Messrs. Dickeson of the Capital and Counties Bank drawing their attention to the overflow from the cesspit on their premises. (The building involved is now known as Harcourt House which was built as a bank and later converted to apartments). A dozen years were to pass before anything was done about Ludgershall's sewage disposal problem, and in the meantime cesspits continued in widespread use.

The next initiative came from the County Medical Officer of Health in 1927. He forwarded a report on sanitary conditions in the village with a detailed list of houses which were considered either satisfactory or unsatisfactory. The report stated that the Sanitary Inspector had visited two-hundred and fourteen houses: in one hundred and twenty-eight of these night soil and refuse was collected; eighty-six houses had no collection done at all and of the sixteen houses unsatisfactory for both night soil and refuse collection *'six are houses recently occupied and belong to Pewsey R.D.C.'* This could not be ignored and the Parish Council decided to form a committee consisting of the chairman and vice-chairman, Mark Elkins and J. K. Bridgman of Castle Farm, to visit the premises complained of to see if the owners and occupiers could make some arrangement that would satisfy the authorities and avoid a public scheme at the expense of the ratepayers. It seems that this action did not satisfy the Rural District Council who again wrote to Ludgershall Parish Council saying that the Ministry of Health intended to hold a Public Enquiry. The Parish Council replied that

> *'a compulsory scheme is not wanted and would not be beneficial to the Parish as a volunteer scheme has been carried out for a number of years successfully.'*

Manifestly, it did not want to spend any money.

The Ministry of Health enquiry was held in the Scouts Hall in January 1928 and a solicitor was employed to represent the Parish Council at the enquiry. The verdict was reported to the March meeting of the Parish Council—the compulsory scavenging scheme had been defeated. For the time being, plans for a scheme of sewerage disposal in Ludgershall were shelved, but in March 1940 Pewsey Rural District Council came up with a new plan. Again, the Parish was not happy with it saying,

> *'It is felt that there might have been a more comprehensive scheme to include owners of cesspits and septic tanks who formed a big percentage, under one special rate. The Sanitary Inspector had said that if these tanks etc. used were efficient they did not need emptying especially in Ludgershall where there was a chalk sub-soil.'*

and it was emphasised that a sewerage scheme would require a rate of ninepence in the pound.

The Second World War delayed any further attempts to provide a scheme for the village, but in the summer of 1949 new plans were discussed. Councillor Jack Challis proposed that outlines be displayed in a public place, one to show the Bell Street area and the other for the remainder of the village. Work had already begun on the post-war REEMA houses in May 1949 when the sewerage scheme was being considered, and on adoption the first 'new' installation was at Perham Crescent where the occupants moved into the houses in January 1950. Older houses had to wait while trenches were dug, but by the summer of 1950 the main drains were in place and the village's main employers—Simonds brewery, the NAAFI bakery and the NAAFI store and transport depot also had a modern and hygienic sewerage disposal scheme. In the national perspective, this was a late provision of an elementary service, and the conclusion must be that local resistance to change was the cause.

The three village ponds were outside the *Crown* in the High Street, in Castle Street, and where the telephone box now stands at the junction of Meade Road and the Andover Road, and they became a smelly nuisance after periods of drought. They had to be cleaned out at intervals, and we know that in 1910 the work was done by William Bunce, father of 'Bob' Bunce who worked on the railway and father-in-law of Hilda Bunce who still lives in the village. The ponds in the High Street and Castle Street and the animals that were watered there interfered with vehicle traffic, and following a resolution put to the Parish Council in January 1915 it was decided to fill them in. They were still not completely eliminated in September 1917 when new material was being looked for to level them, but by 1920 they had gone and trees were being planted on the Castle Street site. The third village pond at Meade Road continued in use until January 1950 when the Parish Council made enquiries about ownership as Pewsey Rural District Council proposed to incorporate the land in a garden. This pond was eventually filled, although a depression survives to show its position. The site of the other ponds can nowadays only be traced by using the photographs published by Barbara Humphrey in her two excellent books about the village in years gone by.

Finally, we come to electricity and gas. Again, electric power was a late arrival, and in dealing with the school it was noted that the St. James' Street did not get artificial lighting until 1942. Houses built in the 1930s had electric light as a matter of course, but the older dwellings were only slowly uprated. In Bell Street, for example, where the houses dated from 1901, number 22 did not get electric power until 1945. By and large, gas is still only readily available to houses south of the railway line, although at the time of writing there are indications that a supply will eventually be available to those who can contribute to the cost of bringing a gas main in under the railway embankment. In looking at the provision of utilities over time there is a pattern of lags and delays, and the two reasons appear to be the relative isolation of the village and the innate conservatism of the leaders of the community in the recent past.

SOURCES FOR CHAPTER NINETEEN

BUNCE, Hilda	Personal reminiscences.
BURROWS, J. (ed.)	*The New Forest and the Strong Country*. (Strong, Cheltenham and London, 1952).
FABER, David	Personal reminiscences.
HUMPHREY, Barbara	*A Pictorial History of Ludgershall*. (Holmes, Andover, 1989).
HUMPHREY, Barbara	*Ludgershall Then and Now*. (Holmes, Andover, 1991).
	Records of Ludgershall Parish Council.
SCOTT, Wilf	Memorandum on Bell Street—original in possession of author.

CHAPTER TWENTY

Fire!

Mediaeval and Tudor buildings were chiefly constructed of timber, wattle and daub and thatched so that fire was a constant hazard, while the closeness of village dwellings meant that blazes tended to spread rapidly when a strong wind was blowing. Bringing water from wells and ponds in domestic containers was a slow business, and in dry summers house fires were difficult to control. We know from a list of church collections taken to relieve the distress of burned-out cottagers that there were serious fires in Ludgershall in 1679 and 1681, while John Capps reported on 26 July 1753 that there had been:

> *'a great fire at Penton which burned down six dwelling houses, six barns, several stables and other buildings with above one-hundred quarters of Malt and two hay ricks and almost all house-hold goods to the amount of £2,000 damage.'*

Major fires of the type described above were attended in the late nineteenth-century by the Everleigh House privately-run brigade captained by Percy Curtis and having a horse-drawn manual pump and fourteen men in all. The Savernake Estate also had a fire engine, and both brigades went to a serious fire at the *Windmill Inn* and adjoining cottages in Collingbourne Kingston in January 1881. It cannot be said that Everleigh House brigade was entirely effective because the house burned down in December of the same year despite the attendance of its own brigade and those from Pewsey and Netheravon. Manual pumping on this occasion seems to have been a strenuous business as the bill for liquid refreshment for the firefighters came to £27 in an era when good beer stood at twopence a pint. Minor fires at Ludgershall were attended by the Pewsey and Andover municipal brigades, with no station in Ludgershall until the present century when mains water became available. The local brigade was founded in December 1913 after an agreement two months earlier to spend £20 on a stand-pipe, branch-pipe, nozzle and hose, and the first Captain was William Perry, the Sub-Captain was J. W. Brooks and the Secretary was George Bryan. Fire hydrants were being put in by the water company as part of their bargain with the Parish Council, and at the Annual Parish Meeting in 1914 it was announced that £19-18s had been spent on additional hose, with £14 of the sum taken from the Coronation Fund and the rest raised by a concert. Captain Beale of the Andover Brigade volunteered to give a display, and the Rector promised to find space behind the Rectory for an appliance. (At this period the incumbent lived at what is now Erskine House). Before going off to France as a soldier, William Perry was able to report that several practices had been held although the water pressure was *'quite insufficient'*. Sadly, the newly-appointed Captain was killed and, with most able-bodied men in the armed forces, it fell to George Bryan to take charge and attempt to train Boy Scouts as firemen.

After 1919 several individuals tried to re-form the brigade and Captain Beale came out from Andover to offer his services in a training role. He advised that more hydrants were needed and additional hose with a coupling, spanners and a stronger turn-key were required. These items were ordered by Ludgershall Parish Council, but the Andover brigade was always called when fires occurred in the village. The most serious incident of the 1920s was on 7 August 1927 and involved the Temperance Hotel next door to the *Queen's Head* (and then known as the Queen's Hotel) in the High Street. Two shops filled the frontage of the Temperance Hotel, and the account in the *Andover Advertiser* began with the experiences of the shopkeeper's families.

> 'On Saturday night Mr. Sweet locked up his shop all secure, as he thought, and left the village for the week-end. Members of Mr. Wiles' family, who had been on a British Legion outing, returned home some time before midnight, and the household which included Mrs. Wiles, Mr. and Mrs. Wilkins (his son-in-law and daughter) and his sons retired to rest. A few minutes to one o'clock, Mrs. Wilkins, who was sleeping in the bedroom over Mr. Sweet's shop, roused her husband as she could smell smoke. He alerted the house-hold who escaped in their night-attire within minutes of the burning floor falling below. The Andover Fire Brigade, under Captain Beale arrived in remarkably quick time, but the stand-pipe, the vital necessity before the brigade get to work, could not be found and anxious minutes were spent looking for it. Salvage work continued and it was deemed prudent to remove furniture from the (at it was called at this time) Queen's Hotel. After about twenty mintues Mr. Curtis, a signalman on the G.W.R., found a stand-pipe in an out-building of the nearby Rectory, and the brigade set to work. After thousands of gallons of water had been poured on the fire by 3.30 am the danger to the Queen's Hotel seemed averted and furniture was returned there having sustained £100 worth of damage in the hasty evacuation. The fire brigade left Ludgershall shortly before 8.00 am'.

One consequence of the 1927 fire was that the standpipe and parish hose were thereafter put in a glass-fronted cupboard in the Scouts Hall so as to give ready access in an emergency, and they were next used in 1931 when a fierce blaze in the High Street caused £10,000-worth of damage to two garages, some workshops and the premises of E. E. Roy. Pewsey brigade turned out on that occasion, and the same unit tackled a fire in Winchester Street (Andover Road) when two shops and two cottages went up in 1934. Pewsey Rural District Council took the opportunity to ask Ludgershall for a contribution towards the cost of the fire trailer in May of that year, but received the answer that Ludgershall already had hydrants, standpipe and hose and that, in any case, Andover and Bulford were closer at hand and generally quicker to respond. The Parish Council did *not* say that there was another alternative provision in hand, although within two months its own brigade was to be re-born.

In July 1934 the revived village fire brigade had Mr. Read as Captain and Mr. Power as Sub-Captain. Mark Elkins, Mr. Colliss, Mr. Harfield, Mr. Harding and Mr. Laurie Beaves served on the Fire-Brigade Committee, and the stipend was set at £1 1s. for Mr. Read and £1 for Mr. Power. Ludgershall continued with a volunteer fire-fighting force until the passing of the Fire Brigades Act in 1938 when Pewsey Rural District Council assumed control for attending fires in their district. Suggestions were made that Ludgershall Parish Council provide a place where the trailer pump and towing vehicle plus the necessary ancillary equipment could be housed, and the site of the old *Crown* pond was thought to be suitable. The Parish Council replied that they had other ideas for the site, and in turn proposed that Pewsey Rural District Council make use of its own ground in Ludgershall between the blocks of council houses on the main road. It seems that the Parish Council was not pleased at having control of its fire brigade taken away.

In March 1939 the Clerk to the Parish Council was instructed to send letters to Messrs. Read and Power thanking them for their services as Chief and Assistant Chief Fire Officers for Ludgershall, but to note that from March 31st the fire service was to be taken over by Pewsey R.D.C. They both, in point of fact, became members of the newly-formed unit in Ludgershall, which was listed as Section Leader Cecil Vane, Station Officer A. Read, First Engineer E. Hogan, Second Engineer F. Rawlings and Firemen J. Power, I. Hawkins and Laurie Beaves. All was not yet running smoothly, for in September the Parish Council wrote to Pewsey R.D.C. pointing out that there was an urgent need of a building to be used as a fire-station as soon as possible because the engine was being housed at great inconvenience in a private building. Also, as they indicated, *'there is need for placing a warning siren in position at once'*. Their request was acted upon almost immediately and work was begun on the new fire station situated at the old *Crown* pond site. The contract price was £234 4s. 6d., but at the last minute, the contractor became worried about escalating costs and the solution appeared to be to have the tower constructed in timber instead of steel and galvanised iron. The final amount saved by this substitution was £1. Trials had taken place at Pewsey of various sirens and one was installed there in July 1938, but in Ludgershall the men were summoned by the ringing of an alarm bell situated outside the fire-station. In 1940 the ringing of the church bells was suspended because they were only to be used in the event of an invasion of England by enemy parachutists, and the Police at Ludgershall requested Section Leader Vane not to ring his bell to alert the brigade to a fire. This ban on the use of the fire-bell led to much discussion in the Parish Council until the Clerk ruled that there was no ban on the use of a bell for such a purpose, and instructed Mr. Vane to carry on ringing.

It was in 1940 that Percy Herbert, known as Bert, Bale joined Ludgershall Brigade and in 1949 he was promoted to be Officer-in-Charge of the station. He made history by becoming one of the few men to continue in the post with one leg. After an unfortunate shooting accident in 1957 he had to have his leg amputated, but when he had recovered from the operation he took, and successfully passed, a fitness test which involved climbing ladders. Mr. Bale went on to receive the British Fire Services Association Medal for twenty year's service and the Queen's Medal for Exemplary Service. He also served both as a Parish councillor and as a District councillor. In his profession as a builder, Bert Bale built the houses in Hei-lin Way, whose rather eastern-sounding name was derived from a combination of the names of his young daughter Heidi, and his secretary's daughter, Linda.

Ludgershall's firemen made national headlines in January 1946 when they went, with others from Marlborough, to an explosion and fire at an ammunition dump in Savernake Forest. There were further explosions as they dealt with the original fire, and Cecil Vane, Laurie Beaves and Robert Winstone were injured. The latter remembers very clearly being blown off the tender, and recalls that his helmet was found two miles away. The gallantry of the Ludgershall men at this incident resulted in the award of the George Medal to Cecil Vane and the MBE to Laurie Beaves. Jack Challis, well-known for his many years as a Parish and District councillor, was among those present, and sheltered Robert Winstone from shrapnel as he lay on the ground. Robert Winstone went on to become the longest-serving fireman in Wiltshire, and was granted his long-service medal in 1965 and the only Silver Jubilee medal awarded to a Wiltshire fireman in 1977.

In the post-Second World War years the National Fire Service ceased to be and control passed to the Wiltshire Fire Brigade. The station at the *Crown* pond site was closed and then demolished; men and appliances moved to the new station in Castle Street. Wiltshire County Council recently gave the go-ahead for Ludgershall to become a two-engine station, and to employ fourteen men. The station covers Tidworth and Ludgershall, and much of the surrounding area. One thing is certain. There will be no shortage of brave men willing to protect the community from the ravages of fire.

SOURCES FOR CHAPTER ONE

	'Andover Advertiser' 12 August 1927.
BALE, Christa	Personal reminiscences.
CAPPS, John	Diary. Copy in possession of author.
CHALLIS, Jack	Personal reminiscences.
HUMPHREY, Barbara	*Ludgershall Then and Now.* (Holmes, Andover), 1991.
MYNORS, A. B.	'A List of Briefs from the Register Books of Langley Burrell'. *WAM*, volume XXXVI, 1912, 455.
	Records of Ludgershall Parish Council.
SMYTH, John	*The Story of the George Cross.* (Arthur Barker Ltd., London), 1968.
THORPE, Peter	*Moonraker Firemen.* (Wiltshire Library and Museum Service, Trowbridge), 1979.
WINSTONE, Robert	Personal reminiscences.

CHAPTER TWENTY-ONE

Chapels, Halls and Monuments

The publication of the Authorised or King James Version of the Bible in 1611 marked the high water of the Protestant ascendancy, with the Church of England virtually controlling all aspects of religious thought. The Catholic challenge had been met, and the only cloud on the horizon in the theological context was that presented by the Baptists. The sect shared the general beliefs of the Church of England, but believed in total immersion as a profession of faith. The first English Baptist church was put up in Spitalfields in London in the same year that the Authorised Version appeared, and by 1689 a Toleration Act allowed Baptists to put up their own chapels and choose their own pastors. In 1815 there was enough local support for a chapel in Ludgershall, and one was built in what is now Chapel Lane with a burial ground alongside it. The building was demolished in 1909, but the burial ground may still be seen as a grassy patch next to the Scouts Hall. The Strict Baptist Union pays a small sum annually to the Parish Council for its upkeep, and the bath used for immersion survived until 1960. For many years it was used as the inspection pit for Elkins' Garage prior to the move to the Andover Road site. John Walcot, grocer, draper and insurance man in the 1830s, was a pastor for some time, and Robert Mower of Shipton Bellinger preached at the chapel in the latter half of the nineteenth-century. At least three, and perhaps four, other chapels sprang up at this time, and the competition probably led to a withering away of the Chapel Lane congregation.

Information about the other chapels is sparse, and a brief summary follows. Mrs. D. M. Taylor's *Short History of the Village of Ludgershall* published in 1958 says that:

> '*on the site where the Castle Club stands stood one of three chapels, Primitive Methodist.*'

and Methodist influence in the countryside is mentioned by John Capps in a diary entry of 1737. He wrote:

> '*And likewise in this year sprung up a new religion called methodism, The leader of which was one Whitefield and bred up at Oxford and hath that university education who soon as he came from thence began to spread his enthusiastic doctrine and poisoned the morals of numbers of the common people in all parts of the Kingdom especially the western parts, where some of very good fashion and fortunes become his hearers as I have been credibly informed especially at Bristol, Bath and Salisbury etc. and preached to them in highway fields upon stools to numerous audiences.*'

George Whitefield and John Wesley made open-air preaching a fundamental part of Methodism, and we know that there was no dissenting chapel in Ludgershall in 1786 when the Rev. John Selwyn made his report to the bishop. The 1815 building seems to have been the first, with the remainder coming into existence at the end of the nineteenth and the beginning of the twentieth centuries. The *Andover Wesleyan Circuit Magazine* of August 1909 reported that a Methodist Mission Hall existed in Ludgershall, being run by adherents from Collingbourne and Andover on alternate

Sundays, and in 1960 it was said that this hall later became the Territorial Drill Hall and stood in the Andover Road opposite today's Boys Club. The same building was used for Catholic services from 1933 to 1942, but was subsequently demolished. Another chapel was situated on the site of today's Kennet car park near the *Crown*, and photographs of it appeared in the book *Ludgershall Then and Now* by Barbara Humphrey in 1991. The building is substantial and pleasing in appearance, and we know from the 1878 survey map of Ludgershall that it was a Primitive Methodist chapel. The fourth chapel or hall is well-documented and continues in use.

Mr. Henry Tasker, whose family owned the ironworks and who ran the Anna Valley Workman's Hall Mission, held an open-air gathering in Ludgershall in 1892 and was so encouraged at the response that he resolved to build a hall in the village. A plot of land on the Andover Road was purchased for £150 and the hall opened for worship in 1904 but, as the Minute Book shows, open-air meetings were still held. One preacher, famous in her day, was Phyllis Thompson who was dubbed *'The Chinese Missionary'* in press reports and drew large crowds to hear her speak. In 1913 a fence and a gate were placed around the hall, and with the outbreak of the First World War an emergency meeting was held to decide the best use to which it might be put. It was decided to open the hall to all the members of H. M. Forces in the area, and the hall became known as the *'Soldiers Welcome'* with Mr. Gray in charge supported by a devoted band of ladies. A similar establishment was opened in Andover at this time, and from local newspaper reports it can be seen that the Mission Halls were eagerly frequented by soldiers from the various camps in the neighbourhood. Refreshments, entertainment, games and writing materials, which were supplied free of charge, were much appreciated by the men and their families who were gladdened to receive news of them. Henry Tasker died in 1929; he lived to see the hall registered as a place of worship in 1921. Another death which was seen as a great loss to the Mission was that of Mark Elkins who had been connected with its work for twenty-four years. In 1938 the hall was re-seated with pews, but with the coming of the Second World War the Open Air Mission took over the hall once more and again it was used as a *'Soldiers Welcome'*. The original building was dilapidated by the end of World War Two, and in 1948 the former mission hall at Tangley was brought to Ludgershall and set up on the site. The hall continues to attract a small but devoted band of worshippers, and there are hopes of celebrating the centenary early in the next century.

Ludgershall's most unusual place of worship is the now-disused Catholic church in Doctor's Meadow. The building started as the Catholic Women's League canteen during World War Two with the land owned by Clifton Diocese and the structure provided by the War Office. Opened by the Bishop of Clifton in March 1943, the hut had folding double doors at one end so that the canteen and chapel could be combined for larger congregations and kept separate for small ones. The chapel was subsequently fitted with an Italianate altar skillfully painted and decorated, and members of the U.S. Forces worshipped there. Clifton Diocese bought the building from the War Office in 1949, and it continued in use as a church until 1990 when it was badly damaged by fire. Its future is uncertain at the time of writing, but as there are plans to put a ring road through Doctor's Meadow and build either houses or industrial units on the site it looks as though demolition will be its eventual fate.

The oldest street monument in the village is the shaft of a market or preaching cross now on display behind railings outside the *Queen's Head*. It is generally reckoned to be fifteenth-century work; the decoration is badly worn but it can be seen that on one face is carved Christ's descent from the cross in relief. It is a composite cross in four parts, of which only the base and part of the shaft remain. A water-colour painted by John Buckler in the early nineteenth-century shows it standing on a large square base of four layers of well-dressed stone—since removed—and with an open downland background. The railings that protect it from damage were erected in 1897 to commemorate the Diamond Jubilee of Queen Victoria, and were made by three village blacksmiths—William and Charles Crouch and Charles Hailstone—while the work was designed and paid for by Mr. Alfred Henry Huth who then lived at Biddesden House. In recent years part of the railings have been damaged in traffic accidents, but English Heritage has restored and replaced them and adhered closely to the original design. The Market or Preaching Cross remains in the ownership of Ludgershall Parish Council. The head and top part of the shaft have been missing since at least 1813, and the most likely explanation is that the upper part was mutilated during the English Civil War when Cromwell's supporters reacted fiercely to any carving that seemed to foster idolatry.

The Preaching Cross

At the end of the First World War communities all over the country gave consideration how best to remember the fallen. A meeting of the Parish Council in November 1918 accepted a proposition by the Rector, the Rev. Henry Byrde, that *'a war memorial be raised'*, and a committee was formed that comprised Jack East, Doctor Herbert Williamson, J. Stidston of Castle Farm, H. G. Rawlings and Mark

Elkins. The Triangle at the junction of the High Street and the Andover Road was chosen as the best site and the design was entrusted to Captain R. H. Cowley, an engineer officer stationed at Perham Down. Captain Cowley's drawings envisaged a four-side obelisk in Bath stone, and when the monument was unveiled in June 1920 there were originally thirty names on the eastern and western faces of the memorial. When we look at the memorial nowadays it bears thirty-two names, and by comparing the list compiled in 1920 with the present inscriptions it may be seen that the name A. Peck was added at the top of the eastern face and that of F. Davidge at the bottom of the western face at a later date. After the Second World War the north face was used to record the twenty names of those from Ludgershall who died in the conflict, and there is some correspondence of names. The Worsdell, Peck and East families lost a son in each war; the Lansleys lost a family member in one war and two in the next one. Two Perry men died in the first war: a small stone on the south side at ground level commemorates Sid Perry who tended the memorial until his death in 1972. A full list of the dead of both wars named on the monument appears in Appendix Eleven, together with three Second World War names that are in the church record but not on the memorial.

The Memorial Hall standing in the Andover Road was conceived as a fitting remembrance of those men who had served their country in the Second World War. In the immediate post-war years domestic building took precedence, but in January 1950 a committee was chosen to consider the scheme. A suitable site was found facing the road, then called Winchester Street, bounded on one side by Laurel House (now demolished and the site of Gateways Food Store), and where some old thatched houses once stood. Mr. H. G. Rawlings, who owned the land, was willing to sell at a reduced price and Lord Moyne, who was the guiding spirit in this endeavour, had commissioned his architect to draw up the plans. These included an auditorium, a library, a clinic, reading rooms, dressing rooms, projection room and kitchen, and with one hundred and ten feet of frontage, and being set back seventy feet from the road, there was ample space for parking. In March 1950 the Parish Council agreed to accept the trusteeship of the site so that plans could go ahead to purchase. At a further meeting in June, which was attended by Lord and Lady Moyne and some seventy villagers, the plans were displayed and Mr. G. L. Kennedy, the architect, was asked to speak on them.

Meanwhile, many of the village people were busy organising fund-raising events, but with local labour, skilled and unskilled, being in very great demand so that even the building of the bus-shelters had to be postponed and the long-awaited public conveniences not completed until 1952, it was to be seven more years before the Hall was built with the extremely generous help of Lord Moyne. Built by the firm of Challis and opened in 1957 by Lady Moyne, it is administered by a committee made up of laymen and councillors whose guiding rule is that the property is to be:

> 'held upon trust for the purposes of physical and mental training and recreation and social and moral and intellectual development through the medium of reading and recreation rooms, library, lectures, classes, recreations and entertainments or otherwise as may be found expedient for the benefit of the inhabitants of the Parish of Ludgershall aforesaid and its immediate vicinity without distinction of sex or of political, religious or other opinions . . .'

The hall is the focal point of the village with day-to-day management in the capable hands of a committee headed by John Newman and Mary Neve, Arthur White and many other caring inhabitants. It has recently been designated a community building, and the activities range from harvest suppers to bingo; dances and pantomimes, wedding receptions and church fetes. It houses the local library and the Parish Council chamber, is used during elections and for every kind of public meeting. A village of under five thousand people has a facility that many towns with ten times that population would envy.

The War Memorial

SOURCES FOR CHAPTER TWENTY-ONE

	Andover Advertiser. 19 March 1943 and 11 June 1920.
	Andover Wesleyan Circuit Magazine. August 1909.
BRITTON, John	*The Beauties of Wiltshire*. Volume II, London, 1801.
BUCKLER, John	Set of watercolours held at WANHS.
CAPPS, John	Diary. Copy in possession of author.
CHURCHILL, Winston S.	*A History of the English Speaking Peoples*. Volume II. (Cassell, London), 1956.
COLLINS, Sheila	Personal reminiscence.
HUMPHREY, Barbara	*Ludgershall Then and Now.* (Holmes, Andover), 1991.
LEVELL, Eric	Personal recollection.
	Ludgershall Parish Council records.
MARPLES, B. J.	'Mediaeval Stone Crosses' *The Hatcher Review*. Volume II, No. 17. 1984.
	Memorial Hall deeds.
	Minute Book of the Mission Hall.
OLIVER, R. W.	*The Strict Baptist Chapels of England*. Volume V. London, 1968.
	Parish Records in St. James Church.
PEVSNER, Nicholaus (ed.)	*The Buildings of England; Wilts.* (Penguin, Harmondsworth), 1963.
TAYLOR, D. M.	*Short History of the Village of Ludgershall.* Pamphlet published in 1958—copy in Ludgershall Public Library.
	'True note and terrier of all Tythes . . .'. Document dated 1786; original in WRO.
	Ordnance Survey map of 1880 from a 1878 survey. Original in WRO.

CHAPTER TWENTY-TWO

Roads, Streets, Councils and Land

Ludgershall's main road is the A342 from Andover to Devizes, and this ancient route was, in the early nineteenth-century, a turnpike road with a gate near the present-day Karamand Hair Studio, formerly the Bungalow Stores, in Faberstown. Turnpikes were run by trusts and collected fees from through traffic, although there is plentiful evidence that a popular rural pastime was for young men mounted on good horses to jump the gate and get by without paying the keeper who lived in the nearby toll-house. The other roads in the village were parish roads, and prior to the takeover by Wiltshire County Council these roads were the responsibility of Surveyors of the Highways who paid out rate money for materials and labour. In 1792, for example, the surveyors in Ludgershall were Thomas Everett and Thomas Batt and they paid William Dobbs eighteen shillings for picking up and transporting thirty-six loads of stone with another seven shillings for seven days' work on the roads. Ann Cook was also paid sixpence a load for stones, and it seems that most road maintenance consisted of filling potholes with stones and allowing the traffic to consolidate the surface. The County Council took over just before motor traffic was beginning to be a source of danger, and as early as 1905 the Clerk to the Parish Council was writing to the County Council drawing attention to the excessive speed of motor cars through the village and asking for *"danger boards"* to be put up at the bend in Castle Street and on the Tidworth side of the railway bridge. Congestion caused by parked goods vehicles was another early problem, and in 1916 there was a complaint about horse-drawn vehicles such as *'carts left in front of blacksmiths and carpenters shops in Castle Street, Chapel Lane and other parts of the village'*. Prior to the post-World War Two housing boom there was hardly any change in the road pattern, although the building of the complex now called Castledown School led to two improvements for pedestrians. The footpath along the Tidworth Road was built first, and in 1943 the footbridge over the railway line was put in place to parallel the existing road bridge. Older residents will recall that a range of corrugated-iron shops lined the approach to the footbridge, among them a coal order office and a tattooist.

At a time when the village consisted chiefly of houses bordering main roads there was little necessity to place name-boards in the streets, and even in the 1930s it was dismissed as not necessary despite new building at Astor Crescent. In March 1946, however, the Parish Council asked the County Council to name and adopt new streets. In the following year the reply came that the cost of making up the roads on the Astor Estate would be £930 and at Bell Street it would be £200. The owners of property in Drove Road were asked for £40 each. As may be seen today, the people on the Astor Estate voted for a council-maintained street; owners of the nine houses in Drove Road and the inhabitants of Bell Street voted the other way. The naming of streets was passed back to the Parish Council, and councillors N. J. Colliss, H. H. Beaves and H. R. Workman were entrusted in 1950 with the task. Some decisions were easy: Castle Street, the High Street and Dewey's Lane were already known by these names, and the last is an ancient one because it derives from James Dewy, member of Parliament in 1658–69. Short Street and Perham Crescent were names given to new council housing, while Meade Road commemorates the services of Royston ("Roy") Meade who had been active in local and district politics in the 1940s. This mixed naming pattern continued in later years. Spray Leaze and Woodpark are historic names; Colliss Terrace and Challis Court recall councillors prominent in the recent past. Local doctors, kings and queens and Boer War towns have all been the impetus for street names.

Abbatts Close derives from Dr. Phillip Abbatt who lived in the house in St. James Street now occupied by Dr. Richard Wells. Dr. Abbatt was a keen motorist and took pride in owning the latest models, he died in the spring of 1994 after a long retirement. Hyson Close is named after another doctor who also lived at the house in St. James Street; The parents of Dr. George Hyson founded the firm of the Adjutants Press in Butt Street and lived in the now demolished cottage called "Missy Lodge" which was at the corner of St. James Street and Butt Street. Capt. George Edmond Hyson gained the M.C. and D.C.M. for his services during the First World War. The printing works which were continued by Michael Bulpitt have moved away to Weyhill but the building, now unused, still stands. Dr. Hyson married Kay Bridgman daughter of Mr. J. K. Bridgman who farmed at Sweet-apple Farm and subsequently at Manor or Castle Farm. They now live in happy retirement at Marlborough.

Pretoria Road and Graspan Road in Faberstown were named for a headquarters and victory that occurred in the Boer War in which Capt. Faber served. Royalty is well-represented in the street names of Ludgershall; Empress Way and Clarence Close commemorate the Empress Matilda and the Duke of Clarence who have associations with the royal castle here while the names Prince Charles Close and Lady Diana Court speak for themselves.

The Local Government Act of 1888 made the County Council the driving shaft of local administration, with the Rural District Council as the axle and Parish Councils the spokes of the wheel. The earlier Public Health Act of 1872 had put Ludgershall into the Andover Rural District area but it was transferred to Pewsey in 1879 and the first meeting of the newly formed Ludgershall Parish Council took place at the Old School House in Butt Street on 4 December 1894. A few days later the elected councillors took office. Dr. Herbert Williamson was chairman of the meeting, a post which he continued to fill for the next twenty years. On 7 November 1907 Dr. Williamson was elected Mayor of Ludgershall and a very successful dinner was held at the *Crown* Hotel in honour of the event. He continued to serve the community both as a doctor and administrator. He lived at and practised from Ivy House in Andover Road, he was Medical Officer of Health and Public Vaccinator of Number 5 District and a certifying factory surgeon for the Pewsey district and also as a churchwarden at the Church of St. James. Appointed churchwarden in 1890, he continued to serve in that capacity for fifty years until his death in 1940 aged eighty-one, and he is buried in Doctor's Row in the churchyard.

At the first meeting of the Parish Council, Colonel Rowland Hill Fawcett was vice-chairman, William Crouch became Clerk and the other councillors were Caleb Dudman, John Joseph Fox, William Piper, John Saunders, John Snelgrove and Nathaniel Young who was the last lord of the manor of Ludgershall. As is often the case today, the emphasis at that meeting was on the allotments and the recreation ground, and an early decision was made to acquire additional allotment land and set up a committee to apportion it. The tenant of Castle Farm was approached by the Rector, the Rev. William H. Awdry, and the former agreed to let land at £8 a year. The rules drawn up in 1897 for allotment holders appear on the adjoining page, and by March 1903 all the land had been taken up. I want to follow the story of Ludgershall's allotments down to the purchase of the land by the Parish Council in 1928 as it illustrates clearly the complicated relationship between the then War Department, two sets of allotment holders, the Parish Council and Pewsey Rural District Council in the early years, and the passions aroused by the tenure of land.

At the Annual Parish Meeting in March 1922 Mr. J. Stidston of Castle Farm, who had continued to let out the allotment land at £8 per annum to the Parish Council since 1897, pointed out that the rent paid to him was insufficient in view of the considerable increase in rates charged for it. Agreement was quickly reached in the May meeting of the Parish Council; Mr. Stidston would continue to be paid £8 but the Council would pay the rates. The resulting difference in price charged for rent at the Deweys Lane and the Bell Street allotments sparked off a controversy that led to the Parish Council eventually buying all the allotment land on both sites from the War Department. The tenants at Bell Street protested in April 1925 that they were paying more for their allotments than Deweys Lane tenants. The Allotments Committee inspected the site; correspondence was sent to and from the War Department, offers were made by the Chief Land Agent of the War Department to let both pieces of allotment land direct to the Parish Council at £2 per acre, and there was haggling over who should fence off the Bell Street site. The Parish Council decided that the Deweys Lane rents could not be raised again to carry out the fencing, and in August 1925 it was decided to take no further action. A letter from Mr. J. K. Bridgman, who had taken over the tenancy of Castle Farm, to the Parish Council in October 1925 informed them that he had been given notice to quit the allotment land in Deweys Lane by September 1926, and pointed out that it was contrary to his agreement with the War Department that he should sub-let the land at all, but that the War Department were willing to let direct to the Parish Council providing that they could come to suitable terms. The information opened up the whole question again; a meeting was held in the school so that the views of the allotment holders could be heard, and Mr. P. Hurd, the local Member of Parliament, attended.

Correspondence with the War Department resulted in their offering again to let the land at £2 per acre. The Parish Council replied with a counter-offer of £1 per acre, and they would pay for the fencing at Bell Street. Letters flew back and forth; the Council's letter to the Land Agent at Durrington regretted that they demanded a rent *"higher than that of the agricultural value"*. (Mr. Bridgman was paying fifteen shillings an acre for the adjoining farmland, as they well knew). The reply that came back in January 1926 from the War Department estate office was quite unrepentant; it pointed out that this was a *"fair rental of the land . . . owing to unauthorised acts of previous tenants (of the farm) the land had been let well below the normal"*. They finished by

LUDGERSHALL PARISH COUNCIL.

Allotment Rules.

1.—All Rents shall be paid on the Saturday previous to October 10th.

2.—The Allotments shall be held for one year only, and an agreement shall be signed by each man on taking his Allotment.

3.—The Parish Council does not hold itself liable for any growing crops left by a tenant.

4.—No Building of any kind shall be allowed on the ground.

5.—No Cattle, Sheep, Horses, Pigs, or any other animal shall be allowed to graze on the ground.

6.—No Allotment Holder shall be allowed to cut the hedges.

W. CROUCH,

Clerk to the Parish Council.

September 30th, 1897.

PRINTED BY J. C. HOLMES, ANDOVER.

Rules for Holders of Allotment Lands 1897

stating once more that the department would consider letting direct to the allotment holders. The Parish Council decided to carry on the fight; letters were sent enlisting the help of Stanley Baldwin, who was the Prime Minister at the time, Edward Ward the Minister of Agriculture, Lloyd George, a former Prime Minister, and their MP. A further letter from the Parish Council thanked Mr. Hurd for his efforts on their behalf by asking a question in the House of Commons on the 23rd February 1926. The immediate result was that the Parish was offered all 13.4 acres of land which comprised both the allotments at Deweys Lane and Bell Street at a rent of thirty shillings per acre. The agreement was signed and sent to the War Department Land Agent in April 1926, but the Parish Council signed *"under protest"*, spurred on by the knowledge that the Pewsey Rural District Council had given *them* notice to quit the land they had let out as allotments because it planned to build six houses on the site.

The matter of the allotments receded into the background temporarily as more urgent matters took the attention of the Parish Council, until March 1928 when it was revealed at a special parish meeting that the War Department had decided to sell off the allotment land and a decision had to be taken almost at once. Did the Council wish to purchase the land and, if so, how best to raise the asking price which was £30 per acre; the total cost being £410? Opinion was strongly in favour of buying, and at a further parish meeting in July a resolution was put that the Parish Council be authorised to apply to the Public Works and Loan Board for a loan of £430 to cover all cost. It got the loan and the outcome was the purchase of the two allotment sites by Ludgershall Parish Council for the use and recreation of the people of the village in perpetuity. Various proposals to develop the allotment land have from time to time been made, but have always been rejected.

A Recreation Ground committee was formed in April 1896, and some of its early decisions read a little strangely nowadays. It was resolved, for example, that the oats growing on the land be sold *"as they stand . . . the person buying the oats should pay ready money before cutting.* Tenders for grazing were issued by the Clerk; sheep were not objected to as their manure had a beneficial effect. A local farmer, William Hutchins, paid £3 3s. for the grazing until Michaelmas 1897, and a further 7s 6d. for the grazing until March 1898. During the following year he was sternly warned to keep his cows off the field, and in 1901 a wire fence was put up to keep his animals out. In 1906 he was called before the Council and severely rebuked by the chairman for leaving a load of turf on the land. It was not until 1908 that the ground was available solely for recreation in the summer, although by 1912 it had a football pitch. There was soon a complaint, echoed again in the 1980s, that the game interfered with free use of the path that ran diagonally across the ground.

When King George V died in 1936 a Memorial Fund was raised and from the proceeds it was decided to build a pavilion on the Recreation Ground. In April 1937 Mr. Peters was asked to prepare a plan for a shelter to cost no more than £40. His plan was accepted and the tenders were submitted for the work. Mr. New a builder from Collingbourne was given the contract and by the summer of 1938 the village had gained proper changing facilities for the sports and games played there. Interestingly enough, the first proposal to install swings and other amusements for children was made in 1916; a play area in the south-eastern corner was not a conspicuous success in the 1980s, but the present play area near the pavilion and put up in the 1990s has prospered. Much of the credit for this latter development must be given to the late Councillor Monty Wells who campaigned long and hard for the facility. The present-day Recreation Ground, which came into village control as long ago as 1853, is one of Ludgershall Parish Council's finest assets.

SOURCES FOR CHAPTER TWENTY-TWO

CHALLIS, Jack	Personal recollections.
General Register Office	*Census 1951 England and Wales; County Report, Wiltshire.* (HMSO, London), 1955.
	Hansard, 23 February 1926
	Kelly's Directory (various dates).
LEVELL, Eric	Personal reminiscences.
	Ludgershall Parish Council records.
	Parish registers held in St. James' Church.
	Road repair records held by Ludgershall Parochial Church Council.

CHAPTER TWENTY-THREE

Village Life Between 1895 and 1939

In 1895, just before the coming of the army transformed Ludgershall, the pattern of village life was relatively simple. There were twenty-one traders, of whom three ran public houses. Henry Norris was at the *Crown,* William Collins at the *Queens Head* and Miss Kate Weeks at the *Prince of Wales Hotel and Railway Inn.* This last establishment stood where the Gothic red-brick *Prince of Wales Hotel* (now apartments in Station Approach) was to arise, and was a modest hostelry whose enterprising owner also ran a posting house and, with her brother, a coal merchant's. John Brangwin was baker, grocer and draper. Thomas Meaby was baker, grocer and had the post office, while Ebenezer Westlake was a grocer and a draper. The shops must have been small and with limited stock because the 1891 population census count gave a mere 476 people in the village. Other tradesmen included William Crouch, blacksmith and Parish Clerk, Charles Brackstone, marine store dealer, John Fox, tailor and press correspondent, and George Beams, the carrier.

Highfield House, home of Mary Ann Selfe

Further up the social scale was Nathaniel Young, lord of the manor, who lived at Castle Farm. William Piper and his son were at Biddesden Farm, and T. J. E. Metcalfe occupied Biddesden House. The Rev. William H. Awdry was

Rector and a Justice of the Peace. Dr. Herbert H. Williamson, prominent as newly-elected chairman of the Parish Council, was the local surgeon. Private residents of means included Lieutenant-Colonel Rowland Hill Fawcett, vice-chairman of the Parish Council, and Miss Mary Ann Selfe, who was probably the most influential woman in the village. She had come to live in Ludgershall with her mother in 1863, and is remembered for her *'Dorcas'* classes which she held in Highfield House on Saturday mornings. The girls of the village came to sit and chat, and to learn to sew. (Dorcas was the trade name of a well-known brand of sewing needle). The garments which they produced were distributed to the needy. Her home at Highfield House included at that time a large garden which extended as far as the present railway bridge and enclosed a lovely croquet lawn in a beech hedge. Numbers 29–33 Tidworth Road now occupy the site. When Miss Selfe died a stained-glass window was put in St. James' Church in her memory, and it shines out in deep reds and blues from the north side of the nave. She has a second memorial. The brass offering plate that usually stands on a table near the church door is dedicated to her. The inscription reads: *'He that giveth to the poor lendeth to the Lord.'*

Poverty was still a feature in 1895, but had been virtually abolished by 1904 when Dr. Herbert Williamson reported that:

> *'owing to the building of the new military camp in the adjoining parish of Tidworth there has been a great demand for labour and in consequence very few persons have been out of work.'*

and the coal and clothing clubs ceased to utilise dividends from the ancient Ludgershall charities from 1898. Charitable funds came from four main sources, of which the combined Everett endowment was the largest. Anna Maria Everett, Martha Everett and Ellen Everett gave a total of £700 between 1843 and 1882, and the income from this capital was used for the benefit of the poor at the Rector's discretion. Peter Blake's will of 1624 left funds providing shoes and clothing to deserving cases, who in this parish were generally plough-boys, and Mundays or Poor's Land Charity relied on the income produced by a parcel of land off The Drove of about two and a half acres. Down to 1828 it paid sixpence yearly to forty poor widows of Ludgershall, but after that date the processes of litigation when the land in question changed hands were so prolonged that in Sir Sandford Graham's time the annual payment of £1 was suspended. Smith's Charity came from Henry Smith, a London alderman who by a deed dated 20 January 1827 assigned the rents of certain lands to be employed by the churchwardens and overseers of the poor of each of a number of parishes, one among them being Ludgershall. Henry Smith gave clear and concise directions as to how the money was to be spent by the trustees;

> *"They should distribute the said rents for the relief of aged, poor or infirm people, married persons having more children born in lawful wedlock than their labours should be able to maintain, poor orphans, such poor people as should keep themselves and families to labour, and should put forth their children to apprentices at the age of fifteen; and that they should take course that a stock should be provided and always in readiness to set such of the said persons to work as should be able to labour and take pains."*

He further directed that the churchwardens of each parish should meet once a month to consider which of the poor should be most in need of relief and that they should enter the accounts . . . *'in a book to be kept for that purpose which should be read annually in church.'* The money paid by Henry Smith's Charity to Ludgershall came from a property in Longstock Harrington, Hants; it consisted of the income from a farmhouse and 778 acres of land. Ludgershall's portion was seven out of one hundred and fifty-nine parts of the property, which in the years 1900–1905 averaged £13 10s per annum. Sadly, this sum was not fully inflation-proofed, and the Annual Parish Meetings over the years when figures are disclosed reflect the stagnation of such funds. If we look outside the period covered in this chapter and go forward to 1947 it can be seen how the charitable sums have been eroded. The payout in 1947 amounted to £14 for Smith's, £20 for Everett's and £1-5s. for Blake's. Alderman Smith's bequest is hardly producing enough to sustain a single labouring family for a month. In 1993 the combined Ludgershall charities awarded £12 to each of the fourteen elderly widows in the village—a reflection of the better management of such funds in recent years.

The Vestry accounts show the tilt of change in the years from 1899 to 1904 as the balance of unspent charity money rose to over £91. Population figures confirm an expansion; the village numbers rising to 526 in 1901 and doubling to 1,117 by 1911 as people moved into the area to take up work. By 1911 the number of tradesmen had tripled to more than sixty, and the goods and services being supplied reflected army demands. There were now two hairdressers, William Beavis and Henry Fryer, two tobacconists, Charles Dudman and Miss Jane Cook. There was a stationer, a newsagents, three butchers, a fruiterer and a greengrocer. Mrs. Mary James had opened a refreshment room, as had Charles Wiles. Henry Burden sold fish and chips, and Albert Schmidt had opened a coffee house. Arthur Duke and James Dowse were cycle agents; the Dowse family later moved to Tidworth and opened a cycle shop there. Joseph Hunt set up as a photographer, and William Worsfold worked as a watch-maker. The Crown Mineral Water Works was established in Crown Lane; the building still stands as a warehouse and bottles bearing marbles in the neck turn up regularly in village gardens. H. G. Simonds of Reading built premises in the road that now bears their names and supplied beer to meet government contracts. Allan Herbert came into the area as an estate agent; descendants still live in Andover where the firm he founded continues to flourish. Prospering businessmen took their ease in the newly-built *Prince of Wales Hotel* where John Russell was the manager, and the advertising described it as the nearest *'high class family and residential hotel'* to Tidworth Barracks, Windmill Hill, Perham Down and Pennings Camp.

The construction of the barracks at Tidworth was virtually complete by 1912, and many of the construction workers remained in the area. The Register of Baptisms reflects two new elements in Ludgershall; railwaymen and builders, with fourteen fathers in 1912 being bricklayers, joiners, painters, carpenters or labourers. The number of soldiers is small; regiments did not encourage matrimony before the First World War, and the policy was strengthened by declining to make married quarters available to private soldiers, reserving that privilege for non-commissioned officers of a mature age. When soldiers arrived in even greater numbers after 1914 there was some friction with the civilian population and considerable overcrowding. Drunkenness was said to prevail in the streets of Ludgershall; the public houses were closed at 9 p.m. to discourage rowdiness but, as was pointed out military canteens remained open until 9.30 p.m. and

"Now that there is so much water and not a small amount of mud about, canvas life is not of the brightest unless interspersed with some rousing concerts at frequent intervals."

The streets of Ludgershall were said to be in an 'abominable condition' in November 1914, the reason being the excess of traffic, mostly timber wagons, for the erection of huts on the Plain. In Castle Street and Winchester Street the roads were reported 'sloppy' but in Butt Street the mud had set and was being shovelled up into the gutters to the depth of a foot. In the same week that this was reported the arrival of about four hundred officers and men of the 19th Division Army Service Corps joined the already overcrowded inhabitants and were billeted in:

'The picture Hall, the Police Court, the Wesleyan and Baptist Chapels and the Scouts Hall.'

The Old Bath House in Butt Street (later the site of the Adjutant's Press), would have been a very busy spot while the railway station was cluttered with

'huge consignment of barrels of beer which very often adorn the up platform. Yesterday there were over a hundred barrels awaiting removal . . .'

In 1916 a complaint was voiced in the parish that *'Australian troops are about the village at all hours of the night'*, and John Wilson, headmaster and Parish Clerk, wrote to the Provost Marshall at Bhurtpore Barracks in Tidworth to request an all-night patrol. However, the prosperity brought by war-time conditions seems to have outweighed any inconvenience, and the opening of the *'Soldier's Welcome'* at the Mission Hall and the regular dispatch of parcels and comforts to the troops testifies to the general good relations between soldiers and civilians between 1914 and 1918.

With the need for wives to provide the manpower in shops, factories and farms while their men were away serving in the armed forces, women began to play a more prominent role in local society. The wholly masculine enclave of the Church Vestry Meetings had been infiltrated by a Miss Riggs in 1912. Encouraged by this step, the Rector's wife Mrs. Byrde, Mrs. Andrews and Mrs. Charles Wigley joined her in attending the annual meeting held in 1913 but it was not until the spring of 1922 that a woman served on the Parish Council. She was the Hon. Mrs. Guy Baring who had been widowed in the war. Wreatha Collins remembers the family, all with 'lovely red hair', coming in to take their seats in the Biddesden Chapel. The family held a garden fête for the village on August Bank Holiday in the grounds of Biddesden House. Mrs. Baring continued to serve on the Parish Council until 1928.

As elsewhere in Great Britain, the immediate post war period gave rise to the slogan *'Homes Fit for Heroes'* and an appreciation that the tumbledown cottages that comprised the bulk of the housing stock were inadequate for modern needs. Additionally, the demolition of the old hospital and accommodation huts at Brimstone Bottom led to much rusty corrugated iron being used to repair the old cob and thatch dwellings and the ugliness of these patches gave the village a very shabby air. Mark Elkins, garage proprietor and former police inspector, told Pewsey Rural District Council that:

'several families are living in places that are not certified for habitation and many of the cottages by two families, thereby causing crowding and high rents'

and the initial response was to put up six houses in what became Central Street. Mark Elkins asked for another twelve, and eventually got them. By 1939 there were council houses in the Andover Road, but the coming of the Second World War led to a housing standstill for almost a decade. In the private sector, the enterprising Leonard Astor Labett was developing land south of the railway line, and Astor Crescent was his creation.

The population had stabilised at 1,259 in the 1931 census, and although the period of fast growth was over the village retained a large service sector catering to military needs. The Adjutant's Press was producing invitation cards, headed stationery, handbills and notices; it was to remain in business until the late 1980s with Mike Bulpitt as proprietor. Herbert Allerton was a boot repairer in the Tidworth road and William Thomas the tattooist was further along the same street. Midland Bank and Lloyds Bank had branches in the village, and John Stewart Menzies lived in the Bank House above Lloyds. Gray's Tea Rooms were on the corner of the High Street and the Andover Road, and faggots and peas was a speciality in the cafe in Station Road. Mrs. Laura Gray was also a confectioner and in competition with James Skerry whose shop was in the High Street. George Rusher sold fish and chips, and the family were in business as coal merchants along with George Rawlings & Son and E. Watton & Sons. Reginald Watton was a poultry farmer at The Drove, and the business later switched to market gardening and then operated as a garden centre. The housewives of Ludgershall had the choice of four grocery shops. Charles Teal traded in the Andover Road, and the Yates family ran the Triangle Cash Stores. The Sarum Stores, proprietor, G. H. Diffey, was nearby, as were the premises of Wiltshire & Sons. There were two social clubs. The Sports Club in the Tidworth Road, founded in 1922 and under the secretaryship of William Midwinter in 1939, survives to this day; the British Legion Club has been replaced by the Castle Club on the same site. Dances were held in the Scouts Hall, and the Women's Institute had a cricket team. Behind what was Rusher's Shop in the Tidworth Road was a cinema/theatre known as the *Palladium* that had certainly been in existence since the First World War. It was used for whist-drives, films, lectures and song-and-dance variety shows, and old inhabitants of Ludgershall recall going to the Twopenny Rush on Saturdays when live variety performers held a matinee. The same twopence would obtain admission to the *Electric Cinema* in Tidworth where serial films and cartoons enlivened wet Saturday afternoons. The rather more up-market *Hippodrome* in Tidworth cost sixpence a visit. For those working on the railway such as Hilda and Bob Bunce, there was cheap travel to Andover, Swindon and Southampton by train or Bartletts bus to Andover on market day.

The shadow cast by the coming war was apparent from 1937 when the Clerk was asked to nominate suitable residents to act as wardens, man first-aid posts and attend anti-gas lectures. In the following year the Air-Raid Committee was formed with Captain C. B. Draper as a leading member. Draper owned the *'Prince of Wales Hotel'*, and on one occasion he rented the shooting rights on the allotments and proposed to station beaters on them to the great alarm of the councillors. Evacuees came in September 1939, but few of them stayed for long. Mrs. Wreatha Collins recalls that a coach-load of children came from London, and her mother took in Winnie and Harry Billings from Walworth. The Phoney War period during which nothing much happened intervened, and the children went back to London. To round off this aspect of things before dealing fully in the next chapter with the war years, it is proper to record that Winnie Billings came back to Ludgershall when the

London Blitz was on and stayed with Mrs. Cunliffe in Short Street because she and Mrs. Cunliffe's daughter got on well together. Many such friendships survived into peacetime, and former evacuees still return to talk over old times with their hosts.

SOURCES FOR CHAPTER TWENTY-THREE

	Andover Advertiser, various dates.
BUNCE, Hilda	Personal reminsicences.
	Church Vestry Accounts held by Parochial Church Council.
COLLINS, Wreatha	Personal reminiscences.
JAMES, N. D. G.	*Plain Soldiering*, (the Hobnob Press, Salisbury), 1986.
	Kelly's Directory, various dates.
	Parish records in the church of St. James.
PUGH, R. B. (ed.)	*A History of Wiltshire. VCH*, volume IV, 1959.
	Records of Ludgershall Parish Council.

CHAPTER TWENTY-FOUR

Ludgershall after 1939

The Air Raid Wardens and Special Constables that had been recruited to cope with the trauma of enemy attacks found that their first duty was to find billets for evacuees, and in September 1939 they got a special vote of thanks at a Parish Council Meeting. There was fear, unjustified in the event, of gas attack, and during the winter of 1939–40 Mr. J. Lovell, in his capacity of group warden, made strenuous efforts to get enough civilian gas masks in cardboard boxes for all the village children. In September 1940 when the Battle of Britain was raging the emphasis turned to fire-watching, and Captain P. T. Elliott and Mr. P. A. Berry, who was a former Parish Council Chairman, organised a force of over fifty men and women to look out for and tackle incendiary bombs. The Parish Council obtained stirrup pumps, and heaps of sand were left near the Police station and in the yard of Perham House. Mr. E. E. Roy, whose furniture business survives in the High Street under the same name but different management, had a tall tower built at the top of his yard overlooking what is now Byron Close, and from this vantage point a watch was kept while bombers were overhead. Eric Levell, the well-known naturalist and writer who has served as Parish Clerk since 1958, describes the strain of these extra duties:

> *'At that time I spent several nights each week fire-watching at Ludgershall and several more with the Home Guard at Collingbourne. In fact, when I did join the Royal Navy I used to say that I did so to get a rest.'*

The air battles overhead had two immediate results: the Spitfire Fund Committee was active in the village, and the spur to giving was that when £5,000 had been raised the aircraft would be named for the donors. Attacks on Bristol, Southampton and Coventry in November and December 1940 drove the populations into the countryside each night and the Southampton children, in particular, were in billets in and around Andover. Itchen Secondary School pupils shared their classrooms with Andover Grammar School students, and many children went onto half-day teaching in their usual classrooms with the rest of their time spent more pleasurably in the playing fields or in the Art School above the Public Library in Bridge Street. Some bombs were dropped in daylight close to Tidworth Station, but eye-witnesses say that the Heinkel aircraft was fleeing fighters at the time and flying so low that dropping the bombs was a panic reaction rather than a warlike one. In any event, no-one was hurt.

The *'Dig for Victory'* slogan was coined at this time, and in January 1941 the Ludgershall allotment holders were called to a meeting and told bluntly;

> *'in the National Emergency the Parish Council expects you to fully cultivate your allotment or . . . the Council will terminate your tenancy.'*

and the threat was a serious one because rationing meant that basic foodstuffs alone were hardly sufficient to maintain health. The amounts varied from time to time, but by 1943 each adult had eight ounces of sugar weekly, four of bacon, two of butter and two of cheese. Ironically, rationing led to the lowest crime rates this century. Everyone had to register at food offices, and however often a criminal changed his address he had to notify the food office to get enough to eat so that policemen making regular calls to see who was new in the area were able to make arrests with ease. There was a shortage of accommodation in Ludgershall because of an influx of workers at the Hedge End depot and the arrival of the wives and sweethearts of soldiers who moved to be near them, and Doctor's Meadow became a temporary caravan site. The local bus service was so crowded that eight standing was permitted on the lower deck and an 8.55 a.m. special left Faberstown daily for Tidworth to relieve congestion on the regular service.

After Pearl Harbour American soldiers came in large numbers. Tidworth Garrison, Perham Down and Warminster Barracks, together with eighteen camps on, or adjacent to, Salisbury Plain were allocated to the Americans. The camps near Tidworth were Park House, Pennings, Windmill Hill and Lopcombe Corner and the headquarters of the United States Second Corps was established at Tidworth under the command of General Mark Clark. By the 22 July 1942 virtually the whole of the garrison was taken over, including the married quarters within the camp.

On 8 August 1942 the First Infantry Division arrived at Tidworth to be followed on the 8th of October by the Twenty-Ninth Infantry Division, while the Second Armoured Division moved in on 27 November 1943. Further Infantry and Armoured Divisions followed in 1944 and stayed for varying amounts of time while they finished training and were organised to take their place on the battlefronts. Dances were held at Tidworth in all the different barracks blocks so that as Wreatha Collins remembers *'it was possible to go to a dance every night of the week.'* She also enjoyed the dances held by the Americans at Everleigh.

> *'They sent transport to pick us up and bring us home; we used to tie up the ends of our coat sleeves on leaving and they would fill up the sleeves with food left over from the supper.'*

The first marriage of an American soldier and a Ludgershall girl took place on 9 November 1943 when Muriel New of 4 Bell Street was married to Robert Fairbanks, and there were four more such marriages in 1944. The highest number of war-time marriages came in 1945 when out of twenty bridegrooms seventeen were British servicemen. The end of the war saw a three-day celebration, with a bonfire and community singing on the Recreation Ground and a tea-party for the three hundred children on the Sports Club field. The older inhabitants had a similar tea-party on the Rectory lawn. The post-war baby boom led to demands for a welfare clinic, and the first mother-and-baby sessions were held in the Catholic church in Doctor's Meadow where orange-juice, cod-liver oil and dried milk were distributed. If anything, rationing was more severe *after* the war was over, with bread joining butter and jam on the list of restricted supplies.

Housing was chronically short, and many desperate young couples moved into the huts at Kangaroo Corner which were, strictly speaking, War Department property. Pewsey Rural District Council put in taps for drinking water, and the hut-dwellers scrounged old army coal stoves for cooking and heating. Some of them, like Mrs. Betty Gamble, lived there for three years until proper accommodation was available and the huts were embellished with rockeries, brick chimneys and porches by the occupants. Swedish timber houses went up in 1947, but it was the building of the REEMA houses in Perham Crescent that broke the logjam in 1950 and began a programme that went on to the building of the Woodpark estate that houses so many people today. The REEMA houses were relatively expensive at twenty-four shillings a week rent, and after thirty years or so of occupation some construction flaws developed so that they had to be largely re-built. The streets were not wholly lit by electricity until 1948, and the reason lay far in the past. The Parish Council had clung fiercely to the provisions of the Lighting and Watching Act of 1833 over the years in order to keep the rates down, and until 1933 there were still thirteen acetylene lamps in the village that had replaced the earlier oil lamps. Pewsey Rural District Council had eventually forced the change to electricity, but the coming of war prevented an up-grading in 1939 and a shortage of raw materials had the same effect after 1945. In the older streets the arrival of indoor electric lighting and outside street lighting very nearly came together.

With steady increase in population in the 1950s and 1960s keeping pace with more and better affordable housing, there occurred an improvement in communal facilities and a change of shopping patterns. The Old Rectory in the High Street was redundant once a new clergy house went up in St. James' Street opposite the lych gate, and it was renovated in 1968 through the good offices of Bryan Guinness, the second Baron Moyne, in memory of Lady Evelyn Erskine, wife of the first Lord Moyne. It was thereafter called Erskine House and used as sheltered accommodation for the elderly. Bartlett House at the north end of Central Street had a similar role; it was a new construction opened by the Duke of Gloucester on 5 May 1982, and named after William George Bartlett, County Councillor, who worked to improve the conditions for the sick and elderly of Ludgershall. The Health Centre next door dates from 1980. In that decade there came an awareness of the environment and architectural worth, and the Department of the Environment began listing buildings worthy of preservation. Perry's Cottage, Erskine House, the two public houses, Biddesden House and houses in Castle Street were among those placed on the list, and the full tally may be found in Appendix Twelve.

In the recent past there has been a dramatic change in the pattern of shopping and consumption. Village grocery shops could not meet the supermarket challenge or match their range of products, and the Bungalow Stores at Faberstown and the Spar Grocery near Bell Street both closed their doors. Hocking and Lovell was an old-fashioned haberdashery store even in the 1950s, and it has given way to a solicitor's office and a hairdressing salon. The Midland Bank has gone; Broad's the butcher has become a Chinese take-away and the useful hardware shop in the High Street has been demolished for a redevelopment that has yet to take place. The founder was Jack Challis, who was for many years active on the Parish Council, Pewsey Rural District Council and Kennet District Council. When interviewed, he gave a concise account of what a lifetime of looking at Ludgershall had taught him.

'the times are completely changed', he said, 'people generally have a better standard of living, better schooling, more entertainment and facilities. As children, the Mission Hall annual coach trip to Bournemouth was the only outing. The Scouts Hall was the only social centre. I do not find that people have changed a lot; it is the circumstances of their lives that have changed beyond all imagining.'

SOURCES FOR CHAPTER TWENTY-FOUR

	Andover Advertiser, various issues.
BARRETT, David	*A Wiltshire Camera, 1914–1945.* (Compton Russell Limited, 1976).
CHALLIS, Jack	Personal reminiscences.
COLLINS, Wreatha	Personal reminiscences.
DIXON, Conrad	Personal reminiscences.
GAMBLE, Betty	Personal reminiscences.
JAMES, N. D. G.	*Plain Soldiering*, (The Hobnob Press, Salisbury), 1986.
LEVELL, Eric	Personal reminiscences.
	Parish registers in the church of St. James.
	Records of Ludgershall Parish Council.
TAYLOR, A. J. P.	*English History, 1914–1945.* (Oxford History of England series, BCA, 1977).

APPENDIX ONE

The first part of this appendix attempts to assign explanations for the origin of the name; the second gives the many versions noted down the centuries.

SUGGESTED MEANINGS

LITLEGARSELE — The name given in Domesday Book—see JONES, W. H. *Domesday for Wiltshire*. Bath, 1865. May be a combination of lytel, meaning small, and gaersheath, a grass heath or retired place. Thus, 'a small and sheltered grazing ground'.

LUTLEGRESHALE — 'Lutgers corner of land'. HASLAM, J. and EDWARDS, A. *Wiltshire Towns; the Archaeological Potential.* (WANHS, Devizes), 1976. No Saxon chief called 'Lutger' or 'Ludger' has been traced.

HLYTEGAERSHEALH — 'A nook of land where pasturage is assigned by lot'. GOVER, J. E. *Place Names of Wiltshire*, (English Place Names Society, Cambridge, 1939).

LUTGAERSHALL — Suggested in a newspaper article in 1954 as 'a grass meadow for which lots (luts) were cast'. *Southern Daily Echo*, 22 May 1954.

SPELLINGS

	Date	Source
LATEGARESHEALE	1015	First recorded name.
LITLEGARSELE	1086	The name in Domesday Book.
LUTTEGRESHALE	1279	Somerset Assize Rolls.
LUTERGARSHALE	1287	Calendar of Close Rolls.
LOTEGARSAL	1135	Calendar of Charter Rolls.
LOTEGARSHAL	1203	Calendar of Patent Rolls.
LOTERGARESHALL	1294	Calendar of Patent Rolls.
LOTEGARSHALE	1254	Calendar of Close Rolls.
LUTEGERSHAL	1257	Forest Proceedings.
LUTEGRASHAL	1281	Placita de Quo Warranto.
LUTGERSHALE	1290	Calendar of Close Rolls.
LUTTEGARSHALE	1327	Placita de Banco.
LUDGARSHALE	14??	Feet of Fines.
LUDGERESHALL	1453	Calendar of Patent Rolls.
LUDGASALL	1519	Catalogue of Ancient Deeds II.
LUDGASSALE	1535	Valor Ecclesiasticus.
LURGASALE	1529	Catalogue of Ancient Deeds VI.

	Date	*Source*
LUGGERSHAULE	1540	Leland Itinerary.
LURGUSHALL	1577	A Calendar of Feet of Fines for Wilts.
LURGISHAL	1595	Gerardus Mercator's map.
LUDGASHALL	1715	John Capp's diary.
LUTGERSHALL	1772	John Capp's diary.
LURGERSHALL	1773	Andrews and Drury's map.
LUDGERSHALL	1833	Survey map.

APPENDIX TWO

Rectors of St. James' Church at Ludgershall

1300	William de Budesden	1468	John Horewode
1306	John Sweteman	1472	Edmund Mosprot
1308	Robert de Pagham	1479	David Myleys
1314	Roger de Pirebrock	1479	W. Iokyns
1316	John de Pirebrock	1498	Willis Stacy
1316	John de Rodborne	1512	Edward Esthed
1318	Geffray de Leyghton	1516	Thomas Haghton
1322	William de Hungerford	1553	William Dawkins
1340	Alan de Aveyel	1556	George Whetstones
1340	Nicholas de Durneford	1620	Bartholomew Parsons
1345	Nicholas de Pryton	1641	Andrew Read
1349	John Bide	1650	John Cusse
1361	Robert de Aadeham	1670	John Trobuck
1364	William de Empyngham	1707	Richard Yalden Yaldwyn
1383	Simon Cosyn	1763	Joseph Bailis
1383	Simon Quarendon	1777	John Selwyn
1407	Robert Pyjon	1824	John Pannell
1410	Hugh Brayles	1872	William H. Awdry
1410	Hugh Bryce	1899	Edward S. Best
1440	John Passlewe	1906	Henry A. W. Byrde
1440	William Helyer	1920	Glenn B. Dalrymple
1446	Nicholas Adam	1923	Alfred W. Watt
1448	John Grene	1943	Richard S. Miller
1454	Thomas Sayer	1949	Frederick A. Oliver
1462	Humphrey Gower	1966	Peter Chesters
1465	Robert Dowbelcy	1983	John Rose-Casemore
1466	John Nutkyn	1994	Malcolm Bridger

Source: Triptych in Church of St. James.

APPENDIX THREE

Members of Parliament for Ludgershall, 1295–1831

1295	Willielmus de Lekford and Johannes Dyeuteyt.
1300–1	Willielmus de Lekford and . . . Kynewyne.
1304–5	Adam Douce and Johannes Dieu te eyde.
1306–7	Willielmus Gerveys and Johannes le Neuman.
1309	No return made.
1313	July 8—Johannes atte Mere and Henricus le Smyth.
	Sept 23—Johannes atte Mere and Johannes Sireman.
1314	Names illegible.
1314–15	Walterus de Lecford and Walterus Douce.
1320	Robertus Lonye and Johannes atte Mere.
1329–30	Johannes le Clerk and Johannes Gibon.
1360–1	No return made.

(In addition to the above there were seventy-seven parliaments summoned between 1295 and 1378 for which no returns from this borough have been found.)

1378	Robertus Monek and Robertus Northbourne.
1379–80	Rogerus Sottewell and Robertus le Monek.
1382	Robertus le Monek and Rogerus Shottwell.
1383	Robertus Monek and Rogerus Sotwell.
1384	Summoned to meet at Salisbury April 29 Rogerus Sotwell and Johannes Sille.
1384	Nov. 12 at Westminster—Rogerus Sottewell and Willielmus atte Moure.
1385	Rogerus Shotewelle and Willielmus atte Moure.
1386	The names torn off the return.
1421	Johannes Denby and Willelmus Bysshopp.
1422	Johannes Sturmy and Johannes Saymour.
1423	Willielmus Gatecombe and Johannes Denby.
1425	No return found.
1425–6	Johannes Skylling, jun. and Ricardus Shotwelle.
1427	Return again torn, the word Henricus only remaining.
1429	No return found.
1430–1	Johannes Gloucestre and Ricardus Briggys
1432	Willielmus Ludlowe and Galfridus Gudelok.
1433	Willielmus Luddelowe and Ricardus Brigges.
1435	Willielmus Ludlowe and Willielmus Hankessok.
1436–7	Willielmus Ludlowe and Johannes Combe.
1439	No return found.
1441–2	Thomas Chamburleyn and Thomas de la Pylle.
1444–5	Returns for county of Norfolk only found.
1446–7	Nicholaus Pystor and Thomas Bartelot.
1448–9	Willielmus Clement and Robertus Spycer.
1449	Johannes Erneley and Johannes Strange.

1450	Thomas Thorp and Johannes Erle.
1452–3	Robertus Dyneley and Willielmus Ludlowe.
1455	Willielmus Ludlowe and Johannes Rogers.
	(For the next four parliaments no returns found.)
1467	Arthurus Ormesby and Willielmus Sturmy.
1469 and 1470—No returns.	
1472	Robertus Sheffeld and Ricardus Kyngesmyll.
1477–8	Willielmus Slyfelde and Willielmus Barett.
	(For the next eleven parliaments no returns at all are found.)
1529	Henricus Bridges and Ricardus Brydgis.
	(From this time till the first year of Queen Mary we have no returns.)
1553	Ricardus Bryges, ballivus burgi de Ludgarshall, and Edmundus Powell.
1554	April 2nd. Johannes Wynchecombe, jun., and Edmundus Powell.
1554	Oct. 27th. Anthonius Browne and Arthurus Alleyn.
	Nov. 19th. Johannes . . . vice Anthonii Browne, who elected to serve for Maldon Essex.
1555	Johannes Storye and Johannes Wynchcombe, Jun.
1557–8	Sir Richard Bridges, Knighte, and Thomas Marten.
1558–9	William Weyghtman and Henry Sharryngton.
1562–3	Griffin Curtis and George Cope.
	(Sir R. C. Hoare gives under date 1570, Christopher Wray, Speaker, and James Colbrand; but there is no record of any parliament having been called between 1562–3 and 1572.)
1572	James Colbrand and Thomas Walkadyn.
1584	John Kingesmyll and Francis Button.
1586	Ambrose Coppinger and John Kyngesmyll.
1588	Carew Rawliegh and Henry Huyde or Hynde.
1592–3	Edward Thornboroughe and Chidiac Wardour.
1597	Edmund Ludlowe and Richard Leake.
1601	Robert Penruddocke and James Kyrton.
1603–4	James Kerton and Henry Ludlawe.
	(1614—No returns found; but Sir R. C. Hoare gives Sir Charles Wilmot Knt. and John Thorp.)
1620–1	Alexander Chokke and William Sotwell.
1623–4	Edward Kyrton and William Sotwell.
1625	Sir Robert Pye, Knt., and Sir Thomas Hinton Knt.
1625–6	Sir Wm. Walter Knt., and Sir Thomas Jay, Knt.
	(The names of Sir Wm. Walter and Robert Mason are also given, but without date.)
	(Another return, dated March 18, gives Sir Thomas Hinton, vice Sir Thomas Jay and Robert Mason, whose election was declared void, and another, dated March 21, gives Sir Thos. Jaye, vice Sir Thos. Jay and Robert Mason whose election was declared void. The *Commons Journals* do not show how this election was finally settled nor has any further return been found.)
1627–8	John Seldon and Sir Thomas Jay.
1640	April 13. William Ashborneham and Sir John Evelyn, Knt.

1640	Nov. 3 (Long Parliament). William Ashborneham and Sir John Evelyn, Knt. (Subsequently we get the name of Walter Long, but without date. He was probably elected in the place of William Ashborneham, who was expelled the House, and afterwards disabled (*Commons Journals* Dec. 9th., 1641 and March 23, 1647–8.)
1653, 1654 and 1656.	No returns found.
1658–9	James Dewy and Richard Sherwyn.
1660	William Prynne and William Thomas. July 31 1660 Silas Titus, vice William Prynne, who elected to serve for Bath.
1661	William Ashbournham and Geoffrey Palmer.
1661	Dec 7th. Sir Richard Browne, sen., Knt. and Bart. Major-General of the army of the City of London, vice Geoffrey Palmer, deceased. Oct. 28th. 1699, Thomas Grey, eldest son of Lord Grey, Baron of Werks vice Sir Richard Browne deceased. Feb 12, 1672–3, George Legge, vice Thomas Grey, deceased.
1678–9	Thomas Neale and John Smith, Jun.
1679	Thomas Neale and . . . Gerard (return defaced). (Sir R. C. Hoare gives John Garrett and Thomas Neale.)
1680–1	Sir John Talbot, Knt., of Laycock, and John Smyth. (Another return, which is torn, gives Thomas Neale and . . . Hartford.)
1685	Thomas Neale and Henry Clerke.
1688–9	John Smith and John Deane.
1689–90	Thomas Neale and John Deane. Jan 16, 1694–5 John Webb, vice John Deane, deceased.
1695	Thomas Neale and John Webb.
1698	John Webb and Walter Kent. (Thomas Neale was returned but by an order of the House dated Feb 11, 1698–9, his name was erased and that of John Webb substituted.)
1700–1	Edmund Webb and John Webb.
1701	Colonel Edmund Webb and Colonel John Webb.
1702	Ditto
1705	Walter Kent and John Webb. (Thomas Powell was returned, but on the 17th Jan. the House of Commons ordered his name to be erased and that of John Webb to be substituted.)
1708	Robert Bruce and John Webb.
1710	John Webb and Thomas Pearce.
1713	John Richmond, alias Webb, Lieutenant-General of the Forces and Robert Ferne.
1714	March 24th. John Ward, vice John Richmond, who elected to serve for Newport, alias Medina, county Southampton.
1714–15	John Richmond Webb and John Ivory Talbott.
1722	General John Richmond, alias Webb and Borlace Richmond, alias Webb.
1724	Dec 12th. Anthony Cornish, vice John Richmond Webb, deceased.

1727	Borlace Webb and Charles Boone.
1734	Peter Delme and Daniel Boone.
1741	Charles Selwyn and Thomas Hayward.
1747	Thomas Farrington and George Augustus Selwyn.
1753	Jan 20th. George Augustus Selwyn re-elected after appointment as Chief Clerk Register and Sole Examiner in the Chancery in the Island of Barbados in America and Clerk of the Crown and Peace there.
1754	Sir John Bland, Bart. and Thomas Hayward.
1755	Nov. 21. Henry Digby vice Sir John Bland deceased.
1761	Thomas Whateley and John Paterson.
1768	John Stewart, commonly called Lord Garlies, and Penistone Lamb. July 2, 1798. Lord Garlies re-elected after appointment as one of the Commissioners of Police in Scotland.
1772	Dec. 5th. Lord Garlies re-elected after appointment as one of the Commissioners for Trade and Plantations.
1774	Jan. 22. Whitshed Keene, vice Lord Garlies, called to the Upper House as Earl of Galloway.
1774	Sir Penistone Lambe, Bart. Lord Melbourne of the kingdom of Ireland and George Gordon, commonly called Lord George Gordon. (This is the Lord George Gordon after whom the No-Popery riots of 1780 were named the 'Gordon Riots' and for which he was tried, but acquitted, on the ground that he was more a dupe than a leader. He was subsequently imprisoned for publishing a libel on the Queen of France, and died in Newgate, Nov. 1 1793.)
1780	George Augustus Selwyn and Penistone, Lord Melbourne.
1784	Jan 3. George Augustus Selwyn, re-elected after appointment as Surveyor-General of the Land Revenue.
1784	George Augustus Selwyn and Nathaniel William Wraxall.
1790	George Augustus Selwyn and William Assheton Harbord.
1791	April 28th. Samuel Smith, vice George Augustus Selwyn, deceased.
1793	June 17th. Nathaniel Newnham, alderman of the CIty of London vice Samuel Smith, deceased.
1796	Charles William Montague Scott, commonly called the Earl of Dalkeith, and Thomas Everett.
1802	Earl of Dalkeith and Thomas Everett.
1804	May 7. Magens Dorrien Magens, vice Earl of Dalkeith, who accepted the Chiltern Hundreds.
1806	Magens Dorrien Magens and Thomas Everett.
1807	Ditto.
1810	Feb 27th. Joseph Hague Everett, vice Thomas Everett, deceased.
1811	April 19th. Charles Winn Allanson, Lord Headley, Baron Allanson and Winn of Aghadoe in Ireland, and Bart. vice Joseph Hague Everett, who accepted the Chiltern Hundreds.
1812	Magens Dorien Magens and Joseph Hague Everett. Dec. 22, 1812. Sandford Graham, vice Magens Dorien Magens, who accepted the stewardship of the Manor of East Hendred; and Joseph Birch, vice Joseph Hague Everett, who accepted the Chiltern Hundreds.

1815	June 26th. Charles Nicholas Pallmer, vice Sandford Graham who accepted the Chiltern Hundreds.
1817	June 18th. Henry Lawes Luttrell, Earl of Carhampton in Ireland, vice Charles Nicholas Pallmer, who accepted the Chiltern Hundreds.
1818	Sandford Graham and the Earl of Carhampton.
1820	Ditto
1821	May 5th. George Charles Pratt, commonly called the Earl of Brecknock, vice the Earl of Carhampton, deceased.
1826	George James Welbore Agar Ellis and Edward Thomas Foley,.
1830	Sir Sandford Graham, Bart. and Edward Thomas Foley.
1831	Ditto

Ludgershall was disfranchised by the Reform Act of 1832.

Sources

HISTORY OF PARLIAMENT TRUST — *The House of Commons.* Published in sections by HMSO and Secker and Warburg between 1964 and 1983.

House of Commons Journal (In OPL in British Library).

APPENDIX FOUR

Principal voters in Ludgershall in 1772 and 1791–98

1772	**1791–98**	
(All freeholders)	(Freeholders marked 'F')	
Joseph Baylis, Clerk	John Baiden	(F)
John Castleman	George Cook	
Thomas Humphreys	Christopher Dobb	(F)
Joseph Munday	William Edwards	(F)
Francis Batt	John Hutchins	(F)
George Church	George Noyes	(F)
Richard Hutchins	William Reeves	
Robert Smith	Henry Spratberry	(F)
Robert Horne	Ephraim Sturgis	(F)
Selwyn Sturgess	John Selwyn	
Mark Cook		
George Augustus Selwyn, Esq.		

Sources

LUDGERSHALL HISTORY SOCIETY	List of Freeholders in 1772. Copy in possession of author.
STALKER, C. (comp.)	*Universal British Directory of Trade, Commerce and Manufacture*, London 1791–98.

APPENDIX FIVE

Landowners and Occupiers of Land in the Parish of Lugershall 1841

Landowner	Occupier	No. Referring to Plan	Description	Cultivation
Bailey John	Lansley George	142	Arable Plot	Arable
,,	,,	143	Garden	
,,	,,	178	House, Blacksmith's Shop & Garden	Homestead
,,	,,	239	Carthouse	
,,	Spackman John	144	Garden	
,,	,,	240	Cottage & Garden	Homestead
,,	Lansley Charles / Sturgess David / Taylor Stephen / Beams James	149	Four tenements and gardens	
Batt	Lansly George	99	Top Lay Field	Arable
,,	,,	100	Middle Lay Field	
,,	,,	101	Bottom Lay Field	
Blackmore Ruth	Williams Thomas	134	Kentons	Arable
Chandler Thomas	Fields John / Coombs Charles	236	Two tenements & Gardens	Homestead
,,	Walters James	234	Cottage & Garden	
,,	Culley Robert	233	Garden	
,,	,,	235	The Crown P.H. Yard & Stables	
Everett Joseph Hague Esq.	Himself	47	Back meadow	Pasture
,,	,,	48	Hedgerow Meadow	Wood
,,	,,	49	The Orchard	Pasture
,,	,,	50	Chapel Copse	Wood
,,	,,	55	Part of Coldridge Down	Down
,,	,,	57a	Row in Timberslade	Wood
,,	,,	58	Row & New Field	Arable
,,	,,	59	Row in in New Field	Wood
,,	,,	60	Mundys Down part of	Arable
,,	,,	61	Row Down part of	Wood
,,	,,	62	Cowleaze	Arable
,,	,,	63	Back Smarland	Arable
,,	,,	64	Row Smarland	Wood
,,	,,	65	Smarland Row	Wood
,,	,,	66	Smarland Barn	Arable
,,	,,	67	Hedgerow	Wood
,,	,,	68	Honey Close	Arable
,,	,,	69	Round Coppice	Wood
,,	,,	70	Eighteen Acres	Arable
,,	,,	71	Row	Wood
,,	,,	72	Plantation	Wood
,,	,,	73	Nine Acres	Arable
,,	,,	74	Waste by side of road	Wood
,,	,,	75	The acre Mead	Pasture
,,	,,	76	Chute Mead	Pasture
,,	,,	77	Flower Garden & Shrubbery	Pasture
,,	,,	78	The Park	Pasture
,,	,,	79	Biddesden House, Offices, Lawns etc.	Homestead
,,	,,	80	Plantations	Wood
,,	,,	81	The Gardens	Garden
,,	,,	82	Stables, Yard Etc.	Homestead

Landowner	Occupier	No. Referring to Plan	Description	Cultivation
Everett Joseph Hague Esq	Himself	83	Plantation	Plantation
,,	,,	84	The Park	Pasture
,,	,,	85	Row	Wood
,,	,,	109	Off New Drove Cottage Gdns.	Arable
,,	,,	269	Cottage Gdns.	Arable
,,	Himself and Sturgess James	176	Tenement and Garden	Homestead
,,	William Evan	5	Part of Forty Acres	Arable
,,	,,	6	,,	,,
,,	,,	7	,,	,,
,,	,,	8	,,	,,
,,	,,	9	,,	,,
,,	,,	96	Layfield	,,
,,	,,	260	Yard, Barns etc.	Homestead
,,	Harrison Richard	19	Row	Wood
,,	,,	20	Field in front of House	Arable
,,	,,	21	Carthouse and Pasture	Pasture
,,	,,	22	Spawleypiece	Arable
,,	,,	23	Hedgerow	Wood
,,	,,	24	Greenacre	Mead
,,	,,	25	The eight acres	Arable
,,	,,	26	Great Burrfield	Arable
,,	,,	27	Little Hatters Close	Arable
,,	,,	28	Wood	Wood
,,	,,	29	Redlands	Arable
,,	,,	30	Rowind	Wood
,,	,,	31	Brickkiln Pit Field	Arable
,,	,,	32	Row and Pit end	Wood
,,	Steele James	33	Picket Healdridge	Arable
,,	,,	34	Great Healdridge	Arable
,,	,,	35	The Six acres	Arable
,,	,,	36	Row of Wood	Wood
,,	,,	37	The twenty-two acres	Arable
,,	,,	38	Shoulder of Mutton Copse	Wood
,,	,,	39	,, Field	Arable
,,	,,	40	Bushy Down	Arable
,,	,,	40a	Roadway	Pasture
,,	,,	41	Bushy Down Copse	Wood
,,	,,	42	Fifteen acres	Arable
,,	,,	43	Home Ground	Arable
,,	,,	44	Homestead	Homestead
,,	,,	45	Paddock	Pasture
,,	,,	46	Upper Biddesden Mead	Pasture
,,	,,	51	Long Breach	Arable
,,	,,	52	Coldridge Hill	Arable
,,	,,	54	Part of Coldridge Down	Down
,,	,,	54a	Part of Coldridge Down	Down
,,	,,	56	Great Breach	Arable
,,	,,	57	Rows in Breach	Wood
,,	,,	86	Long Ground	Arable
,,	,,	87	Row in Ground	Wood
,,	Hutchins Joseph	102	Barn Piece	Arable
,,	,,	114	Sheephouse Mead	Arable
,,	,,	115	Sheephouse Ground	Arable
,,	,,	120	Batts Land	Arable
,,	,,	124	Two Acres	Arable
,,	,,	185	Queens Head P.H. Yard Stables Barn & Gdn.	Homstead
,,	,,	186	Garden	Homestead
,,	,,	187	Garden	Homestead

Landowner	Occupier	No. Referring to Plan	Description	Cultivation
Everett Joseph Hague Esq.	Hutchins Joseph	188	Meadow	Pasture
,,	,,	189	Arable	Arable
,,	,,	190	The Orchard	Pasture
,,	Hutchins John	254	Garden	
,,	Cook James	145	Cottage & Gdn.	Homestead
,,	Beams Jane			
,,	Lansly George	148	Two Tenements & Gdns.	Homestead
,,	Beams William	176	Yard Stable etc	
,,	Beams William }	175	Two Tenements & Gdns.	
,,	Lansley William }			
,,	Coombs David	244	Cottage & Gdn.	Homestead
,,	Cockell James			
,,	Taylor Isaac	168	Gardens	
,,	Cockell James	172	Tenement & Gdn.	Homestead
,,	Cannings James			
,,	Coombs John			
,,	Gudman Thomas			
,,	Richardson George			
,,	Tayler David	191	Ten Tenements and Gardens	Homestead
,,	Sturgess James			
,,	Sturgess Sarah			
,,	Cook James			
,,	Reeves William			
,,	Sturgess Henry			
,,	Crouch William and Joseph	192	Blacksmith Shop and Garden	
,,	Dudman Thomas	185	Garden	
,,	Edwards Francis	207	Cottage & Gdn.	Homestead
,,	Edwards Philip			
,,	Muspratt Joseph	256	Gardens	Homestead
,,	Fuld John			
,,	Edwards Thomas	208	House & Gdns.	Homestead
,,	Hunt Henry			
,,	Beams Jane	135	In New Drove	Arable
,,	Hunt William	152	Tenement & Gdn.	Homestead
,,	Hunt Henry	154	House & Part of Garden	Homestead
,,	Hunt James	252	Barn and Yard	Homestead
,,	Hutchins John			
,,	Williams Evan	205	Two Tenements & Gardens	Homestead
,,	Lansley George	177	Gardens	Homestead
,,	Lansley George	282	Gardens	Homestead
,,	Lansley George			
,,	Lay William			
,,	Sturgess Nancy	195	Four Tenements & Gardens	
,,	Whitmarsh Widow			
,,	Lay James	196	Two tenements & Gardens	,,
,,	Matthew William			
,,	Leaver Richard			
,,	Sollice Widow			
,,	Worsdale Widow			
,,	Smith Betty			
,,	Richardson Henry			
,,	Cook Henry	159	Nine Tenements & Gardens	Homestead
,,	Newman Thomas			
,,	Reeves David			
,,	South Charles			
,,	Leaver Richard			
,,	Spicer James	160	Garden	
,,	Smith Charles			
,,	Phillimore John	204	Cottage & Gdn.	Homestead

Landowner	Occupier	No. Referring to Plan	Description	Cultivation
Everett Joseph Hague Esq.	Purdue Joseph	258	Garden	
,,	Bull George	179	Garden	
,,	Evans Joseph			
,,	Edwards Francis	209	Gardens	
,,	Spicer Robert			
,,	Sturgess James	156	House & Gdn.	Homestead
,,	Spicer William	218	Two Tenements & Gdns.	
,,	Burns John			
,,	Spicer William	242	Garden	
,,	Sturgess William	225	Cottage & Gdn.	Homestead
,,	Tarrant Thomas	130	Cottage & Gdn.	Homestead
,,	Tarrant William	170		Homestead
,,	Tayler William	224	House & Gdn.	Homestead
Everett J. and Hunt H.	Matthews John	217	Cottage & Gdn.	Homestead
Everett J. and Green Charles	Fields Charles	222	Three Tenements	Homestead
,,	Fields John			
,,	Sheppard Jonathan			
Everley Turnpike Trustees of Fowle,		88	Turnpike House & Gdn	Homestead
Sir Henry	Himself	53	Coldridge Coppice	Wood
Graham, Sir Sandford	Crook Jacob	1	The Down	Down
,,	,,	2	Down Ground	Arable
,,	,,	3	Down Ground & Westfield	,,
,,	,,	4	In West Field	,,
,,	,,	10	The sixty acres	,,
,,	,,	11	Coneygre	,,
,,	,,	12	The eighteen acres	,,
,,	,,	13	Long Park & Crowbush piece	,,
,,	,,	14	Bowling Alley Park	,,
,,	,,	15	Wood Park	,,
,,	,,	16	Town Field or East Field	,,
,,	,,	18	West Wood	,,
,,	,,	128	The Seven Acres	,,
,,	,,	129	The eight acres	,,
,,	,,	136	The eleven acres	,,
,,	,,	137	Late Garrards	,,
,,	,,	138	Milk pit Croft etc.	,,
,,	,,	132	Late Hutchins	,,
,,	,,	141	Fishers Field	,,
,,	,,	198	The Ditches	Pasture
,,	,,	199	House & Gdn. etc.	Homestead
,,	,,	200	The Ditches	Pasture
,,	,,	201	The Ditches	Pasture
,,	,,	202	Farm Homestead	Homestead
,,	,,	203	The Ditches	Pasture & Wood
,,	,,	206	Private Road	Road
,,	Burden James	261	Garden	
,,	Crook Evi	107	Earls	Arable
,,	,,	108	Late Hutchins	Arable
,,	,,	111	Four Acres	Arable
,,	,,	130	Kelsey's & three acres	
,,	Coombs Charles	157	Garden	
,,	Dudman Caleb	246	Cottage & Gdn.	Homestead
,,	Lansley George	241	Stable & Yard	Homestead
,,	,,	243	Tullans Garden	Arable
,,	Smith John	197	Tenement & Gdn.	Homestead

Landowner	Occupier	No. Referring to Plan	Description	Cultivation
Graham, Sir Sandford	Reeves William			
,,	Baiden James	262	Garden	
,,	Williams Thomas	182	Ravenscroft	Arable
Gulliver Benjamin	Tayler Thomas	213	Tenement & Gdn.	Homestead
Green Charles Henry	Himself	229	Garden	
,,	,,	230	Garden	
,,	,,	231	House Brewhouse Yard	Homestead
Hutchins Thomas	Crook Evi	90	Bottom Mead	Arable
,,	,,	106	House Barn Stable Granary Gdn & Yard	Homestead
,,	,,	110	At New Drove	Arable
,,	,,	112	Burgess Piece	Arable
,,	,,	125	Burgess Marl Piece	
,,	,,	127	Bottom Piece	Arable
Hutchins William	Himself	131	Adjoining Kelsey & three acres	Arable
,,	,,	133	Windmill Ground	Arable
,,	,,	165	House & Yard	Homestead
,,	,,	166	Garden	Homestead
,,	,,	167	Foals Croft	Pasture
,,	Himself and Curry George and Rockall John	104	Two Tenements Gdn. Stable & Yard	
Hutchins Joseph	Himself	126	Reeves Ground	Arable
,,	Himself and Burbage George	105	Tenement & Gdn.	Homestead
Henry James Esq.	Barnes John	91	South Park	Arable
,,	,,	92	Road and Waste	Road
,,	,,	93	South Park	Arable
,,	,,	94	South Park	Arable
,,	,,	95	South Park	Arable
,,	,,	113	King's Field	Arable
,,	,,	116	Sheephouse Ground	Arable
,,	,,	116a	Roadway	Road
,,	,,	117	Bottom Ground	Arable
,,	,,	118	Pit Ground	Arable
,,	,,	119	Barn, Yard & Plantation	Homestead
,,	,,	121	King's Field	Arable
,,	,,	122	,,	Arable
,,	,,	123	,,	Arable
Hunt James	Himself	139	Windmill & Arable	Arable
,,	,,	140	Tenement, Barn, Stable Yard occupied by Widow Chandler	Homestead
,,	,,	147	House, Yard, Gdn. & Stables	Homestead
,,	Himself, Cannings James Fields Richard	146	Three Tenements & Gdns.	Homestead
Hunt Henry	Himself	155	Yard & Part of Gdn.	Homestead
,,	,,	221	Piece of Waste	Homestead
,,	Himself and Hopgood Thomas	153	Tenement & Gdn. Carpenter's Shop. Yard etc.	Homestead
,,	Bendall Charles Baiden James Dobbs Widow Hiscock John Tayler Charles Cook Widow	215	Six Tenements & Gardens	Homestead
,,	Matthews John	219	Garden	Homestead
,,	Muspratt Joseph Edwards Philip	235	Two Tenements & Gdns.	Homestead
Independents Society of	Walcot John	220	Chapel	

Landowner	Occupier	No. Referring to Plan	Description	Cultivation
Lee Thomas	Himself	151	Cottage, Gdn. Yard & Stable	Homestead
Millett William Dobbs Mary J. H. Everett	Lifeheld under Themselves	194	Two Tenements & Gdn.	,,
Lay John	Himself	103	Cottage & Gdn	,,
Lansly John	Butt George	180	Cottage & Gdn	,,
Lansly John	Hutchens Joseph	181	Garden	,,
,,	Lee John	243	Cottage, Gdn. & Yard	,,
Muspratt George	Himself	253	Cottage & Gdn.	,,
Purdue Joseph	Himself	257	House Gdn. & Yard	,,
Sturgess James	Himself	161	Orchard	Arable
,,	Lay Widow and Happerfield William	158	Two Tenemenets & Gdns.	Homestead
,,	Spicer James and John	162	Two Tenements & Gdns.	,,
Sturgess John	Crouch William	214	Tenement & Gdn.	,,
Sturgess Henry	Himself	171	House & Gdn.	,,
,,	,,	169	Gardens	,,
,,	Cook Anthony	173	Tenement & Gdn.	,,
Smith Richard	Smith Eleanor and Cook Thomas	163	Two tenements & Gdns.	,,
Stanley Thomas	Happerfield James and Dudman Robert	248	Two Cottages & Gdns.	,,
Turner Edward	Culley Robert	97	Layfield	Arable
,,	,,	98	,,	,,
Turner James	Himself	238	Barn & Yard	Homestead
,,	Tarrant Thomas	237	Cottage & Gdn.	,,
Tayler Isaac	Himself	164	,,	,,
Taplin Henrietta	Unoccupied	195	House & Gdn.	,,
Walcot John	Himself	184	House Gdn. & Yard	,,
,,	Himself	223	Meadow	Pasture
,,	Reeves Joseph Smith Thomas	212	Two Tenements & Gdns.	Homestead
William Thomas	Himself	259	Cottage & Gdn.	,,
William Evan	Himself	251	Garden	,,
,,	Crouch Joseph	210	Tenement & Gdn.	,,
,,	Gulliver William	226	Garden	,,
,,	,,	227	Yard & Stable	,,
,,	,,	228	House & Gdn.	,,
,,	Offer Thomas Dobbs William	211	Two Tenements & Garden	,,
,,	Tayler William	250	Cottage & Gdn.	,,
	Commonable	17	Spray Leaze	Down
		89	No Man's Ball	Down & Road
		247	Church and Church Yard	

Note: Where space permits, the number in the third column will be found to correspond with that on the plan in the text.

Source

Apportionment of the Rent-Charge in lieu of Tithes attached to the Tithe Map of 1841. Original in WRO.

APPENDIX SIX (A)

Leading Inhabitants of 1786

John Coombs	Parish Clerk and Sexton	74 years of age
John Edwards	Carpenter	80 years of age
Daniel Dobbs	'the oldest'	91 years of age
Daniel Dobbs	'the elder'	60 years of age
Daniel Dobbs, Junior	Constable	30 years of age
Roger Geator	Churchwarden	30 years of age
John Beale	Senior Overseer of The Poor	60 years of age
John Beale, Junior	Miller	30 years of age
Robert Smith	Freeholder	69 years of age
Thomas Parsons		50 years of age

APPENDIX SIX (B)

'A list of Proper Persons to serve the Office of Surveyor of the High Roads for the Parish of Ludgershall to be returned ot the Justices agreeable to a meeting held in the Parish Church by publick notice 23 Sept 1793.'

James Wilkins	Joseph Hawkins	Thos. Everett, Esq.
Thos. Batt	Thos. Beale	Joseph Shipway
Wm. Edwards	John Hutchins	Henry Spratsbury
Wm. Reeves		

Note: James Wilkins and Joseph Hawkins were appointed in 1793 and 1794; John Hawkins and Thomas Batt in 1795.

Sources:

The 'True note and terrier of all Tythes' in *WRO*.

Road repair records held by Ludgershall Parochial Church Council.

APPENDIX SEVEN

*Stationmasters who served on the
Midland and South-West Junction Railway*

LUDGERSHALL

1882	
1883–1884	J. Manning
1884–1890	S. Lock
1893	W. E. Chitty
1894–1898	A. F. Newman
1899–1901	F. J. Lashbrook
1902–1906	R. M. Davies
1906–1908	E. G. James
1908–1927	G. H. Humphries
1927–1936	S. J. G. Harding
1936–1961	E. F. Vickery

TIDWORTH

1901	Mr. Morris
1901–1906	F. J. Lashbrook
1906–1908	R. M. Davies
1908–1928	E. F. Bodwin
1928–1935	A. E. Jones
1936–1943	L. E. Perrott
1944–1947	V. Edwards
1947–1955	S. G. S. Plummer

Sources:

BRIDGEMAN, Brian, BARRETT, David and BIRD, Dennis — *Swindon's Other Railway*. (Red Brick, Swindon), 1985.

APPENDIX EIGHT

The Midland and South-West Junction Railway—Chronology

Opening of Swindon, Marlborough and Andover Railway Station at Ludgershall	1 May 1882
Remodelling & extension to coincide with the building of Tidworth Military Railway	1900–1902
Double line opened to Weyhill	28 August 1900
Double line opened to Collingbourne	1 September 1901
Tidworth Branch opened for goods	1 July 1902
Tidworth Branch opened for passengers	1 October 1902
Engine Shed opened	1903
5-ton Yard Crane installed	1916
Water tank and columns installed	1916
Engine Shed closed	July 1925
British Railways Southern Region take-over	2 April 1950
Line to Perham Box singled	15 November 1955
British Railways Western Region take-over	1 February 1958
Line to Weyhill singled	29 August 1960
Station closed to passengers	11 September 1961
Line to Swindon closed	11 September 1961
Tidworth Branch closed	31 July 1963
Closed for public goods	24 March 1964

The railway line remains open from Andover as a military siding as far as the Hedge End vehicle depot.

Source:

BARTHOLOMEW, David   *Midland and South Western Junction Railway*. Wild Swan Publications. 1982.

APPENDIX NINE

Burials and Baptisms; 1621–1850

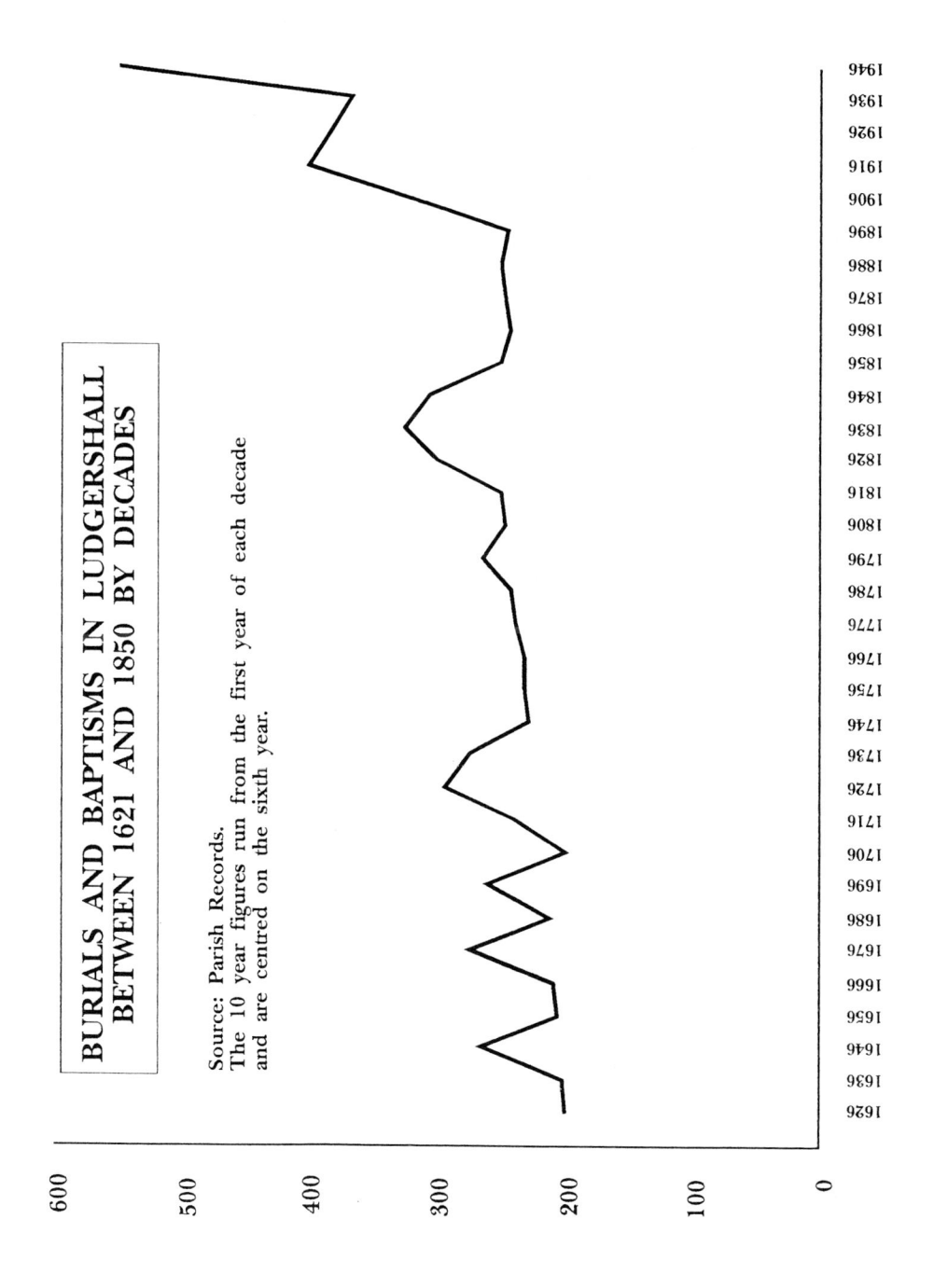

BURIALS AND BAPTISMS IN LUDGERSHALL BETWEEN 1621 AND 1850 BY DECADES

Source: Parish Records.
The 10 year figures run from the first year of each decade and are centred on the sixth year.

APPENDIX TEN

Walter Vavasour Faber entered the Royal Artillery in 1877, and transferred to the Royal Horse Artillery in 1884. Promoted Captain in 1885, he resigned five years later but rejoined for service in the South African War with the Wilts Yeomanry in 1901. He resigned again in 1908, but came back for the First World War, being promoted Major in 1914 and Lieutenant Colonel in 1915. His principal interests were hunting and fishing, and he served as Master of the Tedworth Hunt in 1907–08. Contemporary accounts show that many meets began at his home at Brewery House, Weyhill with the field then riding westwards to draw coverts at Sidbury Hill, Everleigh and Collingbourne. On one occasion while he was Master the hunt made an unusually long run from a covert in Savernake Forest to Etchilhampton, a distance of about thirty miles.

A landowner and partner in Strongs of Romsey, a leading brewery, he was elected the Member of Parliament for West Hants in January 1906, holding the seat for the Conservatives until 1918 and becoming Deputy Lord-Lieutenant of the county. His scheme for Faberstown was imaginative, but it did not mature during his lifetime because it was not until the 1960s that all the sites that had been pegged-out at the turn of the century were finally utilised for housing.

Sources

'The Strong Country' in *Hampshire the County Magazine*. July—December 1966.

Andover Advertiser issues for January 1906.

FABER, David and HOPE, J. F. R.   *The History of Hunting in Hampshire*. 1950.

APPENDIX ELEVEN

Names on the War Memorial

West Face
Lt. Col. Hon. Guy Baring MP DSO
C. C Baiden
D. Barnett
A. Bates
A. J. Boulter
R. Bunce   *First World War*
J. W Conquest
W. H. East
H. W. Elkins DCM
R. J. Freeman
F. C. Hockings
W. C. Keen
C. H. Lansley
R. Loader
F. Davidge

East Face
A. Peck
E. Soper
J. McEvoy
W. J. Millett
R. Perry
W. Perry
J. Pillans
F. W. Pocock
A. H. Rose
E. J. Scanlan
A. G. Smith
W. Taylor
E. C. Walker
G. V. Ward
J. F. Ware
D. F. Worsdell
W. Worsfold DCM

Note: F. Davidge and A. Peck do not appear on a second list in St. James' Church, and as they are top and bottom of their columns it is likely that these names were added after 1920.

North Face—World War Two

J. A. Blackmore
A. T. East
W. V. L. Edwards
W. C. Harper
C. Harland
M. E. Hayward
C. E. Jeremy
T. F. Knight
M. H. Lansley
C. Lansley

E. M. Luff
R. V. Moore
G. A. Peck
R. W. Roberts
E. F. Saunders
V. A. Taylor
R. G. Vockins
G. W. J. Young
A. C. Worsdell
E. R. Hiscocks

Note: The record in St. James' Church also shows:
H. K. Annetts   Albert George Godfrey   Eric Sheldon Shrimpton

175

APPENDIX TWELVE

Listed buildings and structures in Ludgershall

Perry's Cottage, 29 Andover Road. Chalkstone/cob house with thatched roof, eighteenth-century.

Milestone 1M west of village on S. side A342. Eighteenth-century.

Biddesden farmhouse, Biddesden Lane. Flint and chalkstone faced in diaper brick. Late seventeenth to early eighteenth-century.

Farm buildings at Biddesden Farm SE of main building, same date.

Entrance screen and gates at Biddesden House. Eighteenth-century.

Sundial in front of Biddesden House. Early eighteenth-century.

Biddesden House, 1710–11.

Dovecote at Biddesden Park. Flint and brick. Eighteenth century.

Stables and dairy cottage in Biddesden Lane.

Gazebo at Biddesden House, c. 1933.

Cob and flint walls at fruit garden, Biddesden House.

Two cottages, No. 6 and Lynton, north side of Butt Street.

Two houses, 1 and 3 Castle Street.

15, 17, 19 and 20 Castle Street, c. 1690.

Crawlboys Farmhouse, Crawlboys Lane, Eighteenth-century.

Farm buildings S of Crawlboys Farmhouse on N side of Crawlboys Lane.

Ludgershall Cross. Fifteenth-century. Railings from 1897.

Queens Head public house. Sixteenth-century.

Crown Inn. Seventeenth-century.

Erskine House, High Street. Late eighteenth-century.

St. James' Church.

Two chest tombs in churchyard of limestone S of tower.

Chest tomb in churchyard E of chancel.

Highfield House, 27 Tidworth Road, rendered rammed chalk, early nineteenth-century.

Source: Department of the Environment.

General Index

Abbatts Close   136
Abbotts Ann   89
Adjutants Press   136, 146, 147
Air Raid Committee   147
air raids   111, 112, 151
air raid wardens   147, 151
allotments   83, 85–86, 137–139, 147, 151
Amesbury   2, 7, 9, 32, 78
   Abbey   31, 37, 49
American soldiers   112, 128, 152
Andover   3, 55, 63, 65, 77, 128, 136, 151
   Advertiser   97, 122, 133, 149
   Grammar School   109, 151
   Junction station   89
   Road   53, 70, 73, 83, 85, 113, 122
   Workhouse   77–78
Anna Valley   69
   Workmen's Hall Mission   128
archaeological record   23–30
Armoured Fighting Vehicle Depot   85, 98
Army   89–95, 97–100, 143, 145, 146
Army Medical Equipment Depot—see
   D-Med
arson   69–70
artifacts   2–4
assarting   9
Astor Crescent   76, 135, 147
Australian troops   98, 107, 146
Avebury   1, 2
Avon, river   2, 18, 67

bailey   23
bailiff   53, 67, 68
Bank House   147
baptisms   105, 145, 173
Baptist chapels   127, 146
barley   1, 81
Bartlett House   153
Barton Stacey   69
Bath   3, 127
Beacon Hill   90
Beaker Folk   2
Bedwyn   53, 54, 92
begging   68
Bell Street   118, 135, 137, 152, 153
bells   43, 44, 63
Benedictine   37
   monks   9
   order   37
Biddesden   9, 19, 20, 34, 37, 49–52
   Bottom   3

chapel   43
   Farm   76, 83, 143, 176
   House   40, 43, 45, 61, 62, 63, 76, 85, 104,
     107, 143, 146, 153, 164, 176
   Lane   83, 85, 176
Bishop Wordsworth's School   44, 109
Blake's Charity   144, 145
Blenheim, battle of   49
Boer War   136
bordars   4, 9
Bourne, river   2, 115
Bowling Alley Park   86, 167
bread   69, 77
   price of   69, 76, 77
   rationing of   152
brick kilns   76
Brimstone Bottom   91–92, 111, 116
British Legion Club   147
Broad's the butchers   153
Brockenhurst   9
Bronze Age   2–3
Brydges Road   86
buildings   73, 92, 109, 122, 130–131, 135
Bulford   2, 90, 122
Bullock's Mead   85
Bungalow Stores   83, 135, 153
Burbage   8
burgage   50, 62, 65
Burgess Marl Piece   86, 168
Burgess Piece   86, 168
burgesses   53
Burghclere   69
burials   73, 78, 83, 105, 127, 173
Butser Iron Age Farm   3
Butt Street   70, 73, 85, 103, 105, 117, 136,
   146, 176
Byron Close   151

Calne   33, 53
camps   1, 2, 152
   causewayed   1, 2
Canterbury
   Archbishop of   45, 63
   Cathedral   33
Capital and Counties Bank   117
carucate   7–8
Castle   4, 9, 11–34, 67
   Club   127, 147
   Farm   62, 76, 83, 91, 117, 129, 136, 137
     143

Street   73, 76, 103, 118, 135, 136, 146, 153, 176
Castledown School   109, 113, 135
Castle Primary School   113
Catholic   56, 127, 128
  church   109, 128, 152
  Women's League   128
Celts   2–3
Central Street   146, 153
cereals   1, 3
Challis Court   136
Chapel Lane   50, 127, 135
chapels   32, 43, 127–128, 146
Chaplin & Co, parcel agents   92
charities   103, 144–145
Chippenham   53
church records   43, 50, 76
churchwardens   43, 44, 45, 76, 83, 136, 144, 170
Chute   19, 56, 103
  Causeway   3
  forest of   9, 18, 19, 20, 27, 50
Clyffe Pypard   11
coaches   63
coinage   17
Coldridge Down   4, 164, 165
Colliss Terrace   136
Collingbourne   2, 18, 19, 68, 89, 127, 151
  Ducis   19
  Kingston   121
  manor of   8
  Road   97, 116
Common Law   17, 18
Coneygre (field)   86, 167
Conholt   19
  Park   103
constables   53, 67, 68, 70, 151, 170
Continental System   69
Corn Law   69
cottars   4
court leet   53, 67
courts   67–71, 146
Crawlboys   76
  Farm   76, 83, 176
  Lane   83, 85
Cricklade   49, 53
crime   67–71
crops   1
cross   50, 129, 176
Crown Lane   105, 145
Crown Mineral Water Works   145
Crown public house   63, 64, 73, 76, 118, 124, 128, 143, 153, 164, 176

Dallas (house at 13 Butt Street)   73, 85
Danebury Down   13

debt   67
deer   18–20, 67
Defence Medical Equipment Dept (D-Med)   85, 98–99
demesne   7–8
Devizes   12–13, 53, 70
  castle   12, 67
  hospital   116
Deweys Lane   73, 85, 86, 136, 137
diet   69, 77
dissection   68–69
Doctor's Commons   103
Doctor's Meadow   44, 109, 128, 152
Dodsdown   92
dogs   1
Domesday Book   4, 7–9, 18
donjon   23
Downton   53
Drove Road   135
Dublin   51
Durrington Walls   1, 2

Earls (field)   85
East Woodhay   69
Eleanor Court   99
electoral practices   55–57, 61–65
Electric Cinema   147
electricity, supply of   110, 112, 119, 153
Elkins Garage   70, 127
enclosure   47, 81–86
Erskine House   46, 61, 73, 153, 176
evacuees   111, 147–148, 151
Everetts Charity   144, 145
Everleigh (Everley)   55, 152
  fire brigade   121
  House   121
  petty sessions   70
  Turnpike Trust   85, 167
excavation reports   23–30
Exeter   3
  Book   7, 9

Faberstown   85, 115, 135, 136, 152, 174
farming   1, 2–3
Fifield   77
finance   17, 81, 83
fire   70, 121–125, 151
  brigade   121–124
  risks   121
Fisher's Field   85, 167
Fisherton Jail   67, 70
flax   1
Fontevrault   33
  order of   32, 37
footbridge   135
footpaths   92, 111, 135

178

forest   1, 8, 9, 18–20, 34
   clearance of   1, 9
   law   19–20
Four Acres   86
freeholders   163

game   18–20, 67
   law   19–20, 69
gas supply   119
Ghurkas   98
Gloucester   3, 57, 97
Gordon Riots   58
Grafton   89, 92
Grays Tea Rooms   147
Great Bedwyn   62
Great Western Railway   89, 90, 97, 99

Hamstead Marshall   11
Harcourt House   117
Harrowdean   19
Hastings, battle of   7
hatchments   40
Havering atte Bower   33
health   73–74, 76, 104, 110, 112, 116, 117, 152
Hedge End   97, 98, 152
Hei-Lin Way   85, 123
Hembury   1
henge monuments   1, 2
hide   7–8
Highfield House   73, 85, 143, 176
High Street   9, 28, 70, 73, 122, 136
Hippenscombe   19
Hippodrome Cinema   147
Hocking and Lovell, haberdashers   153
houses and housing   4, 73, 98, 128, 146–147, 152–153, 176
hunting   9, 34, 174
Hurstbourne Tarrant   19
Hyson Close   136

In-West Field   85, 167
Iron Age   2–3

jails   67–71
John Hanson School   109
justice   17
   administration of   18
Justices   67–71
   in Eyre   19
   of the forest   19
   of the peace   63, 67, 68, 144

Kangaroo Corner   98, 109, 153–154
keep   26
Kelseys (field)   86, 167

Kennett   73, 128
   and Avon Canal   90
   District Council   153
   river   2
   valley of   11
Kimpton   77, 85
Kings Field   76, 83, 86, 168
kings warden   19

Lady Diana Court   136
Lambourne's Hill   3
land areas   81
landowners   81, 83
Lansdowne Terrace   117
Late Hutchins (field)   85, 167
Laurel House   73, 130
Lavinia Cottage   83, 85
Leeds Castle   33
legislation   65, 69, 77, 81, 89, 90, 97, 105, 122, 127, 136, 153
Lena Close   86
lighting   110, 153
Linden Close   83
Linton Cottage   73–74, 176
London   3, 12, 51, 89, 99, 127
London and North Western Railway   93
London and South Western Railway   89
Long Parliament   55
Ludgershall   2, 7, 9, 11, 50, 53, 62, 63, 69–70, 85, 89, 127–131
   allotments   83, 85, 86, 137–139, 151
   area   7, 81, 83
   borough   40, 53, 62, 65
   Boys Club   128
   castle   4, 9, 11–34, 67
   chapels   32, 33, 43, 127–128, 146
   charities   103, 144–145
   clergy   157
   fire brigade   121–124
   forest of   18–20, 27
   housing   73, 98, 128, 146–147, 152–153, 176
   local history society   23
   manor of   20, 32, 33, 34, 46, 49, 54, 56, 62, 137
   Members of Parliament   39, 40, 53–65, 158–162
   Memorial Hall   51, 109, 130–131
   Mission Hall   70, 127, 128, 153
   monuments   51, 129–131
   Moor   19
   parish clerk   63, 83, 105, 117, 123, 133, 136, 143, 146, 151, 170
   parish council   51, 70, 111, 115–123, 127, 129, 131, 136–140, 151, 153
   parish registers   40, 43, 73, 76, 89

Rectors of   37, 43, 46
recreation ground   85, 137–140, 152
St. James' Church   4, 20, 34, 37–48, 83, 98, 109, 130, 136, 169, 176
schools   40, 63, 103–114
Scouts Hall   50, 109, 113, 122, 127, 146, 153
station   85, 89–94, 97–100, 146
territorial drill hall   128
tithes   47, 81–86
versions of the name   4, 155–156
vestry accounts   141, 145
war memorial   51, 129–130, 132, 175
water supply   115–121
Lynton Cottage   73, 74, 176

Magna Carta   17
Malmesbury   53
Malplaquet, battle of   49
Manchester   89
manoeuvres   90
Marchwood, port of   99–100
Marlborough   11, 13, 53, 54, 89, 136
  castle   14, 67
  grammar school   109
Marlins Farm   83, 85
marriages   152
Meade Road   83, 118, 136
Memorial Hall   51, 109, 130–131
Merle Cottage   73, 75
Methodism   103, 127
Micheldever   69
Midland and South Western Junction Railway   85, 90, 91–93, 97, 99
Midland Bank   147, 153
Mildenhall   3
Mission Hall   127–128, 153
Missy Lodge   136
Mortimer Cross, battle of   34
motte and bailey castles   23, 34
Mundays or Poor's Land Charity   144
murders   68

Navy Army and Air Force Institute (NAAFI)   94, 97, 118
National Agricultural Labourers Union   70
Neolithic Age   1
Newbury   39
  seige of   13, 31
New Drove   85
Newton Villas   85
Nicholas Close   85
Nine Mile River   2
No Man's Ball   83–85, 169
Normans   4
  architecture   23–27, 34, 37
  before their coming   1–4

invasion   4
Norwich   33

occupations   46, 63, 89, 91, 143–144, 145
Old Bath House   146
Old Rectory (Erskine House)   46, 61, 73, 153
Old Sarum   3, 53, 57, 67
Old School House   103–109, 136
Overseers
  of the Highway   135, 170
  of the Poor   76, 105, 170

Palladium   107, 146, 147
parish   76–77, 78, 135
  clerk   63, 83, 105, 117, 123, 135, 136, 143, 146
  council   111, 115–123, 127, 129, 131, 136–140, 146, 153
  nurse   107
  registers   40, 43, 73, 76, 89
Park House Camp   107, 152
parking   130, 135
paupers   77, 78
Pennings Camp   145, 152
Penton Grafton   45, 69, 77
Perham Crescent   118, 136, 153
Perham Down   2, 90, 91, 93, 98, 115, 145, 152
Perham House   97, 151
Perry's Cottage   51, 73, 74, 153, 176
Peter Blake's Charity   144–145
Pewsey   70, 123
  fire brigade   121, 122
  Rural District Council   70, 111, 115, 116, 117–118, 122, 123, 136, 137, 152, 153
  workhouse   77–78
Pickpit Hill   2
pigs   1
Pipe Rolls   17–18
police   67, 70, 123
  station   70, 151
ponds   76, 115, 118–119, 122, 124
poor law   73–78
population   73, 85, 105, 131, 145, 147
Portway   3
Pretoria Road   136
Prince Charles Close   136
Prince of Wales Hotel   92, 117, 143, 145, 147
Prince of Wales Hotel and Railway Inn   92, 143
Princess Mary Gardens   86
public order   69–71

Quarley   69
Queen's Head public house   28, 63, 64, 73, 76, 85, 129, 143, 153, 165, 176
Queenhithe   32

180

railway   89–94, 97–100, 171–172
  freight   91–93, 97, 99, 146
  passengers   91, 93–94, 97, 99
Ram public house   91
Ramilles, battle of   49
rates   71, 76–77, 135, 137
recreation ground   139–140, 152
Red Post Junction   89, 99
reeve   32
Reeves Ground (field)   86
Reform Act   64–65
relieving officer   77
roads   3, 135, 146
Rodbourne Chaney   49
Roman   23
  occupation   3
  remains   3–4, 23, 26
  roads   3
  villas   3–4
royal households   9, 31–34
Rushers Shop   85, 147

St. James' Street   73, 75, 117, 136
  school   104–113
St. Mary Bourne   69
Salisbury   7, 18, 32, 53, 67, 70, 89, 127
  Cathedral   32, 46, 110
  Plain   1, 2, 90
Sarum Cash Stores   147
Savernake   19, 89, 90
  Forest   8–9, 18, 54, 90, 123
Saxons   4, 34
  arrival   4
  remains   4
Scouts Hall   50, 109, 113, 122, 127, 146, 147, 153
Seawell workshop   61, 104
sewerage   118
Shaw Hill   116
sheep   1
sheriff   7, 32, 54, 67
Shipton Bellinger   77, 127
Shoddesden   19, 20
Short Street   109, 113, 136, 148
Shoulder of Mutton Copse   86, 165
Sidbury Hill   2, 31
Silchester   3
Simonds   91, 145
  Brewery   85, 118
  Road   85, 97, 98
Smith's Charity   144, 145
Snail Down   2
Snoddington   77
social conditions   63, 69, 70, 73–74, 76–77, 83, 93, 113, 146, 152
Soldiers Welcome   128, 146

Somme Road   98
Southampton   9, 63, 89, 151
South Park Farm   70, 76, 83, 168
Spar Grocery   153
Speenhamland System   76–77
Spitfire Fund Committee   151
Sports Club   147
sports field   85, 152
Spray Leaze   83, 85, 136, 169
Stable Cottage   70
stained glass   45
Standen, manor of   19
Stapleford   2
Station Approach   99, 143
stationmasters   89, 94
Stonehenge   2
straw hat makers   63
Strong's of Romsey   115
Sunday schools   103
Surveyors of the Highway   135
Sweet Apple Farm   97, 136
Swindon   89, 97
Swindon and Cheltenham Extension Railway   90
Swindon, Marlborough and Andover Railway   89–90
Swing Riots   69–70

Taskers Iron Works   69
Tedworth House   55, 56, 65, 68, 69, 90
teachers   103–113
Territorial Drill Hall   128
Test, river   13
thanes   4
Temperance Hotel   122
Tin Town—see Brimstone Bottom   91, 92
Thruxton   4, 69
Three Acres (field)   86
Tidworth   2, 9, 11, 18, 19, 55, 56, 68, 77, 91–95, 145, 152
  demon drummer of   68
  manor of   8, 55
  Road   73, 85, 92, 98, 135
  Station   93, 94, 151
  tattoo   97
Till, river   2
tithes   47, 81–86
tombs   38–40, 45, 176
Totnes   23
Town Field   85
tradesmen   63
trespass   19, 67
Triangle Cash Stores   147
turnpike   135
  gate   135
  house   85

roads   135
   trust   85
unions
   of parishes   77
   trades   70
Upper Clatford   69
utilities   115–119

vehicle depot—see Armoured Fighting
   Vehicle Depot
verderers   19, 20
Vernham Dean   19, 69
vestry accounts   141, 145
villans (villeins)   4, 9, 67
villas   3–4
virgate   8
voters   56, 57, 61, 65

war memorial   51, 129–130, 132, 175
War Office (War Department)   62–63, 90, 91, 98, 128, 137–139
water   115–121
weather   104, 105, 112, 146
wells   107, 115–117
Wessex House   105
Westminster   9
Wexcombe, manor of   14
Weyhill   3, 69, 77, 89, 136, 174
   Fair   89, 104

wheat   3, 69, 81
Wherwell Abbey   13
wills   39–40
Wilton   53
Wiltshire   7, 69
   Constabulary   70–71
   County Council   111, 135, 136
   Fire Brigade   124
Winchester   3, 9, 11, 12–13, 18, 63, 69
   Street   53, 73, 116, 122, 130, 146
Windmill Hill   1, 68, 91, 97, 99, 111, 145, 152
Windmill Inn   121
windmills   76, 168
Witan   9
Woodcroft   20
Wood Park (Woodpark)   19, 83, 85, 136, 153, 167
Woods Farm   109
workhouses   77–78, 107
Wylie, river   2
Wynendael, battle of   40, 49

Younger, George & Sons, brewers   97

Zouch Manor   68

Index of Names

Aadeham, Robert de   157
Abbatt, Dr. Phillip   136
    Mrs.   112
Adam, Nicholas   157
Addison, Joseph   68
Addyman, Dr. Peter   23–26
Aelfric of Winchester   4
Ailesbury, Marquess of   90, 92
Allanson, Charles Winn   161
Allerton, Herbert   147
Alleyn, Arthurus   159
Aluric, Warden of Savernake   8
Annals, Annie   78
Anne, Queen   55
Anne of Bohemia (wife of King Richard II)   33
Annetts, H. K.   175
Ashbourneham (Ashburnham), William   55, 159, 160
Ashwell, Irene   113
Attewater, Robert   53
Aubrey, John   38
Aveyel, Alan de   157
Awdry, Charles   104
    William Henry   43, 137, 143, 157

Baden, James   63
Bagehot, Walter   65
Baiden, C. C.   175
    Ellen   103–104
    family   57
    James   168
    John   57, 163
Bailey, John   164
Bailis (Baylis), Joseph   157
Baldwin, Stanley   139
Bale, Bert   123
    Christa   125
    Heidi   123
Barett, Willielmus   159
Baring, Guy Victor   50–51, 175
    Hon. Mrs. Guy   107, 112, 146
    Olive   51
Barklie, R. M.   115
Barlow, Jim   94
Barnes, John   168
Barnett, D.   175
Bartelot, Thomas   158
Bartlett, William George   153
Bates, A.   175

Batt, Mr.   163, 164, 170
    Thomas   76, 135
Bayley, Nurse   110, 112
Beal, John   75–76
Beale, Captain   121–122
    John (junior)   170
    John (the miller)   170
    Thomas   170
Beams, George   143
    James   164
    William   166
Beaves, H. H.   135
    Laurie   122, 123
Beavis, William   145
Becket, Thomas a'   14
Bedford, Earl of   34
Bendal, Mary   73
Bendall, Charles   168
Berenger, Raymond (Count of Provence)   31
Berry, P. A.   110, 151
Best, Edwards   104, 157
Betjeman, John   51
Bide, John   157
Billings, Harry   147
    Winnie   147–148
Birch, Joseph   161
Black, James   76
Black Prince, the   33
Blackmore, Clive   112–113
    J.A.   175
    Ruth   63, 81, 164
Bland, Sir John   161
Blund, Gunhilda   18
    John   18
Bohun, Humphrey de   13
Boone, Charles   160
    Daniel   56, 160
Borlase, William   40
Bosham, John   90
Boulter, A. J.   175
Bourne, Win   109, 114
Brackstone, Charles   143
Brangwin, John   143
Brayles, Hugh   157
Brecknock, Earl of—see Pratt   162
Bridger, Malcolm   157
Bridgman, J. K.   117, 136, 137
Brigges (Briggys), Ricardus   158
Brito, Hervey (Earl of Wiltshire)   13
Britton, John   28
Brooks, J. W.   121

Browne, Anthonius 159
    Sir Anthony 56
    Sir George 49
    Henry Cave 44
    Sir Richard 160
Bruce, family 56
    Robert 160
Bryan, George 121
Bryce, Hugh 157
Brydges, Anthony 39
    Edmond 39, 40
    Francis 39
    Henry 50, 54, 159
    James 50
    Lady Jane 37, 38–39, 54, 67
    Sir Richard 37, 38–39, 49, 50, 54, 67, 159
Buckler, John 129, 133
Budesden, William de 9, 37, 157
Bunce, R. 175
Bunce, Bob 118, 147
    Hilda 101, 118, 120, 147, 149
    William 118
Burden, Henry 145
Burgess, Miss 111
Bushap, William 53
Butt, Blanche 103
Button, Francis 159
Byrde, Henry 44, 129, 157
Bysshopp, Willelmus 158

Cannings, James 166, 168
Canute, King 4
Capps, John 45, 50, 56, 68, 81, 121, 125, 127, 133
Carhampton, Earl of—see Luttrell
Carley, Brian 85
    Tessa 85, 87
Cartledge, Marguerite 104
    Peter 104
Castleman, John 163
Challis, Jack 118, 123, 125, 136, 141, 153
Chamburleyn, Thomas 158
Chandler, Thomas 164
Chandos, Dukes of 50
Charles I, King 55
Charles II, King 55
Chesterfield, Lord 68
Chesters, Peter 38, 43, 157
Chichele, Henry (Archbishop of Canterbury) 45
Chitty, W. E. 171
Chokke, Alexander 159
Church, George 163
Churchill, John (Duke of Marlborough) 49
    Randolph 51

Clark, Ernest 107
    James 70
Clement, Willielmus 158
Clerke, Johannes le 158
    Henry 160
Cobbett, William 69, 73
Cockburn, Miss A. 111
Cockell, James 166
Cocker, Rebecca Amelia 78
Colbrand, James 159
Collier, Miss 112
Collins, Sheila 133
    William 143
    Wreatha 114, 146, 147, 149, 152, 154
Colliss, N. J. 122, 135, 136
Combe, Johannes 158
Conquest, J. W. 175
Cooke(e), Ann 135
    Anthony 169
    Elizabeth 73
    family 57, 63, 163, 166, 168
    Jane 76, 78, 145
    John 50, 63
    Mark 163
    Mary 50, 163
    Robert 77
    Thomas 50, 63, 169
Coomb(e)s, Charles 164, 167
    David 166
    John 78, 83, 166, 170
Cope, George 54, 159
Copping, Catherine 103
    Gareth iv
    Jack 103
Coppinger, Ambrose 159
Cornish, Anthony 160
Cosyn, Simon 157
Cowen, Aileen 97
    James 97
Cowley, Clayton 94
    Captain R. H. 130
Cozens, N. H. 110
Croc, the huntsman 8, 18
    Ellis 18
Crook, Evi 44, 81, 167, 168
    Jacob 44, 63, 77, 81, 167
    Joseph 76
    William 138
Crouch, Blanche 103
    Charles 129
    Inspector George James 70
    Joseph 166, 169
    William 56, 129, 136, 138, 143, 166, 169
Cubitt, Miss M. C. 111, 112, 113

Culley, Robert   164, 169
Cunliffe, Mrs.   148
Curtis, Griffin   54, 159
    Mr.   122
    Percy   121
Cusse, John   157

Dalkeith, Earl of—see Scott   161
Dalrymple, Glenn B.   157
Dalston, John   56
David, King of Scotland   12–13
Davidge, F.   130, 175
Davies, R. M.   171
Dawkins, William   157
Deakin, Sir William   39
Deane, John   56, 160
Delme, Peter   56, 160
Denby, Johannes   158
Dewy, James   136, 160
Diffey, G. H.   147
Digby, Henry   161
Dixon, Conrad   97, 101, 154
Dobbs, Christopher   163
    Daniel (the elder)   44, 170
    Daniel (the younger)   63, 170
    Daniel (junior)   170
    family   168, 169, 170
    William   135, 169
Douce, Adam   158
    Walterus   158
Dowbeley, Robert   157
Downe, Bartholomew   39
Dowse, family   145
    James   145
Draper, Captain C. B.   147
Drury, William   68
Dudman, Caleb   136, 167
    Charles   145
    Thomas   166
Duke, Arthur   145
Durneforde, Nicholas de   157
Dyeuteyt (Dieuteeyde), Johannes   158
Dyneley, Robertus   159

Earle, Richard   56
Earles, John   50
East, A. T.   175
    family   130
    Jack   129
    W.H.   175
Edmonds, Denise   98, 99
Edward, I, King   31–32
    III, King   33
    IV, King   34
    VI, King   49
    VII, King   90

    Earl of Hertford   37
    of Salisbury   7–8
Edwards, John   170
    Francis   166, 167
    Philip   166, 168
    William   163, 170
    W.V.L.   175
Eleanor, of Castile (Queen Eleanor)   32
    of Provence (Queen Eleanor)   31, 32
Eleyn, Peter   32
Elizabeth I, Queen   54, 76
    the Queen Mother   109
Elkins, H. W.   175
    Mark   70, 117, 122, 128, 130, 146
Elliott, Captain P. T.   151
Ellis, George James Welbore Agar   162
Elward (the thane)   4, 7–8
Empyngham, William de   157
Engels, Freidrich   70
Erle (Erneley), Johannes   158–159
Erskine, Lady Evelyn   153
Esthed, Edward   157
Esturmy family—see Sturmy   8, 32
Etherington, R. A.   111
Evans, Francis   44, 167
Evelyn, family   55
    John (the diarist)   55
    Sir John (I)   55, 159, 160
    Sir John (II)   55
Everett, Anna Maria   144
    Anne   103
    Charles   50, 63
    Ellen   144
    family   40, 43, 44, 50, 63, 76, 81, 85, 86, 144
    Henry   50, 63
    John   50, 167
    Joseph Hague   40, 50, 62, 63, 161, 164, 165, 166–167
    Martha   144
    Richard Thomas   40, 63
    Thomas   40, 44, 50, 61, 62, 76, 135, 161, 170
Ewras, Walter de   7

Faber, David   120, 174
    Walter Vavasour   115, 136, 174
Fairbanks, Robert   152
Falmouth (Lord)   68
Farrant, Thomas   167
Farrington, Thomas   161
Fawcett, Colonel Rowland Hill   136, 144
Ferne, Robert   56, 160
Ferrers, Earl of—see Shirley   68–69

Fields, Charles   167
    John   164, 167
Fitz-Count, Brian   12, 13
Fitz-Gilbert, family   11
Fitz-Girold, Robert   9
Fitz-Peter, family   18
Foley, Edward Thomas   162
Fookes, Captain Henry   40
Fothergill, Mrs.   51
Fowle, Henry   167
Fox, John Joseph   136, 143
Freeman, R. J.   175
French, Miss H.   104
Fryer, Henry   145
Fuld, John   166

Gale, Bertha   104
Gamble, Betty   152, 154
    family   92
    George   92
Garlies (Lord)—See John Stewart   161
Garrett, John   160
Gatecombe, Willielmus   158
Geator, Roger   170
Geoffrey (son of Walter of Oare)   19
George V, King   93, 106, 109, 139
    VI, King   109
George (Duke of Clarence)   34, 136
George, Lloyd   139
Gerveys, Willielmus   158
Gibbs, Caroline   63
Gibon, Johannes   158
Gloucester, Milo of   12–14
    Robert of   12, 13
Gloucester, Johannes   158
Godfrey, Albert George   175
Godwin, Ernest   94
Gold, Martha   68
Gordon, Lord George   58, 161
Gower, Humphrey   157
Graham, family   37, 62, 81
    James (Third Duke of Montrose)   62
    Sir James   62
    Sir Sandford   62, 63–65, 81, 144, 161, 162, 167
Gray, Laura   147
    Mr.   128
Green, Charles H.   167, 168
Grene, John   157
Grenville, Richard   50
Grey, Lady Jane   50
    (Lord)   160
    Thomas   160
Gribble, George J.   50
Gudelok, Galfridus   158

Gudman, Thomas   166
Guinness, Arthur   51
    Bryan Walter (Second Baron Moyne)   51, 130
Gulliver, Benjamin   168

Haghton, Thomas   157
Hailstone, Charles   129
Hall, Miss G. M.   110
Hankessok, Willielmus   158
Happerfield, James   169
Harbord, William Assheton   61, 161
Harcourt, Simon   39
Harding, Mr.   122
    S.J.G.   171
Harfield, Mr.   122
Harland, C.   175
Harper, W. C.   175
Harrison, Richard   165
Hatcher, Douglas   46
Hawkins, I.   123
    Joseph   76, 170
Hayward, M. E.   175
    Thomas   160, 161
Heathcote, Miss   104
Heyler, William   157
Henrietta Maria (Queen Consort and wife of King Charles I)   55
Henry I, King   9, 11–12
    II, King   7, 14, 17, 37
    III, King   11, 18, 27, 31–32
    IV, King   33
    V, King   33, 45
    V, Emperor of Germany   12
    VI, King   33
    VIII, King   37
Henry, of Blois   12
    James   168
Herbert, Allan   145
Hinton, Sir Thomas   159
Hiscocks, E. R.   175
Hoare, Sir Richard Colt   2, 8, 37, 159, 160
Hockings, F. C.   175
Hogan, E.   123
Horewode, John   157
Horne, James   75
    Robert   57, 163
Howe, Mrs.   105
Howell, Enos   70
Humber, Hazel   110
Hume, Miss   105
Humphrey, Barbara   119, 125, 128, 133
Humphreys, Thomas   163
Humphries, G. H.   171
    Thomas   50

Hungerford, Sir Anthony   39
    William de   157
Hunt, family   63
    George   63
    Henry   63, 166, 167, 168
    James   63, 76, 85, 145, 166, 168
    Jane   73
    Joseph   145
    Kate   103, 104
    William   63, 166
Hurd, P.   137, 139
Hutchins, Allen Boardman   63
    family   57, 63
    John   163, 166, 170
    Joseph   63, 165, 166, 168, 169
    Richard   163
    Sarah   63
    Thomas   81, 85, 168
    William   50, 63, 139, 168
Huth, Alfred Henry   50, 129
    Mrs.   104
Hutton, William   39
Hynde, Henry   54, 159
Hyson, family   136

Iokyns, W.   157
Isabella (Countess of Bedford)   33

James II, King   49
James, E. G.   171
    Mary   145
    Ralph, J. H.   110, 111
Jay, Sir Thomas   159
Jenkins, John   112, 114
Jeremy, C. E.   175
Joan (of Navarre)   33
Joan, Queen   45
Job, Frederick   107
John, J. E.   111
John, King   17–18, 31
John, (le glasiere of Calne)   33
    of Worcester   11
    the Marshal   11–17, 31
    V (Duke of Brittany)   33
Johnson, Thomas   70
Jones, A. E.   171
    Dr. James E.   45–46

Keeble, A. J.   92
Keen, W. C.   175
Keene, Whitshed   161
Kelk, Sir John William   90, 91
Kempe, John   33
Kennedy, G. L.   130
Kent, Walter   160

Kingsmill, (Kyngesmyll), John   54, 159
    Richard   54, 159
Kitchener, (Lord)   106
Knight, Robert   39
    T.F.   175
Kynewyne (a Member of Parliament)   158
Kyrton, Edward   54, 159
    James   159

Labett, Leonard Astor   147
Lamb(e), Sir Penistone (Lord
    Melbourne)   161
Langford, Sir John   54
Lansley, C.   175
    C.H.   175
    Charles   164
    Elizabeth   63
    family   63, 130
    George   63, 81, 164, 166, 167
    John   169
    Miss   104
    M.H.   175
    Thomas   63
    William   76, 166
Lashbrook, F. J.   171
Lay, James   166
    John   169
    widow   169
Leake, Richard   54, 159
Leaver, Richard   63, 166
Lecford (Lekford), Walterus de   158
    Willielmus de   158
Lee, John   169
    Thomas   169
Legge, George   160
Leland, John   25
Levell, Eric   133, 141, 151, 154
Lever, Richard   63, 166
Lewis, Mrs. G.   110
    William   50
Leyghton, Geoffrey de   157
Lightfoot, Sheila   112
Littlecott, Gordon   112
Loader, R.   175
Lock, S.   171
Long, Walter   160
Lonye, Robertus   158
Lovatt, Henry   91
Lovell, J.   110, 151
Ludlow, Edmund   159
    Willielmus   158, 159
Luff, E. M.   175
Lush, Lucy   103
Lutegarshale, John de   32
    Richard de   32
Luttrell, Henry Lawes (Earl of
    Carhampton)   162

Mackarell, Thomas 44
Magens, Magens Dorien 62, 161
Malet, Sir Henry 90
Mandeville, Geoffrey de 12
Manning, J. 89, 171
Marlborough, Duke of—see Churchill 49
Marshal, William (Earl of Pembroke) 11, 13, 31
Marten, Thomas 159
Mary, (Prioress at Amesbury and sister of the Black Prince) 32–33
Mary, Queen 39
Mason, Robert 159
Matilda (Countess of Boulogne) 11
Matilda, Empress 11–13, 31, 136
Matthews, John 167
    Robert, 89
Maund, W. H. 62
McDougal, Sergeant-Major and Mrs. 77
McEvoy, J. 175
Meaby, Thomas 143
Mead, Ena 107
    Mrs. 112
Meade, Royston 136
Meadows, Sir William 103
Melbourne, Lord—see Penistone Lamb 161
Menzies, John Stewart 147
Mere, Johannes atte 158
Merlin 14
Mervyle, John 53
Metcalfe, T. J. E. 50, 63, 143
Midwinter, William 147
Miller, Richard S. 43, 157
Millett, W. J. 169, 175
Mitford, Diana 51
Mompesson, family 68
    John 68
Monek, Robertus 158
Monmouth, Duke of 49
Mo(u)re, William atte 53, 158
Montrose, Dukes of 62
Moore, R. V. 175
More, Johannes atte 158
Morris, Mr. 171
Mosprot—see Muspratt
Mower, Robert 127
Moyne, Lady—See Elizabeth Nelson
Moyne, Lord—See Bryan Walter Guiness
Munday (Mundy), Edmund 68
    Henry 39
    Joseph 57, 74, 163
    Peter M. 44, 57
    William 57
Muspratt, Edmund 157
    family 81
    George 81, 169

    Joseph 81, 166, 168
Myleys, David 157

Neale, Thomas 56, 160
Nelson, Elizabeth (Lady Moyne) 51, 130
Neuman, Johannes le 158
Neve, Frederick 109
    Marjorie 109, 114
    Mary 109, 131
Nevill(e), Jollan de 18, 19
    Hugh de 18
New, Muriel 152
Newman, A. F. 171
    Charles 44
    Elizabeth 68
    John 131
    Roger 68
Newnham, Nathaniel 61, 161
Norholt, Inger 38
North, John 53
    Margery 53
Northbourne, Robertus 158
Norris, Henry 143
Noyes, Farmer 68
    George 163
Nutkyn, John 157

Oare, Geoffrey of 19
    Walter of 19
Offer, Thomas 169
Oliver, Frederick A. 157
Ormesby, Arthurus 159

Pagham, Robert de 157
Pallmer, Charles Nicholas 162
Palmer, Geoffrey 160
Palmerston, Lord 69
Pannell, John 157
Parsons, Bartholomew 157
    Thomas 170
Passlewe, John 157
Paterson, John 161
Patrick (Constable of Salisbury Castle) 11
Peachey, William 69
Pearce, Thomas 160
Pearson, John Loughborough 43
Peck, A. 130, 175
    family 130
    G.A. 175
Pecksall, Sir Richard 39
Pelham, Sir John 33
Pembroke, Earls of—see also William Marshal 11–17, 31
Penruddocke, Robert 159
Perrott, L. E. 171

Perry, family   130
    R.   175
    Sid   130
    W.   175
    William   121
Pevsner, Nicholaus   37, 38
Philemore, Charlotte   63
Phillipa of Hainault (Wife to Edward III)   33
Phipps, Thomas Webb   56
Pillans, J.   175
Pille, John   53
Pipard, William   11
Piper, family   45
    Jane   63, 73
    John   110
    William   44, 45, 116, 136, 143
Pirebrock, John de   157
Plantagenet, Geoffrey   12
    Henry   12
Plummer, S. G. S.   171
Pocock, F. W.   175
Pollard, Mr.   92
Powell, Edmundus   159
Power, J.   122, 123
Pratt, George Charles (Earl of Brecknock)   162
Prince, Albert   98, 99
    Denise   98, 99, 101
    Herbert   98
Protheroe, Mr.   103
Prynne, William   160
Pryton, Nicholas de   157
Purdue, Joseph   63, 167, 169
Pye, Sir Robert   159
Pyjon, Robert   157
Pylle, Thomas de la   158
Pystor, Nicholas   158

Quarendon, Simon   157

Rawleigh, Carew   159
Rawlings, F.   123
    George   97, 147
    H.   110
    H.G.   129, 130
Read, A.   122, 123
    Andrew   157
Reeves, family   166
    Henry   73, 76
    Joseph   63, 169
    Mary   76
    Sarah   73
    William   163, 166, 168, 170
Reginald (of Cornwall)   13
Richard I, King   17
Richard II, King   33

Richmond, Earl of   33
Roberts, R. W.   175
Rodborne, John de   157
Rogers, Johannes   159
Rose, A. H.   175
Rose-Casemore, John   157
Roy, E. E.   91, 92, 122, 151
Rusher, family   147
    George   147
Russell, John   145

Sabbe, John   53
Sarisberiensis, Edwardus—See Edward of Salisbury   7–8
Saunders, E. F.   175
    E.M.   111
    John   136
Sayer, Thomas   157
Saymour (Seymour), Edward   54
    family   54
    Johannes   53, 54, 158
    Roger   54
Scanlan, E. J.   175
Schmidt, Albert   145
Scott Charles William Montague (Earl of Dalkeith)   161
    George Gilbert   43
    Wilf   120
Selfe, Mary Ann   143–144
Selwyn Bridget   46
    Charles   57, 161
    family   37, 46–47, 57, 76
    George Augustus   46, 57–58, 61, 62, 161, 163
    Colonel John   46, 56, 57
    Rev. John   46–47, 61, 76, 81, 103, 127, 157, 163
    Miss   103, 113
Seymour—see Saymour
Sharryngton, Henry   159
Shaw, Inspector Harry   70
Sheffield, Robertus   159
Sherwyn, Richard   160
Shirley, Lawrence (Fourth Earl Ferrers)   68–69
Shore, John   78
Shotwelle, Ricardus   158
Shrimpton, Eric Sheldon   175
Sibyl (Wife of John the Marshal)   11, 31
Sille, Johannes   158
Sıreman, Johannes   158
Skeate, Anne   40, 49, 50
    Richard   76
Skerry, James   147
Skylling, Henry   56
    Johannes   158

Sleat, Richard 63
Slyfelde, Willielmus 159
Smith, A. G. 175
    E.S. 111
    Eleanor 169
    First Class Constable 70
    Henry 144
    Hugh C. 51
    John 160, 167
    John (the Speaker) 55–56
    Richard 74–75, 169
    Robert 163, 170
    Samuel 61, 161
    Thomas 55, 76, 169
    Thomas Assheton 65, 69
Smyth, Henricus le 158
Sneddon, Brian 112
Snelgrove, John 136
Sollis, Elizabeth 63, 166
Soper, E. 175
Sot(t)well, Rogerus 158
    William 159
South, Walter 53
Spackman, John 164
Spargo, Mrs. 112
Spencer, Stanley 51
    Wylyam 39
Spicer (Spycer), James 166, 169
    John 169
    Robertus 158
    William 63, 167
Spratberry (Spratsbury), Henry 163, 170
Stacy, Willis 157
Stanley, Thomas 169
Steele, James 81, 165
Stephen, King 11, 12–13, 17, 23, 31
Stewart, John (Lord Garlies) 161
Stidston, J. 129, 137
Storye, Johannes 159
Strachey, Julia 51
Strange, Johannes 158
Sturges(s), A. S. 45
    Elizabeth 45
    Emma 45
    Ephraim 45, 163
    family 166
    Henry 166
    James 45, 63, 78, 167, 169
    John 56, 63, 169
    Mary 76
    Selwyn 45, 163
    Thomas 63
    William 45, 167
Sturmy (Sturmid), family 8
    Henry 32
    Johannes 53, 54, 158

    John 54
    Matilda 54
    Ricardus 8
    Willielmus 159
Sutherland, G. K. 110
Sweet, Mr. 122
Sweteman, John 157
Sybil of Salisbury—see Sibyl 11, 31
Sydney (Lord)—see Thomas Townsend 46, 61–62

Talbot(t), John 160
Taplin, Henrietta 169
Tarrant, Thomas 167, 169
    William 167
Tasker, family 128
    Henry 128
Tayler, William 167, 169
Taylor, Mrs. D. M. 127, 133
    Isaac 166, 169
    Thomas 168
    V.A. 175
    William 175
Teal, Charles 147
Thackeray, William Makepeace 40, 49
Thomas, Brother 18
    Duke of Clarence 45
    William 147, 160
Thompson, Phyllis 128
Thornboroughe, Edward 159
Thorp, John 159
    Thomas 159
Titus, Silas 160
Townsend, Peggy 87
    Thomas (Baron Sydney) 46, 61
Trobuck, John 157

Vane, Cecil 123
Vickery, E. F. 171
Villett, Thomas 40
Vockins, R. G. 175

Walcot, John 63, 127, 168, 169
    Samuel 63
Waleran, (the huntsman) 8
Walker, Bill 94
    E.C. 175
Walleran, Robert de 8
Walters, James 164
Ward, G. V. 175
Wardour, Chidiack 54, 159
Warwick, Earl of 34
Waters, Miss 111
Watt, Alfred 110, 157
Watton, E. 147
    family 147

Reginald   147
Webb, Borlase (Borlace)   49, 56, 160
    Catherine   40
    Edmund   49, 160
    Henrietta   40, 49
    John   160
    John Richmond   40, 49, 56, 160
Weeks, Kate   143
Wellington, Duke of   64
Wells, James   44
    Monty   140
    Dr. Richard   136
Wesley, John   68, 127
Westlake, Ebenezer   143
Westprei, Philip   32
Weyghtman, William   159
Whateley, Thomas   161
Whetstones, George   157
Whitefield, George   127
Whitmarch, Eliza   166
Wiles, Charles   145
    Mr. and Mrs.   122
Wilkins, Henry   69–70
    James   76, 170
    Mr. and Mrs.   122
William the Conqueror   7, 9
    the Marshal   11, 13
    of Salisbury   13
    of Ypres   13
Williams, Dick   94
    Evan   44, 165, 166, 169
    Thomas   81, 164, 168, 169
Williamson, Dr. Herbert Holdrich   44, 107, 110, 129, 136, 144
Wilmot, Sir Charles   159
Wilson, John   105–110, 146
Winstone, Robert   123, 125
Wordsworth, Bishop John   44
Workman, H. R.   135
Worsdell, A. C.   175
    D.F.   175
    family   130, 166
Worsfold, William   145, 175
Wraxall, Nathaniel William   161
Wray, Christopher   54, 55, 159
Wyclif, John   33
Wynchecombe, Johannes   159

Yaldwyn, Richard Yalden   46, 157
Yates, family   147
Young, G. W. J.   175
    Nathaniel   62, 137, 143